California's Coastal Parks

A DAY HIKER'S GUIDE

John McKinney

WILDERNESS PRESS · BERKELEY, CA

California's Coastal Parks: A Day Hiker's Guide

1st EDITION October 2005
   2nd printing April 2006

Copyright © 2005 by The Trailmaster, Inc.

Front cover photos copyright © 2005 by Ed Cooper
Maps designed by: Hélène Webb
Cover design: Larry B. Van Dyke
Book design: Emily Douglas
Book production: Larry B. Van Dyke
Book editor: Cheri Rae

ISBN 0-89997-388-4
UPC 7-19609-97388-1

Manufactured in the United States of America

Published by: **Wilderness Press**
               1200 5th Street
               Berkeley, CA 94710
               (800) 443-7227; FAX (510) 558-1696
               info@wildernesspress.com
               www.wildernesspress.com

Visit our website for a complete listing of our books and for ordering information.

Previously published as *Coast Walks: 150 Adventures Along the California Coast* by Olympus Press. Portions of this book have appeared in the author's hiking column in the *Los Angeles Times*, as well as in *Sunset* magazine.

Cover photos: *(clockwise from top left)* Lighthouse at tip of Pont Reyes Peninsula, Point Reyes National Seashore; Palm Trees at Refugio State Beach; Rhododendron and redwoods, Del Norte Coast Redwoods State Park; Mendocino Headlands State Park

SAFETY NOTICE: Although Wilderness Press and the author have made every attempt to ensure that the information in this book is accurate at press time, they are not responsible for any loss, damage, injury, or inconvenience that may occur to anyone while using this book. You are responsible for your own safety and health. The fact that a trail is described in this book does not mean that it will be safe for you. Be aware that trail conditions can change from day to day. Always check local conditions and know your own limitations.

ACKNOWLEDGMENTS

For their cooperation, field- and fact-checking and for generously sharing maps and interpretive information, the author wishes to thank the rangers and administrators of California's state parks and national parks. A tip of the hiker's cap also goes to the many dedicated interpretive association volunteers who donate countless hours to caring for the California coast. U.S. Forest Service, Bureau of Land Management and State Coastal Conservancy officials were quite helpful also.

PHOTO CREDITS

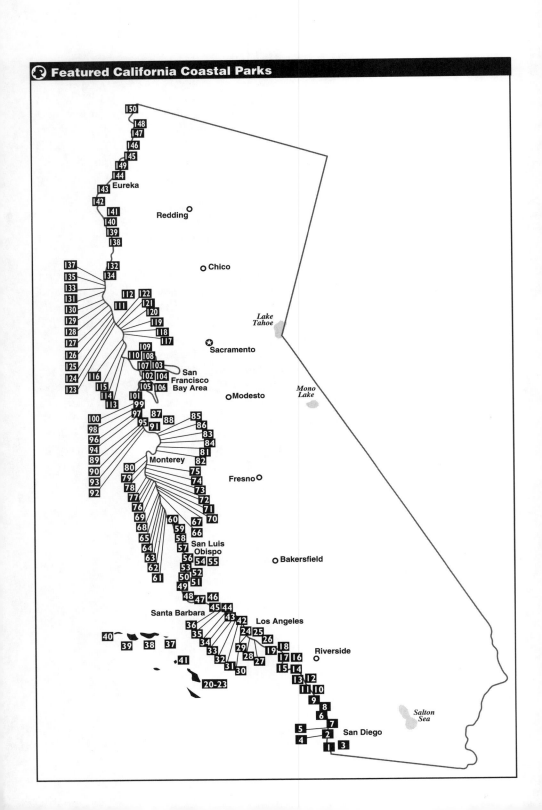

🌐 Key to Locator Map

CHAPTER 1: SOUTH COAST

1 Border Field State Park
2 Tijuana River Estuary
3 Sweetwater Marsh
4 Cabrillo National Monument
5 Mission Bay
6 Torrey Pines Beach
7 Torrey Pines State Reserve
8 Del Mar Beach
9 San Onofre State Beach
10 San Clemente State Beach
11 Crystal Cove State Park
12 Corona del Mar
13 Balboa Island
14 Newport's Back Bay
15 Bolsa Chica Lagoon
16 Long Beach
17 Cabrillo Beach
18 Palos Verdes Peninsula
19 Palos Verdes Hills
20 Catalina: Out of Avalon
21 Catalina: Black Jack
22 Catalina: Little Harbor
23 Catalina: West End
24 Paseo Miramar
25 Malibu Beach
26 San Fernando Valley to the Sea
27 Pt. Dume
28 Nicholas Flat
29 Leo Carrillo Beach
30 Point Mugu State Park
31 La Jolla Valley
32 Port Hueneme Beach
33 Silver Strand
34 McGrath State Beach
35 San Buenaventura State Beach
36 Emma Wood State Beach
37 Anacapa Island
38 Santa Cruz Island
39 Santa Rosa Island
40 San Miguel Island
41 Santa Barbara Island
42 Carpinteria Beach and Bluffs
43 Summerland Beach
44 Santa Barbara's East Beach
45 Arroyo Burro Beach
46 Ellwood Beach
47 El Capitan State Beach
48 Jalama Beach
49 Ocean Beach
50 Guadalupe Dunes

CHAPTER 2: CENTRAL COAST

51 Guadalupe Dunes North
52 Pismo Beach
53 Pt. San Luis Lighthouse
54 Montaña De Oro State Park Bluffs
55 Montaña De Oro Dunes
56 Morro Bay Sand Spit
57 Morro Bay State Park
58 Moonstone Beach
59 San Simeon State Park
60 William Randolph Hearst State Beach

61 Silver Peak Wilderness
62 Sand Dollar Beach
63 Kirk Creek
64 Limekiln State Park
65 Cone Peak
66 McWay Falls
67 Julia Pfeiffer Burns State Park
68 Partington Cove
69 Big Sur River
70 Pfeiffer Big Sur State Park
71 Pfeiffer Beach
72 Andrew Molera State Park's Beach
73 Andrew Molera State Park's Backcountry
74 Pt. Sur Light Station State Historic Park
75 Soberanes Point
76 Garrapata State Park
77 Pt. Lobos State Reserve's Cypress Grove
78 Pt. Lobos State Reserve's North Shore
79 Carmel River State Beach
80 Jacks Peak County Park
81 Monterey Bay
82 Asilomar State Beach
83 Salinas River State Beach
84 Marina State Beach
85 Elkhorn Slough
86 Moss Landing Wildlife Area
87 Butano State Park
88 Forest of Nisene Marks State Park
89 Henry Cowell Redwoods State Park
90 Big Basin Redwoods State Park
91 Pogonip
92 Natural Bridges State Beach
93 Wilder Ranch State Historic Park
94 Año Nuevo State Reserve
95 Cascade Creek
96 Bean Hollow Beach
97 Pescadero Marsh
98 Half Moon Bay
99 Fitzgerald Marine Reserve
100 McNee Ranch State Park

CHAPTER 3: NORTH COAST

101 Sweeney Ridge
102 San Bruno Mountain
103 Land's End
104 Golden Gate Promenade
105 Presidio
106 San Francisco Bay National Wildlife Refuge
107 Candlestick Point State Recreation Area
108 Golden Gate Bridge
109 Alcatraz Island
110 Angel Island State Park
111 China Camp State Park
112 Olompali State Historic Park
113 Tennessee Valley
114 Stinson Beach
115 Mt. Tamalpais
116 Muir Woods

117 Muir Beach
118 Bolinas Ridge
119 Palomarin
120 Bear Valley
121 Pt. Reyes Lighthouse
122 Drakes Estero
123 Tomales Point
124 Tomales Bay State Park
125 Bodega Head
126 Sonoma Coast State Beach
127 Fort Ross State Historic Park
128 Salt Point State Park
129 Kruse Rhododendron State Reserve
130 Gualala Point Regional Park
131 Van Damme State Park
132 Angelo Coast Range Preserve
133 Mendocino Headlands State Park
134 Russian Gulch State Park
135 Pt. Cabrillo Preserve
136 Jug Handle State Reserve
137 Ten Mile Beach
138 Usal Beach
139 Bear Harbor
140 Needle Rock
141 Kings Peak
142 Mattole River
143 Ferndale's Russ Park
144 Patrick's Point State Park
145 Tall Trees Grove
146 Prairie Creek Redoods State Park
147 Lagoon Creek
148 Del Norte Coast Redwoods State Park
149 Humboldt Lagoons State Park
150 Pelican Bay

Point Reyes Lighthouse.

CONTENTS

Introduction: Walking California's Coast 1
California Coastal Trail 4
How to Use This Book 5
Equipping for a Coast Walk 7
About the Maps 7
Precautions in the Surf 9
Coast Walking and Coastal Conservation 10
Adopt a Beach 11
Conservation of Marine Life 12

SOUTH COAST   13

Border Field State Park 14
Beach-walking and bird-watching at America's southwest corner

Tijuana River Estuary 17
More than 170 bird species visit this wetland; you should, too

Sweetwater Marsh 19
San Diego Bay's largest remaining wetland

Cabrillo National Monument 21
Old Pt. Loma Lighthouse, San Diego Bay strolls

Mission Bay 22
San Diego's mega-marine playground

Torrey Pines Beach 24
Famous Scripps Aquarium, infamous Black's Beach

Torrey Pines State Reserve 26
Exploring the last stand of Pinus torreyana

Del Mar Beach 28
A train and a trail where the surf meets the turf

San Onofre State Beach 29
Bluffs Beach and a Bryce Canyon by the sea

San Clemente State Beach 31
San Clemente, Trestles Beach, San Mateo Point

Crystal Cove State Park 34
Moro Canyon and other surprises of the San Joaquin Hills

Corona del Mar 36
Crown of the Sea Trail to Big and Little Corona, Crystal Cove

Balboa Island 38
Newport Pier, Balboa Beach, colorful coastal history

Newport's Back Bay 41
A valuable wetland and bird habitat

Bolsa Chica Lagoon 42
With a little help from its friends, a marshland recovers

Long Beach 44
Long Beach Aquarium of the Pacific, Belmont Shores, Naples

Cabrillo Beach **47**
Cabrillo Marine Museum, Pt. Fermin tidepools, Royal Palms

Palos Verdes Peninsula **50**
Rock-hopping to secret coves and shipwrecks

Palos Verdes Hills **52**
Portuguese Bend, Peacock Flat, vistas from the Eagle's Nest

Catalina: Out of Avalon **54**
Botanical Garden, Wrigley Memorial, Hermit Gulch

Catalina: Black Jack **56**
Black Jack Mountain, Mt. Orizaba (Catalina's highest), Little Harbor

Catalina: Little Harbor **57**
Boar, Buffalo, a Tale of Two Harbors

Catalina: West End **59**
Catalina's West Side Story: happy trails

Paseo Miramar **60**
Los Liones Canyon, The Overlook

Malibu Beach **62**
Malibu Lagoon, Malibu Colony and the Zonker Harris Accessway

San Fernando Valley to the Sea **65**
Lemming Trail links metropolis to the beach

Point Dume **67**
Waves of Zuma, Whales of Dume, Paradise Cove

Nicholas Flat **68**
Peaceful pond, bold backcountry of Leo Carrillo State Park

Leo Carrillo Beach **71**
Lights, camera, action on L.A. County's northernmost beach

Point Mugu State Park **72**
Monarch butterflies and incomparable sycamores

La Jolla Valley **74**
Native grassland, peaceful pond, stalking the elusive chocolate lily

Port Hueneme Beach **76**
Mixing business with pleasure

Silver Strand **78**
Boat-watching from a beach between harbors

McGrath State Beach **80**
Santa Clara River, McGrath Lake, Hollywood Beach

San Buenaventura State Beach **81**
A beach where planning is everything

Emma Wood State Beach **83**
Mouth of the Ventura River, Seaside Wilderness Park

Anacapa Island **84**
Giant coreopsis, the "Light of the Channel Islands"

Santa Cruz Island **86**
Roaming the unusual backcountry of California's largest island

Santa Rosa Island **88**
Cherry Canyon, Lobo Canyon, rare Torrey pines

San Miguel Island 89
Elephant seal congregation, Cabrillo's final resting place

Santa Barbara Island 91
Seabirds and sojourns on small, but spectacular isle

Carpinteria Beach and Bluffs 93
Could it really be "The Safest Beach in the World"?

Summerland Beach 95
Sand Strands and spiritualism south of Santa Barbara

Santa Barbara's East Beach 97
Chase Palm Park, quintessential Santa Barbara

Arroyo Burro Beach 99
The local's favorite beach, Hope Ranch, Goleta Pier

Ellwood Beach 101
Bird-watching in the slough, remembering World War II

El Capitan State Beach 103
Monarch butterflies, Refugio and Coral beaches

Jalama Beach 105
Point Conception, the geographic "end" of Southern California

Ocean Beach 107
A (military) secret beach, Sea Rocket Trail

Guadalupe Dunes 109
To Mussel Rock, the West Coast's highest sand dune

2 CENTRAL COAST   113

Guadalupe Dunes North 115
Oso Flaco lakes, the Dunites revisited

Pismo Beach 117
Clams, coreopsis, Oceano Dunes Natural Preserve

Point San Luis Lighthouse 119
Guided walking tour of Pt. San Luis Lighthouse and long-forbidden coast

Montaña De Oro State Park Bluffs 122
Spooner's Cove, Grotto Rock and a "Mountain of Gold"

Montaña De Oro Dunes 123
Magnificent coastline of reefs, ravines, and dunes

Morro Bay Sand Spit 125
Long, lonely sand spit on the edge of bountiful Morro Bay

Morro Bay State Park 126
Bay views from atop an ancient volcano

Moonstone Beach 128
Cambria Pines and a walk for rock hounds

San Simeon State Park 129
Hearst Castle's rich backcountry

William Randolph Hearst State Beach 131
Castle views from breathtaking San Simeon Bay

Silver Peak Wilderness 133
Salmon Creek and California's southernmost stand of redwoods

Sand Dollar Beach 135
Pacific Valley and some mellow Big Sur Bluffs

Kirk Creek 136
Vincente Flat and other charms of Big Sur's backcountry

Limekiln State Park 138
Inspiring redwoods, a historic trail, a curious coastal industry

Cone Peak 139
Most abrupt pitch of country on the Pacific Coast

McWay Falls 141
Only major California waterfall to tumble into the Pacific

Julia Pfeiffer Burns State Park 144
Ewoldsen Trail tours McWay Canyon redwoods and dramatic ridges

Partington Cove 145
Otter-watching at historic "doghole" port

Big Sur River 146
Ventana Wilderness adventure to Sykes Hot Springs

Pfeiffer Big Sur State Park 148
Through the redwoods to Pfeiffer Falls

Pfeiffer Beach 150
Sea stacks, arches, blowholes, and The Sandpipers

Andrew Molera State Park's Beach 151
Big Sur River Mouth, Molera Point, Creamery Meadow

Andrew Molera State Park's Backcountry 153
Redwood-shaded canyons, grassy ridges, Ventana Wilderness vistas

Point Sur Light Station State Historic Park 154
Touring a tombolo and Big Sur's guardian light

Soberanes Point 156
Whale of a view from Whale Peak

Garrapata State Park 158
Soberanes Canyon's redwoods, Rocky Ridge vistas

Point Lobos State Reserve's Cypress Grove 159
Some call it "the greatest meeting of land and sea in the world"

Point Lobos State Reserve's North Shore 161
Old Veteran Cypress, Guillemot Island, Whaler's Cove

Carmel River State Beach 161
The river mouth and Monastery Beach

Jacks Peak County Park 163
Native Monterey pine cloak peninsula's high point

Monterey Bay 165
Historic waterfront, Cannery Row, the Monterey Bay Aquarium

Asilomar State Beach 167
Sand dunes, rich tidepools, historic Asilomar Conference Center

Salinas River State Beach 169
Monterey Bay's intriguing sand dunes

Marina State Beach 170
Wooden boardwalk and nature trail explore dune ecosystem

Elkhorn Slough 170
Record bird-watching in a large wetland

Moss Landing Wildlife Area 172
Salt ponds attract thousands of brown pelicans

Butano State Park 174
Native Americans called it "a gathering place for friendly visits"

Forest of Nisene Marks State Park 175
A redwood forest regenerates in the Santa Cruz Mountains

Henry Cowell Redwoods State Park 177
Tall trees and tranquility

Big Basin Redwoods State Park 179
Famed Skyline to the Sea Trail leads from redwoods to the coast

Pogonip 181
The wild side of UC Santa Cruz

Natural Bridges State Beach 183
North America's largest concentration of monarch butterflies

Wilder Ranch State Historic Park 185
Old Landing Cove, historic ranch house, Four Mile Beach

Año Nuevo State Reserve 186
An up-close look at the awesome elephant seals

Cascade Creek 188
Wildflower-dotted dunes, Franklin Point's rich tidepools

Bean Hollow Beach 189
"Creek of the Beans" and a shoreline of polished stones

Pescadero Marsh 190
Haven for birds, heaven for bird-watchers

Half Moon Bay 192
Four bayside beaches: Roosevelt, Dunes, Venice and Francis

Fitzgerald Marine Reserve 193
Reef to remember: wonder-filled tidepools studied for generations

McNee Ranch State Park 194
Marvelous vistas from Montara Mountain

3 NORTH COAST   197

Sweeney Ridge 199
San Francisco Bay Discovery Site

San Bruno Mountain 200
Last of the wild—South San Francisco-style

Lands End 201
Cliff House, China Beach, Baker Beach

Golden Gate Promenade 204
San Francisco's engaging northern waterfront

Presidio 206
Old Army post becomes a fabulous new park

San Francisco Bay National Wildlife Refuge 209
Tidelands Trail tours the nation's largest urban wildlife refuge

Candlestick Point State Recreation Area 211
Windy walk along the bay in the shadow of old Candlestick Park

Golden Gate Bridge 212
Across the "Bridge at the Edge of the Continent"

Alcatraz Island 214
A park, a prison and plenty of birds on "The Rock"

Angel Island State Park 217
A walk for islophiles and military historians

China Camp State Park 219
Hiking past the haunts of Chinese fishermen

Olompali State Historic Park 221
A walk through 4,000 years of California history

Tennessee Valley 223
A mellow walk to Tennessee Beach

Stinson Beach 225
A descent from Mt. Tam on aptly named Steep Ravine Trail

Mt. Tamalpais 227
Top of the world coast views from the top of Mt. Tam

Muir Woods 229
Majestic redwoods preserved in "the best tree-lovers monument"

Muir Beach 231
Coyote Ridge, Green Gulch, and Redwood Creek Lagoon

Bolinas Ridge 232
GGNRA's most remote landscape

Palomarin 234
Pt. Reyes Peninsula's "Lakes District"

Bear Valley 235
From Pt. Reyes Visitor Center to the sea

Point Reyes Lighthouse 238
Beacon on the West Coast's foggiest fringe

Drakes Estero 240
Wildlife-watching and the legend of Sir Francis Drake

Tomales Point 242
Wandering with the tule elk to north tip of Pt. Reyes

Tomales Bay State Park 244
Heart's Desire Beach and a rare stand of Bishop pine

Bodega Head 245
Bodega Bay, Bodega Dunes, and the hole in the head

Sonoma Coast State Beach 248
Goat Rock, Shell Beach, Blind Beach via Sonoma Coast Trail

Fort Ross State Historic Park 249
Czarist Russia's California foothold

Salt Point State Park 252
Sandstone cliffs, sandy coves, sea stacks and sea caves

Kruse Rhododendron State Reserve 253
A path of pink blossoms

Gualala Point Regional Park 254
Earthquake-shaped Gualala Creek, a peek at the infamous Sea Ranch

Van Damme State Park 256
Strange flora: Fern Canyon and Pygmy Forest

Angelo Coast Range Preserve 258
Ancient old-growth forest along the Eel River

Mendocino Headlands State Park 260
An intriguing town and its bold blufftops

Russian Gulch State Park 263
A lush coastal canyon and a waterfall

Point Cabrillo Preserve 264
Picturesque lighthouse on wave-battered peninsula

Jug Handle State Reserve 266
A rare "ecological staircase" and the Mendocino Pygmy Forest

Ten Mile Beach 267
Miles to remember: Ten Mile Dunes, Inglenook Fen, Cleone Lake

Usal Beach 269
Introducing the Lost Coast

Bear Harbor 271
An unusual railroad, an uncommon redwood grove

Sinkyone Wilderness State Park 273
Spiritual inspiration on the way to Whale Gulch

Kings Peak 275
Grand views from rooftop of the King Range

Mattole River 277
Black sand beaches, the historic Punta Gorda Lighthouse

Ferndale's Russ Park 279
Quaint Victorian Ferndale's wild side

Patrick's Point State Park 281
Rim Trail to Wedding Rock and Agate Beach

Tall Trees Grove 283
Along Redwood Creek to the world's tallest tree

Prairie Creek Redoods State Park 285
Fern Canyon, Gold Bluffs, wandering with the Roosevelt elk

Lagoon Creek 287
Hidden Beach, Sitka spruce forest, Klamath River vistas

Del Norte Coast Redwoods State Park 288
Last Chance Trail explores state and national park land

Humboldt Lagoons State Park 290
Big Lagoon, Dry Lagoon, Stone Lagoon and more

Pelican Bay 292
Point St. George, lakes Earl and Talawa

Longer Coastal Trails 294
Information Sources 303
Index 306

The California Coast ranges from long and narrow strands to wild and rugged shores.

INTRODUCTION

WALKING CALIFORNIA'S COAST

Creative types and adventurous spirits have long been attracted to the California coast. It's the land the great landscape photographer Ansel Adams called home; it's the place that prompted John Steinbeck to write *Cannery Row* and other novels. The wild geography of Pt. Lobos inspired landscape artist Francis McComas to call it "the greatest meeting of land and sea in the world."

With all due respect to both a renowned artist and a prominent point, many such "great meetings" of shore and sea take place along California's coast, best explored by short walks and long.

I say this with some authority, having walked the entire California coast and written a narrative of my journey, *A Walk Along Land's End: Discovering California's Living Coast.* In what became an "adventure of a lifetime," I trekked some 1,600 miles from Mexico to Oregon along the edge of California.

It was my assignment, on behalf of the nonprofit California Coastal Trails Foundation, to design a system of interconnecting beach and mountain range routes into one continuous state-long walking trail. But the noble idea of a California Coastal Trail was not what finally kept me walking. The coast worked its magic on me and I evolved from a sportsman with something to prove to a traveler with something to learn. The joys of creation displaced those of recreation.

California's coast works that kind of magic. Walk a sandy beach or bold bluff and you'll likely find that your feet and heart will reach some surprising places.

Other states have snowy peaks, evergreen forests and vast deserts, but only California has a coastline of such length and diversity. This is a book about walking that coastline, from the Mexican border to the Oregon border, an invitation to walk along land's end for one mile or ten, a chance to experience what you, too, may consider to be the greatest meeting of land and sea in the world.

This book describes 150 of my favorite coastal hikes—around precious wetlands, along precipitous bluffs, across white sand beaches, around bays, across islands, to lighthouses and through redwood forests. Walkers will find days, weekends and weeks of exploration and recreation along one of the most unique environments on earth.

Hikes in this guide explore dozens of state beaches, marine refuges and reserves. Other walks climb inland through the chaparral-cloaked Santa Monica and Santa Ynez Mountains, through the Santa Lucia Mountains of Big Sur and over the Santa Cruz Mountains, the hills around San Francisco Bay and the precipitous King Range of Humboldt County.

Some hikers will enjoy meeting up with a colony of boisterous elephant seals at Point Año Nuevo. Others will delight in trekking the trackless Nipomo Dunes. Still others will find hearts uplifted with spiritual sojourns among the redwoods of the Santa Cruz Mountains and Big Sur.

Millions of visitors a year drive through Malibu, Monterey, Mendocino and a hundred more communities on scenic Highway 1. The long, winding road gives drivers and their passengers visual inspiration from the glorious landscapes and seascapes glimpsed through windshields. But there's so much more to the coast than what can be seen from a car.

A more intimate connection with the coast can be made by walking to and along the shore, getting close-up views of that otter grabbing mussels off the rocks, that cormorant diving for a fish. A little effort yields big rewards: wildflowers, wildlife and wild beaches hidden from the highway.

True, blue and gray are dominant coastal colors, but that makes seasonal splashes of more lively hues all the more striking. Walk a path of pink blossoms in Kruse Rhododendron Reserve or behold the fields of mustard and poppies that gave Montaña de Oro State Park its "Mountain of Gold" name. Check out the bright yellow giant coreopsis, or tree sunflower, on Anacapa Island.

California's coast offers plenty of wildlife to watch—from colorful insects to giant sea creatures. In autumn, migrating monarch butterflies arrive by the millions to winter in the sheltered groves along the coastal strip from Santa Monica Bay to Monterey Bay. Natural Bridges State Beach's eucalyptus grove hosts the largest gathering of monarch butterflies in America; Sycamore Canyon in the Santa Monica Mountains, Morro Bay and Pacific Grove are other spots where the monarchs reign supreme.

Truly enormous elephant seals (males reach lengths of 16 feet and weigh three tons) arrive at Año Nuevo Point in December and come ashore to breed. Walkers are treated to a wildlife drama that attracts visitors from all over the world—a close-up look at the largest mainland population of elephant seals.

Much of the Central Coast's offshore waters are part of a designated sea otter refuge. Otters can often be seen bobbing in the surf or floating on their backs. During the winter months, migrating California gray whales can be viewed from many places along the coast.

In addition to abundant natural attractions, many coastal hikes have great historical or cultural interest. From the Old Pt. Loma Lighthouse on San Diego Bay to the Pt. Cabrillo Lighthouse on the rugged bluffs north of Mendocino, from Pt. Vicente to Pt. San Luis to Pt. Sur to Pt. Reyes to Pt. Cabrillo to Punta Gorda, lighthouses are beacons for walkers looking for grand vistas and insight into the lonely lives of generations of lighthouse keepers. Coast walkers can visit "the light of the Channel Islands" on Anacapa Island and tour the Pt. Reyes Light Station, which shines over some of the foggiest waters in North America.

Hearst Castle (Hearst San Simeon State Historical Monument) offers four fabulous walking tours of the palatial estate of the late newspaper tycoon William Randolph Hearst. A walk through Old Monterey explores early California's first capital, the once-bustling sardine trade on Cannery Row and the underwater world revealed at the famed Monterey Bay Aquarium. If you want to take a walk on the wild side of a college campus, hike Pogonip Park next to the UC Santa Cruz or Goleta Beach alongside UC Santa Barbara.

Outings in this guide are oriented for walkers of every age and ability. Easy "leg stretchers" are a perfect antidote to that sometimes frustrating drive along the Coast Highway. Many trails are suitable for families with small children. And serious hikers will find a number of challenging routes.

Lastly, and perhaps most importantly, this book is about the California coastline, its sand strands and cobble shores, its wondrous redwood forests, its fists of mountains rising above the surf, its tides and tidepools, its past, present and its future.

Humboldt County's Lost Coast.

Experience the many "coasts" of California, and you will begin to under-stand the entire coastline. The more you hike, the more varied habitats you encounter, and the more you realize how interdependent they are. These habi-tats are links in a single chain, dependent on us for their continued survival. Coast walking provides a microview of the coastline, a slow-motion study of land and sea, a link between ourselves and the edge of the continent.

California Coastal Trail

For decades hikers have dreamed of a continuous trail along the beaches and bluffs, and across the mountain ranges of the California coast. Proposals for a "Pacific Coast Trail" and a "Coastal Trail" have surfaced before, only to become buried in bureaucracy.

California dreamin' at its best. Surfers take to the trails to reach their favorite spots.

It's my hope and the hope of thousands of hikers, surfers, fishers and coast lovers of all sorts, that before too many years pass, an opti-mum route will be developed with the cooperation of state officials. This would be a signed and sanc-tioned trail, with rights to hike the coast, coastal bluffs and coast range unequivocally established.

When completed, the California Coastal Trail (CCT) will guide ambitious hikers from Mexico to Oregon along a 1,600-mile system of interconnecting beach and coastal range trails. For the less ambitious, the trail will provide days, weekends and weeks of explo-ration and recreation along one of the most unique environments on earth.

Beginning in the early 1980s, I took my turn at launching this trail by founding the California Coastal Trails Foundation and by scouting a route for the California Coastal Trail. I even wrote a book outlining a temporary route for this trail, *California Coastal Trails* (1983, Capra Press). At the turn of the twenty-first century, the governors of each of the fifty states nominated a Millennium Legacy Trail, one that reflected the essence and spirit of their particular state. The California Coastal Trail was designated the state's official Millennium Trail.

Now others have taken up the cause, including the State Coastal Conservancy and a nonprofit organization called Coastwalk that champions the trail and leads summer walks along the state's shores.

When completed, CCT will visit nearly every natural attraction (and many unnatural ones) on the California coast. As the trail winds its way from Border Field State Beach on the Mexican border to Pelican State Beach on the Oregon border, it passes through a hundred state parks and beaches, plus a few hundred more reserves, county beaches, city beaches and national park lands.

But don't wait for trail signs to go up before you walk the coast. Thanks to the California Coastal Commission, the State Coastal Conservancy's splendid coastal access program and thousands of dedicated citizen conservationists, hundreds of miles of coast can be traveled by the sojourner afoot. Undeveloped beaches and bluffs, urban/suburban waterfront and coastal range wilderness are among the diverse environments awaiting exploration by the curious coast walker.

How to Use This Book

Hikes in this guide are grouped by geography into three chapters—South Coast, Central Coast and North Coast—then further organized roughly in south-to-north order.

Political pundits are fond of dividing the state in half—Northern California and Southern California—though no two agree about the dividing line. We veteran coast-walkers find that California, as a walking province anyway, is better divided into thirds. You "I ♥ L.A." boosters and San Francisco chauvinists take note: the Central Coast is a land, a people and an outlook all its own. Between the Bay Area and the Southland are four coastal counties—San Mateo, Santa Cruz, Monterey and San Luis Obispo—that offer some of the most memorable walking in the West.

Distance, expressed in round trip mileage figures, follows each destination. The hikes in this guide range from 0.5 to 15 miles; the majority are less than 5 miles. Elevation gain follows the mileage listing.

In matching a hike to your ability, consider both mileage and elevation as well as condition of the trail, terrain and season. Hot, exposed chaparral or miles of beach boulder-hopping can make a short hike seem much longer.

Hikers vary a great deal in relative physical condition, but you may want to consider the following: An easy walk suitable for beginners and children is less than 5 miles with an elevation gain of less than 700 to 800 feet. A moderate hike is in the 5- to 10-mile range, with less than 2,000 feet of elevation gain. You should be reasonably fit for these. Preteens may find the going difficult. Hikes of more than 10 miles and those with more than a 2,000-foot gain are for experienced hikers in top form.

Season is the next item to consider. California's coast offers four-season hiking. Almost all of the trails in this guide are accessible all year, but use common sense about local conditions. The Southland's summer heat and the North Coast's heavy winter rains, for example, mean you won't necessarily have a pleasant hike—unless you enjoy those weather-intense experiences.

An introduction to each hike describes what you'll see in a particular park, preserve or forest area, and what you'll observe along the trail: plants, animals, panoramic views. You'll also learn about the geologic and human history of the region.

DIRECTIONS TO TRAILHEAD take you from the nearest major highway to trailhead parking. For trails having two desirable trailheads, directions to each are given. A few trails can be walked one way, with the possibility of a car shuttle. Suggested car shuttle points are noted.

After the directions to the trailhead, you'll read a description of **THE HIKE**. Important junctions and major sights are pointed out, but I've left you to discover the multitude of little things that make a hike an adventure. Options allow you to climb higher or farther or take a different route back to the trailhead.

What could be more romantic than a sunset stroll along the California coast?

These 1910 coast walkers had fewer apparel options than today's beach hikers.

Equipping for a Coast Walk

A long discussion of hiking wear and hiking equipment is beyond the scope of this guide. However, coast and coast range hiking creates some special equipment needs.

Footwear: Most of the higher quality, modern lightweight hiking boots are adequate for the vast majority of the hikes in this guide. A disadvantage of some of these lightweights is that they're not very waterproof—a consideration if you're hiking a coast range trail in the rainy season. They are water repellent, however, and will get you through wet meadows and mudflats. For very wet hikes and shoreline strolls, consider all-terrain sandals that offer support and good traction.

Clothing: A t-shirt and a cotton shirt that buttons down will give you a lot of temperature-regulating possibilities. Add a wool sweater or synthetic pile pullover, along with a windbreaker with a hood, and you'll be protected against the sudden changes of temperature that often occur along the coast and in the coast ranges.

Shorts are useful much of the year. For cooler days or hikes through brushy country, a sturdy pair of long pants is necessary.

Hats offer protection from the sun, and protect against heat loss when the weather is cold. Sunglasses are a must for those hikes over white sand or across hot, exposed coastal slopes. Make sure you buy a pair that provides adequate UV protection.

Quality rainwear is a good investment. True, some of the new breathable, high-tech fabric laminates are expensive, but they offer superb foul-weather protection. If you stay fairly dry during a coastal storm, a hike in the rain can be a fantastic experience.

About the Maps

The maps in this book support the author's mission, which is to provide an introduction for the day hiker to the state's best state, national, coastal and desert parklands.

Many of the Golden State's parklands are regarded by rangers, administrators—and most importantly by hikers—as true "hiker's parks." These footpath-friendly parks offer miles and miles of maintained trails, with plenty of options for great day hikes. For these adventures, in contrast with, say, easy "walks in the park," route descriptions are described in more detail and accompanying maps highlight more trails and park features.

It's a delight for me to share some of my favorite, often carefully selected, shorter California trails, too. Among these short but scenic paths are nature trails and history interpretation trails, as well as beach trails and informal foot-paths along a river. These short hikes have correspondingly short route descriptions, and the accompanying maps chart a minimal number of features. A handful of the selected hikes are so short, and the on-the-ground orientation for the hiker so obvious, that mapping them would not add anything to the visitor's experience and, in a few instances, would be downright silly.

Fellow hikers, do give us a heads-up about any trail changes you notice or any discrepancies you observe between the map and territory.

For reasons I can't explain, during the 20-plus years that I've been chronicling hiking trails, you hikers have been lots more vigilant about pouncing on errant or out-of-date prose and telling me about it than you have been about pointing out the need for any trail map updates. (Jeez, I can't even misidentify a rare plant or obscure bird without hearing about it from so many of you...) Anyway, your cartographic input is always welcome.

Sea lion.

Precautions in the Surf

Stingrays may be encountered, particularly in summer. They lie about the bottom in the surf zone and, if stepped on, may inflict a painful wound. If stung, cleanse the area thoroughly to avoid infection.

Sea urchins appear in rocky tidal zones. Armored with brittle purple spines, they grow two to six inches in diameter. If you step on an urchin, the spines break off. Remove the mildly poisonous spines with great care; if allowed to remain under the skin, they'll make the wound hurt for a long time. Dissolve the spines, which are made of calcium carbonate, in a weak acid such as vinegar, lemon juice, or, uh...uric acid. The latter remedy suggests a possible first aid procedure on an isolated beach.

Jellyfish are common in the summer months. Avoid them. Their clear blue or purple umbrella-shaped floats are less than a foot in diameter, but their stinging tentacles may dangle ten or fifteen feet below the surface. Traditional first aid is to rub the affected area with wet sand, wash it with ammonia, and apply burn ointment.

Tide Tables: For reasons of both safety and enjoyment, consult a tide table prior to hiking the beach.

Two high tides and two low tides occur every 24 hours and 50 minutes. (It would be convenient for hikers to make it an even 24 hours, but the tides are governed by the gravitational pull of the moon and the sun—over which we have no control.)

The times of these high and low tides are predicted and published by the U.S. Hydrographic Office. Newspapers usually publish the times of high and low tides. Local tide booklets are available free from many marine hardware stores, dive shops and sporting good stores. Having the right tide table in your possession is important because some coast hikes are difficult, even impassable, at high tide.

As you travel the coast, you must pick up a new tide booklet every hundred miles or so, for a tidebook issued for Mendocino has no more value in San Diego than a Utah road map. Last year's tide table is no more useful than last year's calendar.

The time to go coast hiking, tidepool exploring or seashell collecting is at low tide. Plan your day so that you begin hiking a few hours before low tide and finish a few hours after.

Coast Walking and Coastal Conservation

If, with a wave of a wand, one could magically link together the 1,000 or so miles of coastal trail described in this book, the result would be a splendid California Coastal Trail. This trail would be an urban-rural wilderness-collage—the best of far western civilization plus the best of what has remained untouched by far western civilization.

Unfortunately, quite a number of missing links remain and a completed California Coastal Trail will by necessity visit a lot of places coast lovers would probably rather not see. The hikes in this guide for the most part steer away from the worst of this coastal carnage and toward the most engaging natural environments. For example, I have deliberately led the reader away from places such as Laguna Beach, where a Maginot Line of barbed wire and concrete thwarts the coast hiker. I have avoided nuclear power plants, condo-contaminated coastline, and broccoli fields patrolled by cranky farmers.

But we must consider the bad and the ugly along with the good, must enjoy and preserve California's coastline.

To be sure, all is not pristine along the 150 hikes described in this book. In Orange County, you'll encounter a wetland that, after years of oil-drilling activity, is slowly being restored. From Kings Peak, high atop Humboldt County's Lost Coast, you'll overlook a lot of bald hills, shorn by destructive clear-cut logging operations.

Good coastal trails are a precious commodity. Besides a trail's obvious recreational and educational value, a trail can often be seen as an indicator of environmental conditions. People who hike a beach, bluff or coastal ridge trail comprise a constituency that cares about the past, present and future of the land this trail crosses. When a trail is closed or coastal access denied, however, you can bet that some land abuse or misuse will soon follow.

While out coast hiking, if you happen across a neglected, hazardous or overgrown trail, or a path being massacred by mountain bicyclists, please report it to the relevant ranger or administrator.

Similarly, if you notice a water-polluting storm drain, sewer pipe or viaduct, report the problem to the appropriate water conservation authority. The rate of beach closures caused by water contamination increased at alarming rate during the 1990s. Monitoring water pollution sources (usually inland in origin) is critical to ocean life and to the health of swimmers, surfers and all who enjoy the Pacific. Only if you make your feelings known will conditions improve.

The coast's future depends not only on lawmakers and Coastal Commissioners, but to a large extent on citizens adopting a new visualization, another way of looking at land and sea, a vision of the coastline not as a sandbox for play, but as a living thing placed in our trust. When this new visualization is accepted, the problems of zoning, population density, cliff collapse, sewage discharge and oil drilling will be easier to tackle.

One very good way to develop an ecologically sound vision for the coastline is to hike it—to see the shore in its many moods and manifestations. I hope that, in some modest way, this book contributes to a new vision.

Adopt a Beach

It's a way of saying thank you for summer pleasures. It's a way to protect ocean creatures great and small. It's a way to make a good beach better.

What it is is California's annual Adopt-a-Beach program, held during the third weekend in September. Each year, thousands of volunteers haul away tons of debris from 1,600 miles of California coastline, from Border Field State Park on the Mexican border to Pelican State Beach on the Oregon border.

The event, sponsored by the California Coastal Commission, with the help of other governmental agencies, nonprofit organizations and businesses, aims not only to clean up beaches but to instill a sense of pride in California citizens in one of the world's most splendid coastlines.

For good reason, California's beaches get lots of visitors, and for no good reason, these visitors leave plenty of debris. Before dawn, huge mechanized sand rakes scoop up trash along the popular strands by the state's big coastal cities. And, while these machines do an adequate job of picking up after sloppy beach-goers, they miss a lot too, and the only way to clean California's little pocket beaches is by hand. That's where the Adopt-a-Beach program comes in.

Each of California's 15 coastal counties has a coordinator, numerous beach captains and hundreds of volunteers. Kayak clubs scoop up offshore flotsam and jetsam, and dive clubs clean dump sites of the deep.

The sheer quantity of trash picked up in a day is amazing. In not particularly big, not particularly dirty Ventura County, usually about 1,000 volunteers pick up more than 10 tons of trash. Statewide, volunteers scoop up more than 700,000 pounds of trash and recyclables in a single day. That weighty number includes 20,000 bottles, 50,000 fast-food wrappers and 250,000 cigarette butts.

But the problem is more than the amount of debris that piles up; it's the type of trash. Coastal debris not only is displeasing to humans, it's deadly to marine wildlife. Giant 300-pound sea turtles swallow plastic bags and asphyxiate. Baby sea otters playfully poke their heads through six-pack rings, then

California Coastal Trails Foundation members clean Goleta Beach.

slowly strangle as they grow. Birds ingest Styrofoam and plastic objects with disastrous consequences.

Adopt-a-Beach is now a year-around program. Groups now commit to carrying for a beach throughout a year and cleaning it at least three times. Participate in this worthy program by calling (800) COAST4U or visit www.coastal.ca.gov/publiced/aab/aab1/html.

Conservation of Marine Life

Some general rules should be remembered whenever one is observing marine organisms. Rocks which have been turned over should be replaced in their original position, otherwise the plants and animals which were originally on the upper surface are now on the bottom and will die; the same, in reverse, holds for tidepool inhabitants that were originally on the bottom of the rock.

Whenever digging in the sand or mud for clams or other creatures, the material should be shoveled back into the hole because many organisms die when their habitat is disturbed. Avoid provoking, poking or prodding the beautiful creatures that cling to rocks or wiggle into the sand. Life is difficult enough for them.

CHAPTER ONE

SOUTH COAST

For more than a century, the shores of San Diego, Orange, Los Angeles, Ventura and Santa Barbara counties have served as resort areas for California residents and visitors from across the nation and around the world. Many of the "watering places" of old are still popular—La Jolla, Carlsbad, Balboa Island, Laguna, Venice, Ventura and Santa Barbara.

Each Southern California beach has its own character—best surfing, clearest water, panoramic view, most birdlife. The air and water temperatures are Mediterranean, the place names Spanish. It's easy to see why the coastline is an attraction for visitors from around the globe, who come for the sun, sand and historical romance.

The typical mass-use Southern California beach includes acres of hot sand, waves ranging from the gentle to the inspired, a lifeguard stationed every few hundred feet, and a boardwalk full of skaters, restaurants and boogie board rental establishments.

Millions flock to the promised sand, and most cluster blanket-to-blanket on the same few beaches. Less-accessible beaches, bluffs and coastal ridges are left to those willing to walk.

For the coastal hiker, the south coast offers not only those white sand beaches depicted on postcards, but a wide variety of shoreline features—the palms of La Jolla and Santa Monica and the cliffs of Torrey Pines State Reserve and Palos Verdes Peninsula. Above Santa Barbara, the Santa Ynez Mountains march toward the Pacific and at Point Mugu, the Santa Monica Mountains do likewise.

Northern San Diego County is one of the south coast's special places to hike. A shoreline of sandy beaches and sandstone bluffs is broken up by scattered lagoons. Many of California's valuable wetlands are here: Penasquito, Buena Vista, Batequitos. A grove of the rare Torrey pine grows on the bluffs south of Del Mar, in a reserve that shelters a remnant of the south coast of two hundred years ago.

Southern California is blessed with several islands. Located 22 miles offshore, Catalina, with its steep brush- and cactus-covered ridges, clear waters and beautiful coves, is a hiker's delight. Most of the island, except for the resort town of Avalon, is rural—the domain of buffalo, boar and backpackers.

Ventura Harbor is the home of Channel Islands National Park. Visitors sail to San Miguel, Santa Rosa, Santa Cruz, Santa Barbara and Anacapa islands to view elephant seals, enjoy the giant coreopsis in bloom and watch the migrating whales.

Another highlight for the coastal hiker is the Santa Monica Mountains, the nation's only relatively undeveloped mountain range that bisects a major metropolitan area. The mountains stretch from Griffith Park in the heart of Los Angeles to Point Mugu, 50 miles away. State and national parklands host a rich pastiche of nature paths, scenic overlooks, fire roads and horse trails leading through diverse ecosystems: native tall grass prairie, fern-lined canyons, rugged, rocky ridgetops.

The south coast hiker will find one sandy and mellow beach after another. But expect some surprises. Though a huge metropolis crowds the shoreline, there are still some amazingly tranquil and attractive places awaiting your discovery.

■ BORDER FIELD STATE PARK
Border Field Trail
From Border to Tijuana River is 3 miles round trip; to Imperial Beach is 6 miles round trip

At the very southwest corner of America is a monument marking the border between Mexico and California. When California became a territory at the end of the Mexican-American War, an international border became a necessity. American and Mexican survey crews determined the boundary and the Italian marble monument was placed in 1851 to mark the original survey site. Today the monument stands in the shadow of the Tijuana bullring and still delineates the border between the United States and Estádos Unídos Mexicanos.

During World War II, the Navy used Border Field as an airfield. Combat pilots received gunnery training, learning to hit steam-driven targets that raced over the dunes on rails called Rabbit Tracks. Despite a variety of real estate schemers, the Navy retained control of Border Field until the land was given to the state in the early 1970s.

Before you hike down the bluffs to the beach, take in the panoramic view: the Otay Mountains and the San Miguel Mountains to the east, Mexico's Coronado Islands out to sea, and to the north—the Tijuana River floodplain, the Silver Strand, Coronado.

Much of the Tijuana River Estuary, one of the few salt marshes left in Southern California and one of the region's most important bird habitats, is within Border Field State Park's boundaries.

Stop in at the visitor center and check out the natural history exhibits that interpret this unique environment.

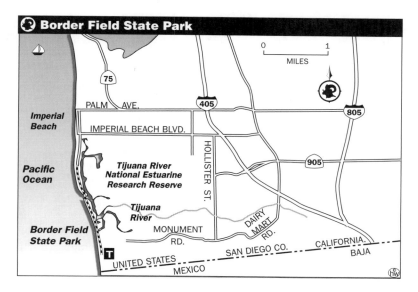

This hike explores the dune and estuary ecosystems of the state park and takes you to wide, sandy Imperial Beach. Wear an old pair of shoes and be prepared for the soft mud of the marsh.

DIRECTIONS TO TRAILHEAD From Interstate 5 just south of Chula Vista and a few miles north of the border crossing, exit on Coronado Avenue and immediately head south on Hollister Avenue, which leads 2.4 miles along the edge of the Tijuana River Valley to Monument Road. Turn right and drive 1.5 miles to a dirt parking lot near the east boundary of the state park.

On weekdays, because of construction activity and security considerations, this lot is where you need to park, because the park road is closed to private vehicles. On weekends, continue another mile or so to road's end at a large parking lot, where you'll find a picnic area, the boundary marker and, of course, the fenced border between the U.S. and Mexico.

The dirt lot is used primarily by equestrians; they and their steeds ride out from here to explore the open space reserve north of the park as well as a newly constructed bridle trail paralleling Monument Road.

Let's review hiking options. On weekdays, you can hike the park road to the actual border and main park features. With only the occasional Border Patrol vehicle sharing the road with you, it's an okay hike—and a very pleasant bike ride if you happened to bring your wheels.

For weekday hikers, I recommend hiking west on Monument Road for a half mile to a corral and hitching posts. Just as Monument Road turns sharply south, continue straight ahead and join the signed horse trail. Hike this wide sandy trail due west a half-mile to the beach. (At the quarter-mile mark, unsigned Marsh Loop Trail extends north from the horse trail to a wildlife-viewing area.)

Beach-walk down-coast a half-mile to the walkway leading up to the top of the coastal bluffs and the border monument. Hike up-coast 1 mile to the mouth of the Tijuana Slough.

THE HIKE Follow the short bluff trail down to the beach, which is under strict 24-hour surveillance by the U.S. Border Patrol. The beach is usually deserted, quite a contrast to crowded Tijuana Beach a few hundred yards to the south. As you hike north on Border Field State Park's 1.5-mile long beach, you'll pass sand dunes anchored by salt grass, pickleweed and sand verbena.

On the other side of the dunes is the Tijuana River Estuary, an essential breeding ground and a feeding and nesting spot for more than 170 species of native and migratory birds. At Border Field, the salt marsh is relatively unspoiled, unlike so many wetlands encountered farther north, which have been drained, filled or used as dumps.

Take time to explore the marsh. You may spot a marsh hawk, brown pelican, California gull, black-necked stilt, snowy egret, western sandpiper or American kestrel—to name a few of the more common birds. Fishing is good for perch, corbina and halibut, both in the surf along Border Field Beach and in the estuary.

A mile and a half from the border you'll reach the mouth of the Tijuana River. Only after heavy storms is the Tijuana River the wide swath pictured on

Begin your hike up the California coast by the Tijuana bullring and the marble monument marking the border between the U.S. and Mexico.

some maps. Most of the time it's fordable at low tide, but use your best judgment.

Continue north along wide, sandy Imperial Beach, past some houses and low bluffs. Imperial beach was named by the South San Diego Investment Company to lure Imperial Valley residents to build summer cottages on the beach. Waterfront lots could be purchased for $25 down, $25 monthly and developers promised the balmy climate would "cure rheumatic proclivities, catarrhal trouble, lesions of the lungs," and a wide assortment of other ailments.

In more recent times, what was once a narrow beach protected by a seawall has been widened considerably by sand dredged from San Diego Bay. There's good swimming and surfing along Imperial Beach and the waves can get huge. The beach route reaches Imperial Pier, built in 1912 and the oldest in the county.

■ TIJUANA RIVER ESTUARY
Tijuana Estuary Trails
1 to 2 miles round trip

At first glance, Tijuana River Estuary, one of the few salt marshes remaining in Southern California, looks lifeless. But a closer look—or a look through binoculars—might reveal a marsh hawk, brown pelican, California gull, black-necked stilt, snowy egret, Western sandpiper or American kestrel—to name a few of the more common birds.

The estuary, about 1.5 miles north of the border dividing Baja and California, 15 miles south of San Diego, is an essential breeding ground and an important feeding and nesting spot for more than 170 species of native and migratory birds.

A flotilla of land use agencies have shared control of what is officially known as the Tijuana River National Estuarine Research Reserve: the California Department of Parks and Recreation, the California Department of Fish and Game and the U.S. Fish and Wildlife Service.

The greatest challenge facing these agencies—and the biggest threat to the estuary—is sewage discharges from Tijuana. The fast-growing city sometimes empties sewage into the Tijuana River, which in turn empties into the estuary. Border Field State Park and the estuary have been closed to public use several times as a result of such sewage spills. In addition, nearby Imperial Beach and Silver Strand State Beach are occasionally closed due to sewage-related problems.

The various resource agencies staff a fine visitor center (open Wednesday through Sunday) that interprets marshland ecology, including the common plants and birds found in the reserve. The reserve has a regular schedule of guided nature hikes.

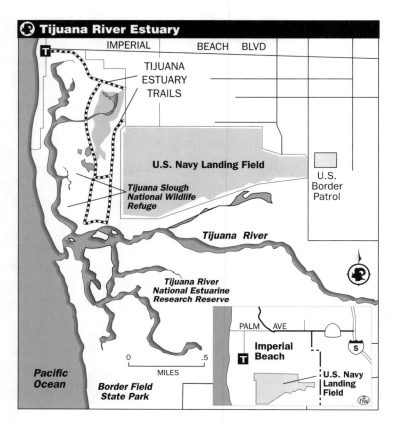

From the visitor center, trails lead into the estuary and continue all the way to the Tijuana River mouth. At times of low water and low tide, the river can be safely crossed, but at times of high water and high tide, crossing can be very dangerous.

At Fifth Street and Iris, a second signed trail leads into the estuary. The path parallels the Ream Field boundary fence. On weekdays, you're sure to see more helicopters hovering over this stretch of trail than appeared in *Apocalypse Now*. Most first-time visitors figure that they must be U.S. Border Patrol copters searching for illegal immigrants crossing the border. Actually, the helicopters from Ream Field are flown by Navy pilots who are practicing their takeoffs, landings and air-sea rescues.

Though the estuary is almost flat, it's not completely flat, and very small changes in elevation bring changes in vegetation. At higher elevations are hillocks of coastal scrub, and at the very lowest elevations are mud flats. Between is a marshland of pickleweed and cordgrass.

For an interesting return route or an addition to your marsh hike, take a walk along wide, sandy Imperial Beach.

DIRECTIONS TO TRAILHEAD From Interstate 5 in Imperial Beach, exit on Palm Avenue. Go west 2.5 miles to Third Street. Turn left and drive half a mile to the visitor center parking lot for the Tijuana River National Estuarine Research Reserve.

■ SWEETWATER MARSH
Center, Cottonseed, Coyote Trails
Around Refuge is 1.5-mile round trip

The Chula Vista—"Beautiful View"—from the observation tower at Chula Vista Nature Center includes a panorama of San Diego Bay, the Silver Strand, Coronado Islands and downtown San Diego. Chula Vista, San Diego County's second-most populous city, gateway to Tijuana and Baja, surprises with its sprawl.

Another beautiful view, for bird-watchers anyway, is that of the considerable native and migratory waterfowl in Sweetwater Marsh National Wildlife Refuge, San Diego Bay's largest remaining wetland. About 90 percent of San Diego Bay's wetlands have been developed or degraded, so the refuge is valuable habitat indeed for the birds and wildlife that feed and breed here.

The 316-acre preserve was established in 1986 to preserve endangered plants and birdlife. One rare and endangered species is the California least tern, the smallest of terns. During the birds' April to August nesting season, they can be glimpsed foraging for food at the mouth of the Sweetwater River. A new nature center exhibit features the rare bird.

The light-footed clapper rail is another protected species. One of the refuge's very rarely seen endangered plants looks like a bird: Salt Marsh's Bird Beak stands eight to

The Chula Vista ("beautiful view") includes many species of birds.

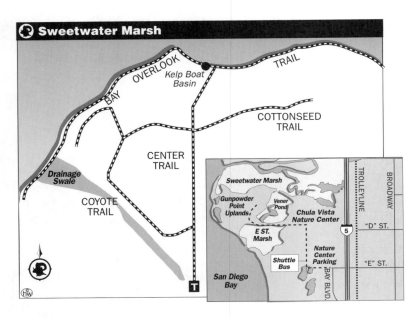

12 inches tall and displays small clusters of cream-colored flowers with yellow tips that look like beaks.

Long before this land became a bird refuge, it was known as Gunpowder Point, the site of the World War I-era Hercules Gunpowder Factory. Harvesters gathered kelp from which the factory extracted acetone; this chemical was used to make cordite, an explosive used for fuses. After the Great War, farmers grew tomatoes and other vegetables on Gunpowder Point.

The city of Chula Vista, in cooperation with the nonprofit Bayfront Conservancy Trust, operates Chula Vista Nature Center, which houses a variety of excellent interpretive displays about coastal wetlands. Children particularly enjoy the fish tanks, videos and interactive exhibits.

A portion of Sweetwater Marsh is accessible by a network of short trails that leave from the Chula Vista Nature Center. Viewpoints offer binoculars-toting hikers (bring your field glasses or rent a pair from the nature center) a chance to view the abundant birdlife. A photo blind helps shutterbugs remain unobtrusive while composing photographs. Guided walks are offered on the weekends.

Getting there can be part of the fun. From Chula Vista's Bayfront Station, a main stop on the San Diego-Tijuana Trolley line, a free shuttle bus carries visitors to the nature center. The Route 708 shuttle (a little bus with a trolley-like design) travels to Chula Vista Nature Center about once every half-hour from 10 A.M. to 5 P.M. There is an admission charge for adults and children over five. The Nature Center and Refuge are closed on Mondays between Labor Day and Memorial Day.

DIRECTIONS TO TRAILHEAD From Interstate 5, about 7 miles south of downtown San Diego and some 7 miles north of the Mexican border, take the E Street exit in Chula Vista. Go west a block to the parking lot and trolley stop.

You can also head east a block on E Street to the Bayfront Trolley Station and Visitor Information Center.

■ CABRILLO NATIONAL MONUMENT
Bayside Trail
From Old Point Loma Lighthouse to National Monument boundary is 2 miles round trip

Cabrillo National Monument, located on the tip of Pt. Loma, marks the point where Portuguese navigator Juan Rodríguez Cabrillo became the first European to set foot on California soil. He landed near Ballast Point in 1542 and claimed San Diego Bay for Spain. Cabrillo liked this "closed and very good port" and said so in his report to the King of Spain.

One highlight of a visit to the national monument is the Old Point Loma Lighthouse. This lighthouse, built by the federal government, first shined its beacon in 1855. Because fog often obscured the light, the station was abandoned in 1891 and a new one was built on lower ground at the tip of Point Loma. (The 1891 lighthouse is still in service today, operated by the U.S. Coast Guard.) The older lighthouse has been wonderfully restored to the way it looked when Captain Israel and his family lived there in the 1880s.

Bayside Trail begins at the old lighthouse and winds past yucca and prickly pear, sage and buckwheat. The monument protects one of the last patches of native flora in southernmost California, a hint at how San Diego Bay may have looked when Cabrillo's two small ships anchored here.

DIRECTIONS TO THE TRAILHEAD Exit Interstate 5 on Rosecrans Street (Highway 209 south) and follow the signs to Cabrillo National Monument.

THE HIKE Before embarking on this easy family hike, obtain a trail guide at the visitor center. The pamphlet describes the coastal sage and chaparral communities, as well as local history.

The first part of the Bayside Trail winding down from the old lighthouse is a paved road. At a barrier, you bear left on a gravel road, once a military patrol road. During World War II, the Navy secreted bunkers and searchlights along these coastal bluffs.

Bayside Trail provides fine views of the San Diego Harbor shipping lanes. Sometimes when ships pass, park rangers broadcast descriptions of the vessels as they pass.

Also along the trail is one of Southern California's most popular panoramic views: miles of seashore, 6,000-foot mountains to the east and Mexico to the south.

The trail dead-ends at the park boundary. Return the way you came.

Old Point Loma Lighthouse

■ MISSION BAY
Mission Bay Trail
From Kendall-Frost Marsh to Sail Bay and Belmont Park is 2 to 6 miles round trip

S ail Bay, Fiesta Bay, Vacation Island and Paradise Island. Is this place named for fun or what?

The fun-in-the-sun place names are highlights of Mission Bay, San Diego's mega-marine playground. Fun comes in many forms here—swimming, sailing, water skiing and cycling.

The walking is pretty good, too. One option is a walk on the wild side through marshland preserves—an ideal opportunity to watch waterfowl. Another kind of wildlife—SoCal beach culture to the max—can be observed from Bayside walk, a walkway on Mission Bay's west side.

Early mariners considered the shallow, marshy bay a hindrance to navigation and repeatedly confused it with more welcoming San Diego Bay. "False Bay" is what 19th-century sailors called Mission Bay.

The bay, a marshland formed by the delta of the San Diego River, deteriorated markedly over the years, and by World War II was even used as a dump. In the early 1960s, the city of San Diego launched an ambitious project to transform the bay into a huge recreational park and world-class resort area. The bay was dredged, waterfront hotels and marinas constructed.

Mission Bay City Park is said to be the largest aquatic park in the world. About 25 percent of the 4,600-acre park, including the famed Sea World, is used for commercial enterprises. The balance, including more than 20 miles of beaches, is for public use.

Prior to the massive dredging and filling that transformed a marshland into a playland, Mission Bay was a haven for resident and migratory birds. Surprisingly, it still is. Loons, egrets, marbled godwits, teals, gulls and many more waterfowl

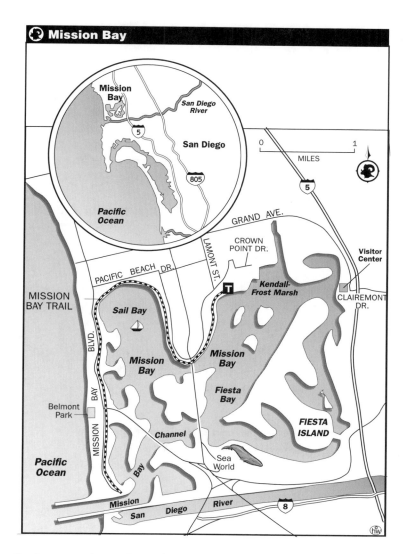

species feed, nest and rest along the bay. The California least tern breeds at a couple of sanctuaries set aside for its preservation.

My favorite Mission Bay hike begins at the Kendall-Frost Marsh Preserve, an environment of cordgrass and pickleweed that hints at how the whole bay may have appeared a hundred years ago. From the preserve, the bayside hike heads into ever-more developed terrain, but definitely fun in its own way.

DIRECTIONS TO TRAILHEAD From Interstate 5 in San Diego, exit on Clairemont Drive. The Visitor Information Center is just west of the freeway. Follow East Mission Bay Drive, then Mission Bay Drive north to Grand Avenue, bearing left (west). Turn left onto Lamont Street and drive to the bay shore at Crown Point Drive. Park in the large lot. Your bay hike adventure begins at the far (east) end of the Crown Point Drive parking lot.

THE HIKE At the east end of the lot is the fenced Kendall-Frost Marsh Reserve, sanctuary for the California least tern. Head southwest along the shell-strewn sand beach, passing water ski take-off and landing areas. The beach, Crown Point Shores, is known for its annual sandcastle building contest.

Your beach path passes below the Ingraham Street overpass leading to Vacation Island, and rounds Crown Point. On the far side of the point, stop to inspect the low eroded cliffs and the old (200,000 years by some estimates) sand dollars poking out of them.

Continue up the beach, known as Riviera Shores here, as you follow horseshoe-shaped Sail Bay. The Bayside Walk begins at Riviera Shores and offers a paved, parallel alternative to beach walking. As you walk south, you'll pass two distinct points—Santa Clara and El Carmel—with a fine sandy beach located between them.

At Mission Bay Drive, visit the long-defunct Belmont Amusement Park, where a huge wooden roller coaster, the Giant Dipper, still stands. A shopping center is the amusement here now.

A good place to relax or unpack your picnic is atop the grassy hillside of Bonita Cove Park. To extend your hike, continue a mile along Bayside Walk to the entrance channel to Mission Bay. For a change of pace, walk the first 2 miles of your return trip along Mission Beach.

■ TORREY PINES BEACH
Torrey Pines Beach Trail
From Scripps Pier to Torrey Pines State Beach is 10 miles round trip

Before or after this hike, check out the Aquarium Museum at Scripps Institute of Oceanography. All manner of local sea creatures are on display in the aquarium. Underwater video cameras provide views of activity in the nearby marine reserve.

Located near the entrance of the aquarium is a dryland tidepool, where the tide rises and falls in two-hour intervals. Kelp planted in the pools provides hiding places for bright orange Garibaldi, rockfish and red snapper. Starfish, barnacles and sea anemones cling to the rocks. A wave generator simulates surf conditions.

This walk begins at Scripps Pier, passes along Torrey Pines City Beach, known locally as Black's Beach, once swimsuit-optional, now enforced suits-only. After walking below some spectacular cliffs and along Torrey Pines State Beach, you'll arrive at Torrey Pines State Reserve, home to the rare and revered *Pinus torreyana*.

Plan your hike for low tide.

DIRECTIONS TO TRAILHEAD Exit Interstate 5 on La Jolla Village Drive, and head west. La Jolla Village Drive becomes North Torrey Pines Road in approximately 1 mile. Turn left on Expedition Way. Parking is to your left, at the bottom of the hill. The Birch Aquarium's parking lot offers 3-hour courtesy parking.

THE HIKE As you look south from Scripps Pier, you'll see long and flat La Jolla Shores Beach, a wide expanse of white sand where the water deepens gradually. This is a family beach, popular during the summer with swimmers.

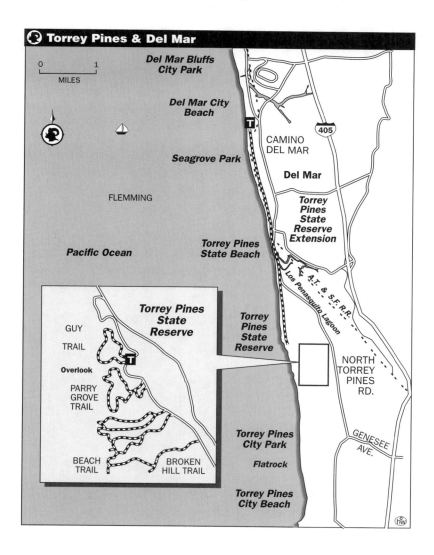

Hiking north, the going is rocky at first; the surf really kicks up around Scripps Pier. Soon the beach widens, growing more sandy, and the spectacular curry-colored cliffs grow higher and higher.

Atop the bluffs is Torrey Pines International Glider Port, where traditional gliders may still be seen flying today.

The 300-foot cliffs tower over Black's Beach, named for William Black, Sr., the oil millionaire who owned and developed most of the land on the cliffs. During the 1970s, Black's Beach enjoyed fleeting notoriety as the first and only public beach in the country on which nudity was legal. Called "a noble experiment" by sun worshippers and "a terrible fiasco" by the more inhibited, the clothing-optional zone was defeated at the polls.

After passing a few more handsome bluffs, you'll spot a distinct outcropping called Flat Rock. Here you may join a bluff trail that leads to Torrey Pines State Reserve.

■ TORREY PINES STATE RESERVE
Parry Grove, Guy Fleming Trails
From 0.4- to 1-mile nature trails

See Map on Page 25

Atop the bluffs of Torrey Pines State Reserve lies a microcosm of old California, a garden of shrubs and succulents.

Most visitors come to view the 3,000 or so *Pinus torreyana,* which grow only here and on Santa Rosa Island, but the reserve also offers the walker a striking variety of native plants.

Be sure to check out the interpretive displays at the park museum and the native plant garden near the head of the Parry Grove Trail. Plant and bird lists, as well as wildflower maps (February through June) are available for a small fee.

Parry Grove Trail was named in honor of Dr. C.C. Parry, a botanist assigned to the boundary commission that surveyed the Mexican-American border in 1850. While waiting for the expedition to start, Parry explored the San Diego area. He investigated a tree called the *Soledad* (Spanish for "solitary") that stood out amidst the surrounding chaparral and other low-lying plant communities. Parry sent samples to his teacher and friend, Dr. John Torrey of Columbia and asked that, if it proved to be a new species, it be named for Torrey. The Soledad pine became *Pinus torreyana,* or Torrey pine, in honor of the famous botanist and taxonomist.

The 0.4-mile loop trail leads past toyon, yucca and many other coastal shrubs. A five-year drought followed by an infestation of the Five Spined Engraver beetle devastated Parry Grove. Only a handful of mature Torrey pines remain, accompanied by saplings planted in 1998.

Broken Hill Trail visits a chaparral-dominated landscape, full of sage and buckwheat, ceanothus and manzanita. From Broken Hill Overlook, there's a

Some 3,000 *Pinus Torreyana* thrive in the state reserve.

view of a few Torrey pines clinging to life in an environment that resembles a desert badlands.

Beach Trail leads to Yucca Point and Razor Point and offers precipitous views of the beach below. The trail descends the bluffs to Flat Rock, a fine tide-pool area.

Guy Fleming Trail is a 0.6-mile loop that travels through stands of Torrey pine and takes you to South Overlook, where you might glimpse a migrating California gray whale.

DIRECTIONS TO TRAILHEAD From Interstate 5, exit on Carmel Valley Road and head west to North Torrey Pines Road (also known as old Highway 101). Carmel Valley Road dead ends at a T; turn left (south) on North Torrey Pines Road. The main entrance to the reserve is at the base of the bluffs, where the park road climbs to a parking area near the reserve visitor center. You can also leave your car along the highway next to Torrey Pines State Beach and walk up the reserve road.

See Map
on Page
25

■ DEL MAR BEACH
Del Mar Beach Trail
From Del Mar Train Station to Torrey Pines State Reserve is 6 miles round trip

Along Del Mar Beach, the power of the surf is awesome and cliff collapse unpredictable. At this beach, permeable layers of rock tilt toward the sea and lie atop other impermeable layers. Water percolates down through the permeable rock, settles on the impermeable rock and "greases the skids"—an ideal condition for collapsing cliffs.

On New Year's Day in 1941, a freight train suddenly found itself in midair. Erosion had undermined the tracks. A full passenger train had been delayed, so the freight train's crew of three were the only casualties.

This walk takes you along the beach, visits the superb Flat Rock tidepool, and detours up the bluffs to Torrey Pines State Reserve. At the reserve, you'll see those relics from the Ice Age, Torrey pines, which grow only atop the Del Mar bluffs and on Santa Rosa Island; no other place in the world.

Consult a tide table and schedule your hike at low tide when there's more beach to walk and tidepool life is easier to observe.

DIRECTIONS TO TRAILHEAD From Interstate 5 in Del Mar, exit on Via de la Valle. Continue west to Highway S21 and turn left (south) along the ocean past the race tracks and fairgrounds to reach the train station, which is no longer an active passenger depot. If you can't find a place to park at the train station, park in town.

Del Mar's cliffs remind some beach hikers of the British seacoast.

THE HIKE From the train station, cross the tracks to the beach and begin hiking south. With the high cliffs on your left and the pounding breakers on your right, you'll feel you're entering another world. Follow the sometimes wide, sometimes narrow beach over sparkling sand and soft green limestone rock. Holes in the limestone are evidence of marine life that once made its home there.

You'll hike past a number of lifeguard towers. When you reach Tower 5, turn left and make a brief detour through the Highway S21 underpass to Los Penasquitos Lagoon, a saltwater marsh patrolled by native and migratory waterfowl. After observing the least terns and light-footed clapper rails, return to the beach trail.

After 3 miles of beachcombing, you'll see a distinct rock outcropping named, appropriately enough, Flat Rock. Legend has it that this gouged-out rock, also known as Bathtub Rock, was the site of a luckless Scottish miner's search for coal. Common tidepool residents housed in the rocks at the base of the bluff include barnacles, mussels, crabs and sea anemones.

Just north of Flat Rock, a stairwell ascends the bluffs to Torrey Pines State Reserve. Torrey pines occupy the bold headlands atop the yellow sandstone; these rare and graceful trees seem to thrive on the foggy atmosphere and precarious footing. The reserve features superb nature trails, native plant gardens and interpretive exhibits.

■ SAN ONOFRE STATE BEACH
Bluffs Beach Trail
From Beach Trail 1 to Beach Trail 6 is 5.6 miles round trip

San Onofre is a place of steep bluffs overlooking a wide, sandy beach. The beach, named for Egyptian Saint Onuphrius, is a joy to walk.

Aptly named Bluffs Beach, part of San Onofre State Beach, is a 3-mile-long sand strand with a backdrop of magnificent, 100-foot high bluffs. The dramatically eroded sandstone cliffs, a kind of Bryce Canyon by the sea, effectively shield the beach from sight and sound of two parallel transportation corridors—the railroad tracks and Interstate 5.

Unfortunately, something of the peaceful ambiance of the park's coastline is diminished by the giant twin spheres of the San Onofre Nuclear Power Plant located just north and Camp Pendleton Marine Base to the south. The nuke and the marines are still very much present, but public access to the splendid beach has loosened up some of late. It's possible to hike a considerable distance both north and south of the power plant.

South of San Onofre State Beach is Camp Pendleton. The camp's beaches are officially off-limits, even if the NO TRESPASSING sign is removed, as it often is. However, the prevailing sentiment among beach-goers is that the military is considerably less proprietary about its surf and turf these days. In the past, some nervous beach-hikers (only half-jokingly) worried about land mines, booby traps or sentries with shoot-to-kill orders.

San Onofre State Beach Campground is actually a length of old Coast Highway with some pull-outs. Charmless it is, but it's popular with surfers and other coastal recreationists who rate beach access over amenities.

And the beach access is first rate. A half-dozen signed trails (Beach Trail 1, Beach Trail 2…) descend from the bluffs to the beach. The paths vary in length from 0.1 to 0.3 mile.

DIRECTIONS TO TRAILHEAD From Interstate 5, a few miles south of San Clemente, exit on Basilone Road. Head west, then south, following the signs to San Onofre State Beach. Park in the first day-use area near the signed trailhead for Beach Trail 1.

THE HIKE I prefer starting with Beach Trail 1 and hiking south along the state beach. From the beaches and bluffs, walkers sometimes spot dolphins, harbor seals and migrating California gray whales.

About 3 miles of beach-hiking brings you to the end of state park property and onto Camp Pendleton's beach. The long sand strand south of the park is popular with nude sunbathers; while it's by no means a legally clothing-optional beach, be advised that many beach-goers opt for none.

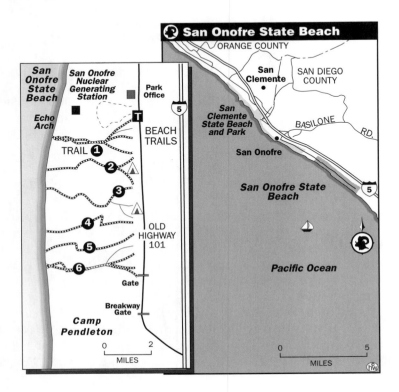

Paths wind among the sandstone bluffs to San Onofre State Beach.

■ SAN CLEMENTE STATE BEACH
Trestles Trail
To San Mateo Point is 3 miles round trip

"Our beach shall always be free from hurdy-gurdies and defilement. We believe beauty to be an asset as well as gold and silver, or cabbage and potatoes."

This was the pledge of Norwegian immigrant Ole Hanson, who began the town of San Clemente in 1925. It was quite a promise from a real estate developer, quite a promise in those days of shameless boosterism a half century before the California Coastal Commission was established.

Thanks in part to Hanson's vision, some of the peaceful ambiance of San Clemente, which he regarded as "a painting five miles long and a mile wide" has been preserved. And some of its isolation, too. Most everyone in the real estate community thought Hanson crazy for building in a locale 66 miles from San Diego, 66 miles from Los Angeles, but today this isolation attracts rather than repels. This isolation was one of the reasons President Richard Nixon (1969–74) established his Western White House in San Clemente.

San Clemente State Beach is a great place for a walk. The beach is mercifully walled off from the din of the San Diego Freeway and the confusion of the modern world by a handsome line of tan-colored bluffs. Only the occasional

train passing over Santa Fe Railroad tracks (located near the shore) interrupt the cry of the gull, the roar of the breakers. The trestles located at the south end of the beach at San Mateo Point give Trestles Beach its name.

Trestles Beach is one of the finest surfing areas on the west coast. When the surf is up, the waves peel rapidly across San Mateo Point, creating a great ride. Before the area became part of the state beach, it was restricted government property belonging to Camp Pendleton Marine Base. For well over 25 years, surfers carried on guerrilla warfare with U.S. Marines. Trespassing surfers were chased, arrested and fined, and on many occasions had their boards confiscated and broken in two. Find a veteran surfer and he'll tell you about escapes from jeep patrols and guard dogs. Many times, however, the cool marines would charitably give surfers rides while out on maneuvers.

This hike's destination, San Mateo Point, is the northernmost boundary of San Diego County, the beginning of Orange County. When the original counties of Los Angeles and San Diego were set up in 1850, the line that separated them began on the coast at San Mateo Point. When Orange County was formed from southern Los Angeles County in 1889, San Mateo Point was established as the southern point of the new county.

The enthusiastic, with the time and inclination, can easily extend this beach-hike several miles south to San Onofre State Beach. Another option worth considering is to take the train to San Clemente and hike south from the Amtrak station.

DIRECTIONS TO TRAILHEAD From the San Diego Freeway (I-5) in San Clemente, exit on Avenida Calafia and head west very briefly to the entrance to San Clemente State Beach or a half-mile to Calafia Beach Park. Expect the usual entrance fee at the state beach, metered parking at Calafia Beach Park.

Northbound motorists on I-5 will exit at Cristianitos Raod, turn left and go over the freeway onto Ave. Del Presidente and drive a mile north to the parks.

Begin this hike from the state beach at the day-use area. Look for two signed beach trails.

THE HIKE From Calafia Beach Park, cross the railroad tracks, make your way down an embankment and head south.

From the state beach day-use area, choose the northern beach access trail which descends the bluffs. You then step over the railroad tracks to the beach. Or take the southern beach access trail, which leads to a pedestrian underpass beneath the tracks to the beach.

As you'll soon see, San Clemente State Beach is frequented by plenty of shorebirds, as well as surfers, body surfers and swimmers.

At distinct San Mateo Point, which marks the border of Orange and San Diego counties, you'll find San Mateo Creek. The headwaters of the creek rise way up in the Santa Ana Mountains above Camp Pendleton. A portion of the creek is protected by the Cleveland National Forest's San Mateo Canyon Wilderness. Rushes, saltgrass and cattails line the creek mouth, where sandpipers, herons and egrets gather.

You can ford the creek mouth (rarely a problem except after winter storms) and continue south toward San Onofre State Beach and the giant domes of San Onofre Nuclear Power Plant. Or you can return the same way.

Or here's a third alternative, an inland return route: Walk under the train trestles and join the park service road, which is usually filled with surfers carrying their boards. The service road takes you up the bluffs, where you'll join the San Clemente Coastal Bike Trail, then wind through a residential area to an entrance to San Clemente State Beach Campground.

Improvise a route through the campground to the park's entry station and join the self-guiding nature trail (brochures available at the station). The path

Trekking to Trestles on the wide sand strand.

descends through a prickly pear- and lemonade berry-filled draw to Calafia Beach Park and the trailhead. The wind- and water-sculpted marine terraces just south of the trailhead resemble Bryce Canyon in miniature and are fun to photograph.

If you want to hike the whole nature trail, you'll walk up to site #70 in the campground, then retrace your steps (100 yards or so) back to the Calafia Beach parking lot.

■ CRYSTAL COVE STATE PARK
Moro Canyon Trail
From Park headquarters to top of Moro Canyon is 7 miles round trip with 700-foot elevation gain

Extending 3 miles along the coast between Laguna Beach and Corona del Mar, and inland over the San Joaquin Hills, 3,000-acre Crystal Cove State Park attracts bird-watchers, beachcombers and hikers.

The backcountry of Crystal Cove State Park is part of the San Joaquin Hills, first used by Mission San Juan Capistrano for grazing land. Cattle raising continued under José Sepúlveda when the area became part of his land grant, Rancho San Joaquín, in 1837. In 1864, Sepúlveda sold the land to James Irvine and his partners and it became part of his Irvine Ranch. Grazing continued until shortly after the state purchased the property as parkland in 1979.

Former Irvine Ranch roads now form a network of hiking trails that loop through the state park. An especially nice trail travels the length of Moro Canyon, the main watershed of the park. An oak woodland, a seasonal stream and sandstone caves are some of the attractions of a walk through this canyon. Bird-watchers may spot the roadrunner, quail, Cooper's hawk, wrentit and many more species.

After exploring inland portions of the state park, allow some time to visit the park's coastline, highlighted by grassy bluffs, sandy beaches, tidepools and coves. The Pelican Point, Crystal Cove, Reef Point and Moro Beach areas of the park allow easy beach access. An offshore area adjacent to the park has been designated an underwater park for divers.

DIRECTIONS TO TRAILHEAD Crystal Cove State Park is located off Pacific Coast Highway, about 2 miles south of the town of Corona Del Mar or 1 mile north of Laguna Beach. Turn inland on the short park road, signed EL MORO CANYON. Drinking water, restrooms, interpretive displays and plenty of parking is available at the ranger station.

Pick up a trails map at the ranger station. At the station, you can consult the schedule of ranger-led interpretive walks, which explore both inland and coastal sections of the state park.

Crystal Cove State Park

0   1
MILES

San Joaquin Hills

MORO
CANYON
TRAIL

Moro Canyon

Pacific
Ocean   Emerald Bay

THE HIKE Below the ranger station, near the park entry kiosk pick up the unsigned Moro Canyon Trail, which crosses the grassy slopes behind a school and drops into Moro Canyon. At the canyon bottom, you meet a fire road and head left, up-canyon.

The walker may observe such native plants as black sage, prickly pear cactus, monkeyflowers, golden bush, lemonade berry and deer weed. Long before Spanish missionaries and settlers arrived in Southern California, a Native American population flourished in the coastal canyons of Orange County. The abundance of edible plants in the area, combined with the mild climate and easy access to the bounty of the sea, contributed to the success of these people; anthropologists believe they lived here for more than four thousand years.

The canyon narrows, and you ignore fire roads joining Moro Canyon from the right and left. You stay in the canyon bottom and proceed through an oak woodland, which shades a trickling stream. You'll pass a shallow sandstone cave just off the trail to the right.

About 2.5 miles from the trailhead, you'll reach the unsigned junction with a fire road. If you wish to make a loop trip out of this day hike, bear left on this road, which climbs steeply west, then northeast toward the ridgetop that forms a kind of inland wall for Muddy, Moro, Emerald and other coastal canyons.

When you reach the ridgetop, unpack your lunch and enjoy the far reaching views of the San Joaquin Hills and Orange County coast and Catalina and San Clemente Islands. You'll also have a raven's-eye view of Moro Canyon and the route back to the trailhead. After catching your breath, you'll bear right (east) along the ridgetop and quickly descend back into Moro Canyon. A 0.75-mile walk brings you back to the junction where you earlier ascended out of the canyon. This time you continue straight down-canyon, retracing your steps to the trailhead.

■ CORONA DEL MAR
Crown of the Sea Trail
From Corona del Mar Beach to Arch Rock is 2 miles round trip; to Crystal Cove is 4 miles round trip; to Abalone Point is 7 miles round trip

In 1904, George Hart purchased 700 acres of land on the cliffs east of the entrance to Newport Bay and laid out a subdivision he called Corona del Mar ("Crown of the Sea"). The only way to reach the townsite was by way of a long muddy road that circled around the head of Upper Newport Bay. Later a ferry carried tourists and residents from Balboa to Corona del Mar. Little civic improvement occurred until Highway 101 bridged the bay and the community was annexed to Newport Beach.

This hike explores the beaches and marine refuges of Big and Little Corona del Mar beaches and continues to the beaches and headlands of Crystal Cove State Park. Snorkeling is good beneath the cliffs of Big and Little Corona beaches. Both areas are protected from boat traffic by kelp beds and marine refuge status.

Consult a tide table. Best beach-hiking is at low tide.

Little Corona and Arch Rock.

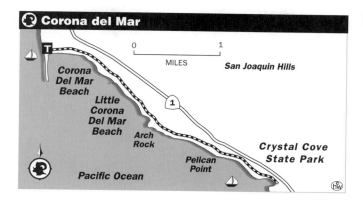

DIRECTIONS TO TRAILHEAD From Pacific Coast Highway in Corona del Mar, turn oceanward on Marguerite Avenue and travel a few blocks to Ocean Boulevard. Turn right and you'll soon spot the entrance to the Corona del Mar State Beach parking lot.

THE HIKE Begin at the east jetty of Newport Beach, where you'll see sailboats tacking in and out of the harbor. Surfers tackle the waves near the jetty. Proceed down-coast along wide sandy Corona del Mar State Beach.

At the south end of the beach, take the paved walkway and ascend to Inspiration Point, an overlook offering excellent views of the Orange County coast. Continue down-coast a few blocks on the sidewalk alongside Ocean Boulevard to the walkway leading down to Little Corona Beach. The highlight of this beach is well-named Arch Rock, which is just offshore and can be reached at very low tide.

The beach from Arch Rock to Irvine Cove, 2.5 miles to the south, is passable at low tide and is part of Crystal Cove State Park. Trails lead up the bluffs which, in winter, offer a good vantage point from which to observe the California gray whale migration.

Continuing your stroll down the undeveloped beach and past some tidepools brings you to the onetime resort community of Crystal Cove, site of a few dozen funky beach cottages. The wood frame cottages, little altered since their construction in the 1920s, are on the National Register of Historic Places. Some of the cottages are being restored and rented out by the night as vacation getaways.

While "Cove" is something of a misnomer here because the beach here shows almost no coastal indentation, it certainly is a pretty place. Rounding Reef Point, you'll continue along El Moro Beach, a sand strand that's sometimes beautifully cusped. The state park is transforming what was once a beach lined with private trailers into a day-use area with beach access from a campground and the other side of Highway 1.

The round dome of Abalone Point lies dead ahead. The point, a rocky promontory located just outside Laguna Beach city limits, is made of eroded lava and other volcanic material distributed in the San Joaquin Hills. It's capped by a grass-covered dome rising two hundred feet above the water.

Return the same way or ascend one of the coastal accessways to the blufftops of Crystal Cove State Park. Blufftop trails offer a scenic alternative for a portion of your return route.

■ BALBOA ISLAND
Balboa Beach Trail
From Newport Pier to Balboa Island is 3 miles round trip

Miles of sandy beach, one of California's largest pleasure craft harbors, and some colorful coastal history are attractions of a walk along Balboa Beach. Balboa—the town, beach and island—was long ago (1906) incorporated into the city of Newport Beach, but has managed to hold onto a different look, feel and vibe than chic Newport.

Local boosters and real estate promoters built the Balboa Pier and Balboa Pavilion in 1905 with hopes of luring both tourists and well-heeled settlers. They succeeded on both counts. Today, Balboa's sand strand hosts huge crowds of surfers and sun-worshipers and as one harbor cruise company boasts, "You'll see some of the most expensive coastal real estate in the world."

On the Balboa beach-hike you'll also encounter two historic piers and a chance to take the ferry to Balboa Island.

By foot and ferry to Balboa Island.

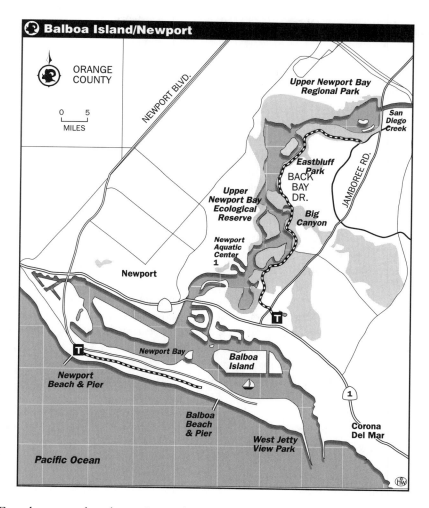

For those weekend warriors who scoff at the mere 3-mile round trip distance between Newport Pier and Balboa Pier, I recommend starting your beach hike at popular Huntington State Beach, 3 miles north.

If you trek this longer option, you'll begin your 10-mile hike by heading down-coast on Huntington Beach, once called Shell Beach because millions of small bean clams were washed up on its sands. In recent years, Pismo clamming has undergone something of a revival here.

At the south end of the beach you'll cross the Santa Ana River on the coast highway bridge. Formerly, the river emptied into the ocean at Newport Bay, but was diverted to shore at this point in order to reduce silting after the bay became a great yacht harbor. Next you'll head shoreward over some sand dunes on the east side of the river, then hike down-coast on Santa Ana River County Beach to Newport Pier.

DIRECTIONS TO TRAILHEAD Head southwest on the Costa Mesa Freeway (Highway 55) toward Newport Beach. In Costa Mesa, the highway empties out onto Newport Boulevard, which you'll follow to its end at the beach. Just as Newport Boulevard angles sharply southeast and puts you on Balboa Boulevard, you'll spot Newport Pier and a number of parking lots. Parking in these parts is mostly metered. Beware that some of the meters give you only an hour; you'll need more time to enjoy this hike.

THE HIKE Begin at the historic Newport Pier, oldest in Southern California. A wharf built here in 1888 served as a railway shipping point for Orange County produce. The railroad also carried passengers here from Santa Ana and helped foster the development of the city of Newport Beach.

Almost a century ago, the Newport Dory fishing fleet began working the waters off Balboa Peninsula. The fishermen are still at it, still headquartered at the foot of Newport Pier. Each dawn, the fleet heads out to sea and returns to the pier in mid-morning to sell its catch of rockfish and sea bass, crab and lobster.

Hike down-coast along the beach. The beach, particularly the stretch north of the pier, looks like a quintessential postcard-perfect seashore, but has occasionally suffered from erosion and lack of sand. Orange County's inland building booms diverted many streams from their normal paths to the sea; the streams were unable to perform their natural function of carrying a cargo of sand to the Pacific. More sand is lost to the Newport Submarine Canyon, located just offshore.

About 1.5 miles of beach-walking brings you to the Balboa Pier, where a plaque commemorates the site of the first water-to-water flight in 1912. Glenn L. Martin flew a hydroplane from the waters here to Avalon Bay at Catalina Island.

Near the pier is Peninsula Park with picnic tables. Hike into town on Main Street, crossing East Balboa Boulevard and coming to the marina. Harbor tour companies are based here. You can join a short cruise of Newport Harbor or do-it-yourself by renting a pedal-boat or kayak.

Walk along the historic Balboa boardwalk. Remodeling and new construction have obliterated most of the early building prompted by the extension of electric railway service from Los Angeles in 1905. Still standing is that landmark of Victorian architecture, the Balboa Pavilion. The Pavilion has served as a Pacific Electric Railway Terminal, a seaside recreation center and a 1940s dancehall. Next to the Pavilion is the Fun Zone, a small collection of rides and arcades.

From the foot of Palm Street, right along the boardwalk, you can catch the Balboa Ferry, which runs frequently. Ferry service was inaugurated in 1907 by a genial African-American boatman named John Watts, who encouraged his open launch, *The Teal,* with great draughts from an oil can. Today's small auto ferries make the 200-yard or so voyage in fewer than five minutes.

On Balboa Island, you can follow a scenic boardwalk to boat slips and small sandy beaches. Balboa Island had its beginning in 1906 when W.S. Collins dredged bay mud onto a sand flat that appeared in Newport Bay during low tide. He subdivided the island and by 1914, more than one half the 1,300 lots were sold.

After you've enjoyed the island, take the ferry back to the peninsula and return the same way.

See Map on Page 39

■ NEWPORT'S BACK BAY
Backbay Trail
Along Upper Newport Bay Ecological Reserve is 3.5 miles one way

Southern California's coastal wetlands have suffered severely from the pressures of the expanding metropolis. But one wetland that has been partially spared from development is Upper Newport Bay in Orange County. In 1974, Orange County and the Irvine Corporation reached an agreement calling for public ownership of Upper Newport Bay, most of which has become a state-operated ecological reserve.

The Upper Bay is a marked contrast to the huge marina complex, one of the world's largest yacht harbors, of the Lower Bay—developments once planned for the Upper Bay. The preservation of Upper Newport Bay is one of Southern California conservationists' success stories.

The wetland is a premier bird-watching spot. Plovers stand motionless on one leg, great blue herons pick their way carefully across the mudflats, flotillas of ducks patrol the shallows. Out of sight, mollusks, insects, fish and protozoa provide vital links in the complex food chain of the estuary.

Upper Newport Bay: A prime bird-watching locale.

This hike follows one-way Back Bay Road which really should be closed to motorized traffic. However, on weekdays, there's rarely much traffic and on weekends, there's seldom more auto traffic than bike traffic. The tideland is fragile; stay on established roads and trails.

DIRECTIONS TO TRAILHEAD From Pacific Coast Highway in Newport Beach, turn inland onto Jamboree Road, then left on Back Bay Drive. The one-way road follows the margin of the bay. Park along the road.

THE HIKE As you hike along the road, notice the various vegetation zones. Eel grass thrives in areas of almost constant submergence, cord grasses at a few feet above mean low tide, salt wort and pickleweed higher on the banks of the estuary. Keep an eye out for three of California's endangered birds: Beldings Savanna Sparrow, the California least tern and the light-footed clapper rail.

Old levees and an occasional trail let you walk out toward the main bodies of water. Also, a trail from the University of California at Irvine extends along the west side of the reserve.

■ BOLSA CHICA LAGOON
Bolsa Chica Lagoon Trail
3 miles round trip

Bolsa Chica Wetlands, a 1,800-acre tidal basin surrounded by the city of Huntington Beach, is one of Southern California's most valuable ocean-front properties. The somewhat degraded marshland was the scene of a long

Oil wells everywhere: Bolsa Chica and Huntington Beach in the 1930s.

dispute between Signal Oil Company, the principal landholder, which desired to develop a marina and suburb, and Amigos de Bolsa Chica, a group that wanted to preserve the marsh as a stopover for migratory birds on the Pacific Flyway and as habitat for endangered species.

For many centuries, the wetlands were the bountiful home of Indians until a Mission-era land grant gave retiring Spanish soldier Manuel Nieto title to a portion of Bolsa Chica. Although the coastal marsh proved useless for farming and ranching to Nieto and succeeding owners, the abundant wildlife attracted game hunters from all over

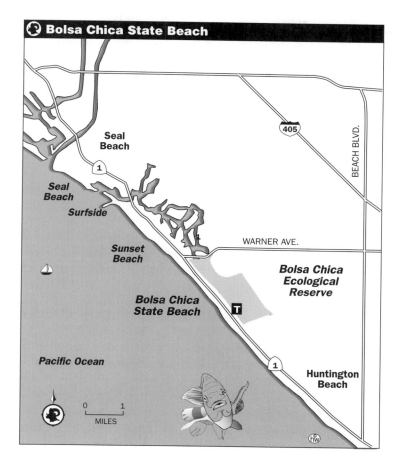

Southern California. In order to stabilize their duck pond, they dammed off the ocean waters, thus starting the demise of the wetland.

During the 1920s, oil was discovered at Bolsa Chica. Dikes were built, water drained, wells drilled, roads spread across the marsh. In fact, oil production is scheduled to continue through the year 2020.

Portions of the marsh bordering Pacific Coast Highway have been restored by the state and are now part of an ecological reserve under Department of Fish and Game management. This loop trail takes you on a tour of the most attractive section. Bring your binoculars. Bird-watching is often quite good here.

DIRECTIONS TO TRAILHEAD Bolsa Chica Ecological Reserve is located just opposite the main entrance of Bolsa Chica State Beach on Pacific Coast Highway. From the San Diego Freeway (405), exit on Beach Boulevard and follow it to the beach. Head north on Pacific Coast Highway for 3 miles to the reserve entrance.

THE HIKE At the trailhead is a sign imparting some Bolsa Chica history. Cross the lagoon on the bridge, where other signs offer information about marshland plants and birds. The loop trail soon begins following a levee around the marsh. You'll pass fields of pickleweed and cordgrass, sun-baked mudflats, the remains of oil drilling equipment. Three endangered birds—Savananna sparrow, clapper rail, California least tern—are sometimes seen here.

At the north end of the loop, you may bear right on a closed road to an overlook. As you return, you cross the lagoon on another bridge and return to the parking area on a path paralleling Pacific Coast Highway.

■ LONG BEACH
Long Beach Trail
From Long Beach Aquarium to Long Beach City Beach is 3 miles round trip; to Belmont Pier is 6 miles round trip; to Naples is 8 miles round trip; to Alamitos Bay is 10 miles round trip

Long Beach Aquarium of the Pacific stunningly recreates the three distinct ecosystems of the Pacific Rim: Southern California and Baja, the Northern Pacific and the Tropical Pacific. Southern California exhibits interpret the tidepools just off Long Beach and a kelp forest. Boisterous seals and sea lions bask on Catalina Island's coast. Puffins and sea otters populate the Northern Pacific exhibit while thousands of brilliantly colored fish swim among coral reefs in the Tropical Pacific galleries.

The new aquarium is having a pronounced ripple effect on the city's economy and waterfront environment. Adjacent Pacific shores have been revitalized—meaning a Long Beach that's easier on the eye and much more pleasant for the adventurer afoot.

From the aquarium, take a short walk along a rejuvenated waterfront now called Rainbow Harbor to the Shoreline Village shopping center or opt for a more ambitious sojourn along long Long Beach. This jaunt travels L.A. County's southernmost coast from just south of the mouth of the Los Angeles River to just north of the mouth of the San Gabriel River.

During the first mile of this shoreline saunter, the walker gets various views of the *Queen Mary,* the largest passenger ship ever built. The 1,000-foot-long British luxury liner was launched in 1934, served as a troop ship during World War II, was retired in 1964 and is now a Long Beach-owned tourist attraction and hotel.

Once past Shoreline Village and the city marina, the Long Beach explorer can continue on the paved beach bicycle/pedestrian path or hit the beach and walk along water's edge.

You can certainly take a very long hike along Long Beach; the well-named strand is very long—and quite wide in places as well. The coastal town was first

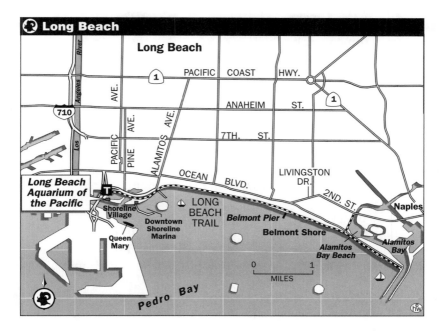

named Willmore City for W.W. Willmore, who developed it in 1880 and colonized it with emigrants from Kansas City. Few lots sold. In 1887, the Long Beach Land and Water Company took over, giving the community its name.

Long Beach City Beach extends nearly 5 miles from the city's downtown marina to Alamitos Bay. The beach, 100 yards wide in places, offers some of the finest and most gentle ocean swimming in Southern California. An ocean breakwater, constructed in the 1940s, protects the shore from all but the most southerly swells.

Those preferring a one-way ramble along Long Beach, can return to the aquarium by Long Beach Transit bus. Catch the westbound Route D bus from the corner of Bayshore Ave. and Second Street and enjoy the inexpensive ride to the corner of 1st and Pine Avenue. Meander the now-trendy Pine Avenue, then board the Route C bus (free) for the short ride back to the aquarium.

DIRECTIONS TO TRAILHEAD Head south on the Long Beach Freeway (710) to its end and follow the Downtown Long Beach/Aquarium signs. The signs lead you onto Shoreline Drive and to the Aquarium's multi-level, 1,500-vehicle parking structure on the right. (A common error for first-time visitors is to look left and mistake that large round building painted with sea creatures for the aquarium; actually, it's the Sports Arena.)

THE HIKE Leaving the wave-shaped aquarium behind, follow the beige- and brown- brick road along Rainbow Harbor. The soothing strains of classical music emanating from the loudspeakers lining the esplanade add to the Oz-like quality of the waterfront.

You'll soon pass the Pine Avenue Pier where *The California*, the state's official tall ship is sometimes berthed.

Follow the promenade as it travels under the pedestrian overpass that links the convention center to the waterfront and you'll soon arrive at Shoreline Village, a waterside shopping center. Two detours beckon: (1) Follow the boardwalk past the shops and eateries of Shoreline Village. (2) Head out on the Long Beach Marina breakwater for good views of the pleasure craft and the *Queen Mary.*

This walk leaves both the breakwater and Shoreline Village behind and continues a less-than-scintillating half mile or so down-coast along the inland side of the marina to a second breakwater and the beginning of Long Beach City Beach. At the south breakwater, the bike-pedestrian path continues beneath the bluffs, but the better, quieter walking is right along the beach.

Walk along the wide sandy beach, sometimes called Long Beach Strand, past the downtown area. On summer weekends, you'll pass brigades of beach-goers; at other times, in other seasons, the walk is a more tranquil one, often in the company of curlews, godwits, sandpipers and other shorebirds.

Continuing along the sand, you'll cross into the trendy Belmont Shores and reach the 1,620-foot-long Belmont Pier. From the pier, a mile's walk brings you to the foot of Bay Shore Avenue. For a fun side trip, follow the avenue a mile around the horseshoe of Alamitos Bay to Appian Way Bridge. Cross the bridge to Naples, a residential community of three islands separated by canals. Explore "Naples of America," via waterfront walkways that lead along the canals, past some intriguing residences and over to Naples Plaza, a palm-lined park off 2nd Street.

The wave-shaped Long Beach Aquarium of the Pacific is a fun place to learn more about the Pacific Rim's coasts and oceans.

(The corner of 2nd Street and Bay Shore Ave. is a good place to catch the bus back to the aquarium.)

Those determined to complete the last leg of the Long Beach walk will head out onto Alamitos Peninsula, which extends from 54th Place to the entrance channel of Alamitos Bay. You can stick with the sandy and rocky beach or join Bay Shore Walk, a public walkway that extends along the bay from 55th to 65th Place.

■ CABRILLO BEACH
Cabrillo Beach Trail
From Cabrillo Beach to White Point is 3.5 miles round trip

This coastal hike has a little of everything: Cabrillo Beach, the only real sand beach for miles to the north and south; the family-friendly Cabrillo Marine Aquarium; historic White Point, an intriguing chapter from coastal SoCal's history.

The mission of the Cabrillo Marine Aquarium is to promote knowledge and conservation of marine life in Southern California and this it does well, with exhibits interpreting the region's mudflats, kelp forest, sandy beach and other environments. The aquarium sponsors tidepool walks and grunion watches and is a coordinating point for whale-watching cruises. Open daily except Mondays, the aquarium attracts scores of school groups.

Nearly all but forgotten today, the rocky cove just down coast from White Point in San Pedro once flourished as a Roaring Twenties health spa and resort. All that remains today are some sea-battered cement ruins and lush overgrown gardens.

White Point was originally settled at the beginning of the 20th century by immigrant Japanese fishermen who harvested the bountiful abalone from the waters off Palos Verdes Peninsula. Tons of abalone were shipped to the Far East and tons more were consumed locally in Los Angeles' Little Tokyo. In a few years the abalone was depleted, but an even greater resource was discovered at White's Point—sulfur springs.

In 1915 construction of a spa began. Eventually the large Royal Palms Hotel was built at water's edge. Palm gardens and a golf course decorated the cliffs above. The sulfur baths were especially popular with the Japanese population of Southern California.

The spa boomed in the 1920s, but the 1933 earthquake closed the springs. The cove became part of Fort McArthur during World War II, the Japanese-American settlers were incarcerated in internment camps and the resort was soon overwhelmed by crumbling cliffs and the powerful sea.

Some maps and colorful local histories refer to White's Point as a place named for a 19th-century sailor who jumped ship and swam ashore to this point. Other sources say the point name honors Senator Stephen White, who

led the fight to locate the Port of Los Angeles in San Pedro. The definitive word from the San Pedro Historical Society is that the white shale of White Point has made it a landmark for generations of mariners, and hence the name.

Look for the new White Point Natural Preserve on the inland side of Paseo Del Mar across from Royal Palms County Beach. Plans call for nature trails and rejuvenation of the coastal scrub and coastal prairie habitats. Other trails will interpret the fascinating local history, explore the hills and lead to overlooks for whale-watching.

DIRECTIONS TO TRAILHEAD Take the Harbor Freeway south to San Pedro and exit on Gaffey Street. Follow Gaffey seaward to 1st Street, turn left and travel a quarter mile to Pacific Avenue. Turn right and travel south 2.5 miles to 36th Street. Fee parking is available in the large lot that serves Cabrillo Beach and the Cabrillo Marine Aquarium.

THE HIKE March up sandy Cabrillo Beach, which has a monopoly on the grunion, since the sand-seeking fish have few other spawning options along

Palos Verdes Peninsula. You'll soon pass the San Pedro breakwater and reach the Cabrillo Bath House.

Just up-coast from Cabrillo Beach is the rocky shoreline of Point Fermin Marine Life Refuge. Cabrillo Coastal Park Trail (a concrete path across the beach and a boardwalk along the cliffs) assists visitors of all abilities to reach the rocky shores of the Point Fermin Marine Life Refuge and the sandy shore of the inner beach.

After rock-hopping among the tidepools, you must double-back on Cabrillo Coastal Park Trail because it is all but impossible to walk around Point Fermin via the shoreline route.

Follow a dirt path or the paved road up to the top of the coastal bluffs; walk steeply uphill along Bluff Place through a residential area to a parking lot at the terminus of Pacific Avenue. Join a blufftop trail, which soon leads past the remains of "Sunken City," a 1930s housing tract built on bluffs that soon collapsed. Palm trees and huge chunks of asphalt are all that remain of the oceanside housing tract.

The dirt path delivers the hiker to Point Fermin Park. Continue on the park's paved pathway past the puzzlingly named Point Fermin Cetacean & Community Building to the handsome Victorian-style Point Fermin Lighthouse. Built in 1874 from materials shipped around Cape Horn, the lighthouse was a welcome beacon to approaching sailors. Lighthouse tours are offered every afternoon except Monday at 1, 2 and 3 PM.

At the up-coast edge of the park, take the walkway paralleling Paseo Del Mar. On the inland side of the roadway lies Joan Milke Flores Park, where paths depart to such attractions as the Korean Friendship Bell and the Fort MacArthur Military Museum, as well as Angels Gate Park and Lookout Point Park.

From atop the landscaped bluff, a coastal access-way at the foot of Meyler Street and another at the foot of Barbara Street lead down to the rocky shores. At low tide, plucky rock-hoppers can reach White Point in this way.

Bluff-top hikers will continue to the end of the linear park and continue another 0.4 mile the White Point Bluff Park. A combination of paved and dirt pathways advance toward White Point. Look across Paseo Del Mar for the entrance to the new White Point Nature Preserve.

An unsigned coastal access-way leads to the cobbled beach on the downcoast side of White Point, however, most hikers will prefer to continue across the bluffs and enjoy the fabulous clear-day vistas of Catalina Island. Along the way, interpretive plaques describe the natural and cultural attractions of White Point. An entry kiosk heralds your arrival at Royal Palms County Beach. Motorists pay for the privilege of driving down to park at the beach, but hikers may enter for free.

Near White Point, you'll see a palm garden with fire pits. Royal Palms Hotel was once situated here until overcome by the sea. Storm-twisted palms and curious cement remains are reminders of the resort and flush times long passed.

Beyond the point stretch the rugged cliffs and cobblestone shores of Palos Verdes Peninsula. Return the same way or, if you have the time and the tide is right, walk on. The difficult terrain will ensure that few follow in your footsteps.

■ PALOS VERDES PENINSULA
Palos Verdes Peninsula Trail
From Malaga Cove to Rocky Point is 5 miles round trip; to Point Vincente Lighthouse is 10 miles round trip

Palos Verdes Peninsula is famous for its rocky cliffs, which rise from 50 to 300 feet above the ocean and for its thirteen wave-cut terraces. These terraces, or platforms, resulted from a combination of uplift and sea-level fluctuations caused by the formation and melting of glaciers. Today the waves, as they have for so many thousands of years, are actively eroding the shoreline, cutting yet another terrace onto the land.

While enjoying this walk, you'll pass many beautiful coves, where whaling ships once anchored and delivered their cargo of whale oil. Large iron kettles, used to boil whale blubber, have been found in sea cliff caves. Spanish rancheros and Yankee smugglers have all added to the Peninsula's romantic history. Modern times have brought white-stuccoed, red-tiled mansions to the Peninsula bluffs, but the beach remains almost pristine. Offshore, divers explore the rocky bottoms for abalone and shellfish. Onshore, hikers enjoy the wave-scalloped bluffs and splendid tidepools.

Hiking this beach is like walking over a surface of broken bowling balls. The route is rocky and progress slow, but that gives you more time to look down at the tidepools and up at the magnificent bluffs.

Check a tide table and walk only at low tide.

DIRECTIONS TO TRAILHEAD Take Pacific Coast Highway to Palos Verdes Boulevard. Bear right on Palos Verdes Drive. As you near Malaga Cove Plaza, turn right at the first stop sign (Via Corta). Make a right on Via Arroyo, then another right into the parking lot behind the Malaga Cove School. The trailhead is on the ocean side of the parking area where a wide path descends the bluffs above the Flatrock Point tidepools. A footpath leaves from Paseo Del Mar, 0.1 mile past Via Horcada, where the street curves east to join Palos Verdes Drive West (see map on page 51).

THE HIKE From the Malaga Cove School parking lot, descend the wide path to the beach. A sign indicates you're entering a seashore reserve and asks you to treat tidepool residents with respect. To the north are sandy beaches for sedentary sun-worshipers. Active rock-hoppers clamber to the south. At several places along this walk you'll notice that the great terraces are cut by steep-walled

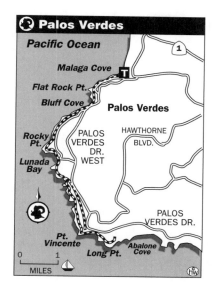

canyons. The first of these canyon incisions can be observed at Malaga Cove, where Malaga Canyon slices through the north slopes of Palos Verdes Hills, then cuts west to empty at the cove.

The coastline curves out to sea in a southwesterly direction and Flatrock Point comes into view. The jade-colored waters swirl around this anvil-shaped point, creating the best tidepool area along this section of coast. Above the point, the cliffs soar to 300 feet. Cloaked in morning fog, the rocky seascape here is reminiscent of Big Sur.

Rounding Flatrock Point, you pick your way among the rocks, seaweed and the flotsam and jetsam of civilization to Bluff Cove, where sparkling combers explode against the rocks and douse the unwary with their tangy spray. A glance over your right shoulder brings a view of Santa Moncia Bay, the Santa Monica Mountains in gray silhouette and on the far horizon, the Channel Islands.

A mile beyond Bluff Cove, Rocky (also called Palos Verdes) Point juts out like a ship's prow. Caught fast on the rocks at the base of the point is the rusting exoskeleton of the Greek freighter *Dominator,* a victim of the treacherous reef surrounding the Peninsula.

Trek around Rocky Point to Lunada Bay, a good place to observe the terrace surfaces. From here you'll walk under almost perpendicular cliffs that follow horseshoe-shaped Lunada Bay. Shortly you'll round Resort Point, where fishermen try their luck. As the coastline turns south, Catalina can often be seen glowing on the horizon. Along this stretch of shoreline, numerous stacks, remnants of former cliffs not yet dissolved by the surf, can be seen.

The stretch of coast before the lighthouse has been vigorously scalloped by thousands of years of relentless surf. You'll have to boulder-hop the last mile to Point Vincente. The lighthouse has worked its beacon over the dark waters since 1926. Guided tours of the lighthouse are available by appointment.

Passage is usually impossible around the lighthouse at high tide; if passable, another half mile of walking brings you to an official beach access (or departure) route at Long Point.

■ PALOS VERDES HILLS
Portuguese Bend Trail

From Del Cerro Park to Badlands Slide Area is 3.5 miles
round trip with 400-foot elevation gain

The little-known and infrequently traveled trails of Palos Verdes Peninsula offer the walker a tranquil escape from metropolitan life. During the spring, the hills are colored an emerald green and sprinkled with wildflowers.

This short loop trip, suitable for the whole family, explores the hills above Portuguese Bend, one of the most geologically interesting (and unstable) areas in Southern California. Earth movement during 1956–57 wrecked approximately 100 homes. The rate of movement was more than an inch a day!

Portuguese Bend takes its name from the men who practiced the risky, but lucrative, business of shore whaling. Most of the hardy whalers who worked the waters off Palos Verdes Peninsula from the 1850s to the 1880s were of Portuguese descent. Many a whale was slaughtered, but the Peninsula whaling operation was abandoned, not for lack of gray whales, but because of a shortage of the fuel necessary to process blubber into oil.

The Palos Verdes Peninsula Land Conservancy and the City of Rancho Palos Verdes are working to purchase and preserve the remaining open space (700 acres) in Portuguese Bend and to create a substantial preserve with more than 20 miles of trails. This comprises the largest unprotected coastal land between Laguna Beach and the Santa Monica Mountains.

The Portuguese Bend area is honeycombed with trails. Just remember, it's all downhill from the trailhead and it's a mighty steep return trip. Some experienced PV hikers descend to the beach to meet friends, who drive them back up to the trailhead.

The route I've dubbed Portuguese Bend Trail links various path and fire roads and offers great clear-day views of the Peninsula and Catalina Island.

DIRECTIONS TO TRAILHEAD From the San Diego Freeway (405) in Torrance, exit on Crenshaw Boulevard and head south. Continue on Crenshaw past Pacific Coast Highway and into the hills of Rancho Palos Verdes. Park at boulevard's end at the side of the road or at nearby Del Cerro Park.

THE HIKE Head down the unsigned fire road, which is officially named Crenshaw Extension Trail. Leaving red-roofed multimillion-dollar residences behind, you'll look ahead to a multimillion-dollar view. The green hills, bedecked with lupine in the spring, roll to the sea. Geology students will observe the Peninsula's unique blend of native brush and imported flora gone wild.

A half-mile descent from the trailhead brings you to a water tank and an unsigned three-way intersection. The leftward trail climbs to a fire station. The trail dead-ahead will be your return route on this walk. Continue right with

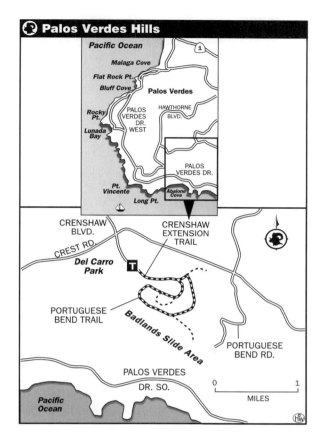

Crenshaw Extension Trail, which soon drops into a wildflower-splashed mead-ow known as Peacock Flats. It's doubtful you'll see a peacock here, but you might here the shrill call of the "watchdog of the Peninsula" from other parts of the trail. The aggressive birds are popular pets around here, but they do get on the nerves of local residents, some of whom favor banishing them from the area.

Above Peacock Flats, two short trails lead up a hill topped with a dozen pine trees. From the crest of the hill, known as Eagle's Nest, you'll have grand clear-day views of Catalina. The nest is close to the southwestern-most point of the Peninsula, meaning Catalina is but 17 nautical miles away; often many of the island's geographical features are identifiable.

Return to the main trail, which heads northwest, then makes a long horse-shoe bend to the southeast. After descending past a stand of eucalyptus and a water tank, you'll begin crossing the geologically unstable terrain known as Badlands Slide Area.

A good turnaround point is at about 1.75 from the trailhead. Enjoy the view, take a deep breath, and ascend back up the hill.

■ CATALINA: OUT OF AVALON
Avalon Canyon, Memorial Road, Divide Road, Hermit Gulch Trails

From Avalon to Botanical Garden is 3 miles round trip with 200-foot elevation gain; return via Hermit Gulch Trail is 6.5 miles round trip with 1,000-foot gain

Botanical Garden is a showcase for plants native to Catalina, and to the Channel Islands. At the head of the canyon is the imposing Wrigley Memorial, a huge monument honoring chewing gum magnate William Wrigley, who purchased most of the island in 1919.

Families with children, and those visitors looking more for a walk than a hike, will enjoy the trip as far as Botanical Garden. More adventurous hikers will undertake the second, more strenuous part of this loop trip; it utilizes fire roads and Hermit Gulch Trail and offers a sampling of Catalina's rugged and bold terrain.

DIRECTIONS TO TRAILHEAD Several boat companies offer ferry service to Catalina, with departures from San Diego, Newport Beach, Long Beach and San Pedro. The 22-mile crossing to Catalina takes about two hours. For more information about ferryboat schedules, island services and accommodations, call the Catalina Island Chamber of Commerce.

If you intend to hike into the Catalina backcountry (anywhere past the Botanical Garden) you must secure a free hiking permit from the Los Angeles County Department of Parks and Recreation. The department operates an information center in the Island Plaza, located at 213 Catalina Street.

Avalon: a short ferry ride from the mainland—and a world apart.

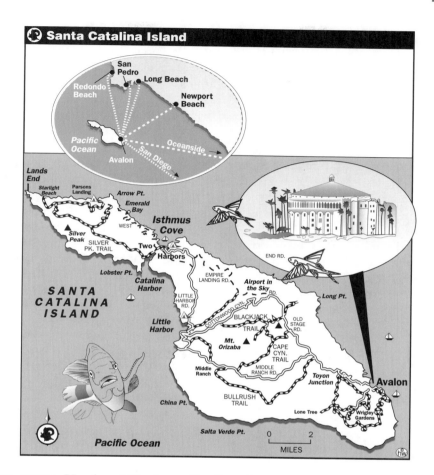

Santa Catalina Island

THE HIKE Head uphill along Catalina Street, which soon joins Avalon Canyon Road, passes a few residences and begins a 1.5-mile ascent toward the Botanical Garden. On your right, watch for one of William Wrigley's many contributions to the island, Bird Park, which once held thousands of unusual birds in the "largest bird cage in the world." Bird Park is now a campground. On the left side of the road, bleacher bums still stop and pay homage to the one-time spring training camp of Wrigley's beloved Chicago Cubs.

At the end of the road is Botanical Garden (fee for entry). The garden began in the 1920s, when Wrigley's wife Ada began planting native and exotic plants in Avalon Canyon. More recently, the garden has greatly expanded, emphasizing native Southern California flora. Particularly interesting are plants endemic to Catalina, including Catalina mahogany, Catalina manzanita, Catalina live-forever and Catalina ironwood.

Proceed up the dirt path to the Wrigley Memorial. At one time, Wrigley's body was entombed here. Climb up the many stairs to the 232-foot-wide, 130-foot-high monument, and enjoy the great view of Avalon Harbor.

At this point, intrepid hikers will pass through the unlocked gate below and to the right of the memorial and stride up Memorial Road. Scrub oak, manzanita and lemonade berry—and many more of the native plants featured in the botanical garden—grow wild along the fire road.

The vigorous ascent on Memorial Road offers better and better views of Avalon Harbor. It's likely your approach will flush a covey or two of quail from the brush. Practiced birders might recognize the Catalina quail, a slightly larger and slightly darker subspecies than its mainland relatives.

Memorial Road reaches a divide and, appropriately enough, intersects Divide Road. Bear right. From the 1,000-foot-high divide, partake of commanding views of both sides of the island and of the mainland.

Continue along the divide, which bristle with prickly pear cactus. The slopes below are crisscrossed with trails made by the island's many wild goats. After about 0.75 mile of walking atop the divide, bear right on unsigned Hermit Gulch Trail. This trail is difficult to spot and the early going is steep. The trail descends 2.4 miles along a waterless canyon back to Avalon Canyon Road, at a point a few hundred yards below the Botanical Garden. Turn left and saunter downhill back to Avalon.

See Map
on Page
55

■ CATALINA: BLACK JACK
Black Jack Trail
From Black Jack Junction to Little Harbor is 8 miles one way
with 1,500-foot elevation loss

Catalina's terrain is rugged and bold, characterized by abrupt ridges and V-shaped canyons. Many of the mountaintops are rounded, however, and the western end of the island is grassland and brush, dotted with cactus and seasonal wildflowers. Bison, deer, boar and rabbits roam the savannas.

This hike is a good introduction to the island; it samples a variety of terrain on the island, inland and coastal. Transportation logistics are a bit complex, but the trail is easy to follow.

DIRECTIONS TO TRAILHEAD From Avalon, travel to the trailhead via the Catalina Island Interior Shuttle Bus (fee), which departs from the information center in Island Plaza. Secure the necessary hiking permit (free) from the center.

THE HIKE At signed Black Jack Junction, there's a fire phone and good views of the island's precipitous west ridges.

The trail, a rough fire road, ascends for 1 mile over brush- and cactus-covered slopes. You'll pass the fenced, but open shaft of the old Black Jack Mine (lead, zinc and silver). On your left a road appears that leads up to Black Jack

Mountain, at 2,006 feet in elevation the island's second highest peak. Continue past this junction.

Ahead is a picnic ramada with a large sunshade and a nearby signed junction. You may descend to Black Jack Camp, which is operated by Los Angeles County. Here you'll find tables, shade and water. Set in a stand of pine, the camp offers fine channel views.

Bear right on signed Cottonwood/Black Jack Trail. A second junction soon appears. Continue straight downhill. The other trail ascends Mt. Orizaba (2,097 feet), Catalina's highest peak.

The trail drops through a steep walled canyon, whose vegetation—chaparral and grassland—is favored by a large herd of wild goats. At the bottom of the canyon, pass through three gates of a private ranch. (Close all gates behind you.)

The trail reaches the main road connecting Little Harbor with Airport-in-the-Sky. You may bear left at this junction and follow the winding road 3.5 miles to Little Harbor. For a more scenic route of about the same distance, turn right on the road. Hike about 200 yards to the end of the ranch fence line, then bear left, struggling cross-country briefly through spiny brush and intersect a ranch road. This dirt road follows the periphery of the fence line on the east side of the ranch to the top of a canyon. You bear left again, still along the fence line. Ascend and then descend, staying atop this sharp shadeless ridge above pretty Big Springs Canyon. When you begin descending toward the ocean, you'll spot Little Harbor.

Little Harbor is the primary campground and anchorage on the Pacific side of the island. It's a good place to relax while you're waiting for the shuttle bus, or to refresh yourself for the hike through buffalo country to Two Harbors.

See Map
on Page
55

■ CATALINA: LITTLE HARBOR
Little Harbor Trail
From Little Harbor to Two Harbors is 7 miles one way

From a distance, the mountainous land on Catalina's east end appears to be separated from a smaller portion on the west end; in fact, it's an optical illusion. The eye is tricked by a low-lying isthmus, the narrowest section of the island. Catalina Harbor lies on the ocean side of this isthmus, Isthmus Cove on the channel side, and together this area is called Two Harbors.

As the Wrigley family opened the island to tourism, Two Harbors pursued a destiny apart from Avalon. During the 1920s and 1930s, it was a peaceful sanctuary for Hollywood celebrities and the elite Southland yachting set.

This hike leads across the island from the Pacific side to the Channel side and offers fine views and a chance to observe buffalo. Your destination is Two Harbors, popular with campers and boaters.

DIRECTIONS TO TRAILHEAD A shuttle bus transports you across the island from Avalon to Little Harbor and can pick you up in Two Harbors for the return to Avalon. If you purchased a ferry ticket from the mainland to Avalon, it's possible to leave the island from Two Harbors if you make arrangements with the ferry company.

THE HIKE From Little Harbor, a onetime stagestop turned popular campground and anchorage, join Little Harbor Road and begin ascending higher and higher into Little Springs Canyon.

Buffalo graze both sides of the canyon and two reservoirs have been developed for the animals. In 1924, when Hollywood moviemakers were filming Zane Grey's classic Western, *The Vanishing American,* 14 buffalo were brought to the island. Recapturing them after filming proved impossible so the beasts were left to roam. The animals adapted well to life on Catalina and quickly multiplied. Today's population is held at 400 to 500, the ideal number for available pasturage.

At an unsigned junction a mile past Lower Buffalo Reservoir, bear left on Banning House Road, which leads 3.25 miles to Two Harbors. (Little Harbor Road continues north, then west, to Two Harbors if you prefer to stick to this road.) Rough Banning House Road ascends very steeply up a canyon roamed by wild boar. At the windswept head of the canyon, hikers are rewarded with superb views of the twin harbors of Catalina Harbor and Isthmus Cove, and can see both the eastern and western fringes of the island.

A steep northeasterly descent brings you to the outskirts of Two Harbors. Improvise a route past ranchettes and private clubs to the ferry building.

Catalina's backcountry: where the buffalo roam.

See Map on Page 55

■ CATALINA: WEST END
West End Trail

From Two Harbors to Cherry Cove is 3.5 miles round trip with 300-foot elevation gain; to Parsons Landing Campground is 14 miles round trip with 800-foot gain

Even the names sound intriguing: Cherry Cove and Parsons Landing, Arrow Point and Emerald Bay. Catalina's west end is a very special place—a series of bold headlands and crescent-shaped coves.

The coastal hills and canyons extending between Two Harbors and Parsons Landing is more botanically intact (i.e. less eaten by feral goats and pigs) than other parts of the island. The windswept oak and chaparral environments are thriving.

The walk from Two Harbors to Cherry Cove is a pleasant family outing on fairly level trail. The jaunt to Parsons Campground, 7 miles west, is a long, but not particularly rugged hike.

DIRECTIONS TO TRAILHEAD Two Harbors is accessible via ferries departing from San Pedro, as well as ferries from Avalon (summer only). If you can work out the logistics with the ferry schedule, you might be able to arrange transportation to or from Parsons Landing and make this a one-way hike.

THE HIKE From Isthmus Cove Beach, look for the trail ascending 50 yards to an intersection with West End Road. Go west. Looking oceanward, you'll spy Bird Rock, a white rock that's a landmark for sailors. Western gull guano gives the rock its distinctive white color.

Geology-minded hikers will pause to look down at the Catalina schist, the fine-grained metamorphic rock that forms the shoreline. You'll pass Fourth of July Cove, a mooring that was the site of Independence Day celebrations held by the Banning family when they owned the island.

A 1.25-mile walk brings you to Cherry Cove named for that large, waxy-leafed native shrub, the Catalina cherry that thrives in the mouth of a wide, V-shaped valley. Through the valley you go, passing, over the next few miles, a number of scout and group camps, as well as private moorings. Particularly beautiful is aptly named Emerald Bay.

Six miles from Two Harbors, you'll pass an intersection with Boushay Trail (a dirt road) on your left. Staying right, walk another 0.5-mile. Leave West End Road as it bends left and join a trail that leads through grassland to Parsons Landing Campground.

■ PASEO MIRAMAR
Los Liones Canyon, East Topanga Fire Road Trails
From Los Liones Drive to The Overlook is 6 miles round trip
with 1,500-foot elevation gain; from Paseo Miramar to The
Overlook is 5 miles round trip with 1,200-foot gain

Rugged Los Liones Canyon is but a mile from Sunset Boulevard, but very much apart from the Westside city scene. "The Overlook" offers grand views of West Los Angeles and Santa Monica Bay.

This walk explores the coastal slopes of Topanga State Park, sometimes billed as "the largest state park within a city limit in the U.S." Your goal is a viewpoint sometimes called Parker Mesa Overlook, sometimes called Topanga Overlook, but most often simply called The Overlook. Views of West Los Angeles and the sweep of Santa Monica Bay are superb. Sunset (the descending day star, not the winding boulevard) views are often inspiring.

Two trails help you reach the inspiring view. Los Liones Canyon Trail travels through its namesake canyon to East Topanga Fire Road which, in turn, leads to Topanga Overlook. Or the walker may head directly for The Overlook via the fire road.

From The Overlook, the ambitious hiker can trek into the main part of Topanga State Park.

Grand views of Santa Monica Bay unfold from Pacific Palisades pathways.

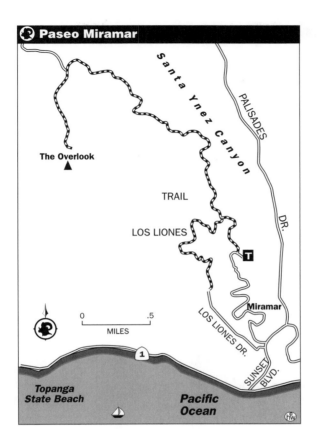

DIRECTIONS TO TRAILHEAD (To Los Liones Drive trailhead) From Pacific Coast Highway in Pacific Palisades, turn inland on Sunset Boulevard for 0.25 mile. Turn left on Los Liones Drive and follow it to road's end and a small parking area. Don't park in the adjacent church lot.

(To Paseo Miramar) From Sunset Boulevard, proceeding inland, the next left after Los Liones Drive is Paseo Miramar. Follow this winding road through a residential area to its end at a vehicle gate across East Topanga Fire Road. Park safely and considerately on Paseo Miramar.

THE HIKE (From Los Liones Canyon) March past the vehicle gate and follow the trail into the canyon. After 0.25 mile, the trail begins to climb in earnest, switchbacking through the chaparral.

After leveling out for a stretch, the path then switchbacks even more earnestly through thickets of ceanothus. Los Liones Trail intersects East Topanga Fire Road about 0.25-mile from the road's beginning at Paseo Miramar.

Turn left (northwest) on the fire road and continue your ascent. For a short while the road travels a cool, north slope and you get good over-the-right-shoulder views of neighboring Santa Ynez Canyon, a canyon that's wild and dramatic in its upper reaches (in the state park) and atrociously subdivided in its lower reaches outside park boundaries.

A two-mile ascent along the fire road brings you to a junction with a trail leading south along a bald ridge. Join this trail, which travels 0.5-mile to The Overlook. Enjoy clear-day panoramas of Westside L.A., Santa Monica Bay, Palos Verdes and Catalina Island.

■ MALIBU BEACH
Malibu Beach Trail
1 mile round trip around Malibu Lagoon; to Corral State Beach is 4 to 6 miles round trip

When Southern California natives say "Malibu Beach" this popular surfing spot is what they mean: the site of beach-blanket movies and Beach Boys songs. The state beach—formerly known as Surfrider—is a mixture of sand and stone. More than 200 bird species have been observed at Malibu Lagoon.

For Frederick Hastings Rindge, owner of 22 miles of Southern California coast, life in the Malibu of a century ago was divine. "The enobling stillness makes the mind ascend to heaven," he wrote in his memoir, *Happy Days in Southern California,* published in 1898.

Long before Malibu meant good surfing, a movie star colony and some of the most expensive real estate on earth, "The Malibu" was a shorthand name for Topanga Malibu Sequit, an early nineteenth-century rancho. This rancho extended from Topanga Canyon on the southeast to Ventura County on the northwest, from the tideline to the crest of the Santa Monica Mountains.

This beautiful locale attracted the attention of a wealthy Massachusetts businessman, Frederick Rindge, who was looking for an ideal spread "near the ocean, and under the lee of the mountains, with a trout brook, wild trees, good soil and excellent climate, one not too hot in summer."

Rindge bought the ranch and proceeded to divide his time between a townhouse in Los Angeles, from which he directed his business affairs—and his beloved rancho. The New Englander-turned-ranchero gloried in rounding up cattle, inspecting citrus groves and walking his St. Bernard along his many miles of private shoreline.

Alas for Frederick Rindge, his happy days ended rather abruptly when a 1903 fire burned his property. He died just two years later. His widow, May Rindge, decided to keep the rancho intact and to keep the public out of her coastal kingdom. Armed guards patrolled the dominion of the woman the newspapers called "The Queen of Malibu." For more than three decades, she not only stopped tourists and settlers, but blocked the state from completing Pacific Coast Highway. Eventually, however, the whole rancho was subdivided

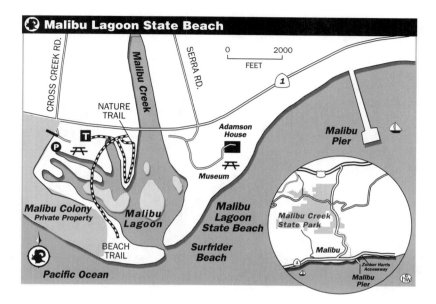

into ocean front lots and 100-acre "ranchos," as well as sites for hotels, yacht clubs and small summer homes.

Malibu Lagoon hosts many different kinds of waterfowl, both resident and migratory. The beach is rock cobble on the ocean side of the lagoon. To the landward side of the lagoon stretches the alluvial fill flatland deposited by Malibu Creek. The town of Malibu is situated here.

Across from the lagoon is a stunning California landmark, the Adamson House, a beautiful Spanish-style home built by Frederick Rindge's daughter, Rhoda Adamson. The house, built in 1929, makes lavish use of ceramic "Malibu Tile." The grounds have been restored to their former beauty, with many ornamental trees and shrubs. Fountains and flagstone pathways wind through the landscaped grounds.

Adjoining the Adamson House is the Malibu Lagoon Museum, which contains a collection of artifacts and rare photographs that depict the various eras of "The Malibu," as this section of coastal Southern California was known.

DIRECTIONS TO TRAILHEAD Malibu Lagoon State Beach is located at Pacific Coast Highway and Cross Creek Road in Malibu.

THE HIKE First follow the nature trails around the lagoon. Next, head down-coast to the historic 700-foot Malibu Pier, built in 1903. It's a favorite of anglers and tourists. Sportfishing boats depart from the pier.

Farther down-coast is Zonker Harris Accessway, long the focus of debate between the California Coastal Commission, determined to provide access to the coast, and some Malibu residents who would prefer the public stay out. The

Sea lion basks on "The Colony" beach.

original sign read ZONKER HARRIS MEMORIAL BEACH, honoring a character from the Doonesbury comic strip whose primary goal in life was once to acquire the perfect tan.

Up-coast, you'll pass Malibu Point; here the strong southwest swell refracts against a rock reef and creates the waves that make Malibu so popular with surfers. Next you walk the narrow and sandy beach lined by the exclusive Malibu Colony residences, home to many a movie star. Toward the west end of The Colony, the beach narrows considerably and houses are built on stilts, with the waves sometimes pounding beneath them.

As you hike along Malibu Beach, rejoice that you do not see State Highway 60, the Malibu Freeway. In the 1960s a plan was hatched to build a causeway along Malibu Beach, supported on pilings offshore. A breakwater would have converted the open shore into a bay shore. The wonderful pounding surf would have been reduced to that of a lake.

The beach is wider and more public at Corral State Beach, located at the mouths of Corral and Solstice Canyons.

■ SAN FERNANDO VALLEY TO THE SEA

Lemming Trail

From Caballero Canyon to Will Rogers State Beach is 12 miles one way with 2,000-foot elevation gain; a pleasant 4-mile round trip walk through Caballero Canyon is a gentler alternative

You won't find any lemmings along the Southern California coast; the furry, short-tailed, mice-like creatures inhabit Arctic, not Mediterranean climes. The Lemming Trail takes its name not from the rodent's presence in the Santa Monica Mountains, but from its proclivity to rush headlong into the sea.

A crisp, cool winter or spring day is a great time to make like a lemming and hike from the San Fernando Valley to the sea. The Lemming Trail offers a grand tour of the Santa Monica Mountains, from Tarzana to Topanga to Temscal to the Pacific on a network of trails and fire roads and rewards the dogged hiker with superb coastal vistas.

Though the Lemming Trail was named for a small rodent, be assured that this is no Mickey Mouse hike. Prepare for a very long and strenuous day.

Caballero Canyon is the starting point for this long journey, but is also a pleasant destination in its own right. It provides a back-door entrance to Topanga State Park. For years conservationists have resisted developments in Caballero Canyon and a proposed extension of Reseda Boulevard. The canyon has been the scene of some lively protests.

DIRECTIONS TO TRAILHEAD This is a one-way walk so a car shuttle or a helpful non-hiking friend to assist with the transportation logistics is necessary. Leave one car at Will Rogers State Beach (fee) or along Pacific Coast Highway (free) near the intersection of the Coast Highway and Temescal Canyon Road. Next proceed up-coast on PCH to Topanga Canyon Road (27) and drive inland through the canyon to Ventura Boulevard. Turn right (east) and head into Tarzana. Turn right on Reseda Boulevard and follow this road to its end. (A quick route to the Lemming trailhead is to exit the Ventura Freeway (101) on Reseda Boulevard and drive east to its end.)

THE WALK From Marvin Braude Mulholland Gateway Park, follow the trail up to Mulholland Drive.

Turn right onto Mulholland and after walking a half-mile, look leftward for the Bent Arrow Trail, which will take you into Topanga State Park. Follow this trail, which at first parallels Mulholland, for 0.5 mile as it contours around a steep slope and reaches Temescal Fire Road (Fire Road 30). Turn left and begin a moderate descent. After a mile and a half, you'll pass junctions with fire roads on your right leading to Eagle Rock and Eagle Spring. Continue straight ahead past these junctions on the sharp ridgeline separating Santa Ynez and Temescal

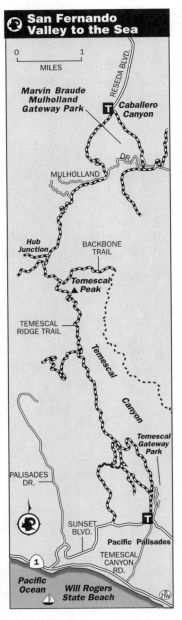

Canyons. You'll pass the junction with Rogers Road which leads to Will Rogers State Historic Park. Near the intersection of Rogers Road and Temescal Fire Road is Temescal Peak (2,126 feet), highest peak in Topanga State Park. If you wish, scramble up a short and steep firebreak to the top for a fine view.

After one and a half miles of mostly level walking beyond the Rogers Road intersection, you'll pass Trailer Canyon Road and a mile farther south, Split Rock Road. A microwave tower, atop what locals have dubbed "Radio Peak," stands halfway between the points.

As you descend along the ridge, you'll see some rock outcroppings. A short side trip off the fire road will bring you to Skull Rock, where you can climb inside the wind-formed (aeolian) caves to cool off or picnic. From the ridgetop, the view to the southwest down at the housing developments isn't too inspiring, but the view of the rough unaltered northern part of Temescal Canyon is superb.

Temescal Fire Road narrows and switchbacks down into Temescal Canyon. You might want to stop and cool off at the small waterfall here at the Temescal Creek crossing at the bottom of the canyon. Your route crosses over to the east side of the canyon and descends the canyon bottom on a trail shaded by oaks, willows and sycamores.

You'll join a paved road and hike through the Presbyterian Conference Center, then join paved Temescal Canyon Road—or improvise a parallel route down canyon through the narrow park.

After crossing Sunset Boulevard, you'll walk an easy mile through Temescal Canyon Park to Pacific Coast Highway. Across Coast Highway is Will Rogers State Beach. Local mountaineering tradition dictates that you emulate the lemming and rush into the sea.

■ POINT DUME
Zuma-Dume Trail
From Zuma Beach to Point Dume is 1 mile round trip; to Paradise Cove is 3 miles round trip

*Z*uma Beach is one of Los Angeles County's largest sand beaches and one of the finest white sand strands in California. Zuma lies on the open coast beyond Santa Monica Bay and thus receives heavy breakers crashing in from the north. From sunrise to sunset, board and body surfers try to catch a big one. Every month the color of the ocean and the cliffs seem to take on different shades of green depending on the season and sunlight, providing the Zuma Beach hiker with yet another attraction.

During the whale-watching season (approximately mid-December through March), hikers ascending to the lookout atop Point Dume have a good chance of spotting a migrating California gray whale.

This hike travels along that part of Zuma Beach known as Westward Beach, climbs over the geologically fascinating Point Dume Headlands for sweeping views of the coast, then descends to Paradise Cove, site of a romantic little beach and a fishing pier.

DIRECTIONS TO TRAILHEAD From Pacific Coast Highway, about 25 miles up-coast from Santa Monica and just down coast from Zuma Beach County Park, turn oceanward on Westward Beach Road and follow it to its end at a (fee) parking lot.

Consult a tide table. Passage is easier at low tide.

THE HIKE Proceed down-coast along sandy Westward Beach. You'll soon see a distinct path leading up the point. The trail ascends through a plant community of sea fig and sage, coreopsis and prickly pear cactus to a lookout point.

From atop Point Dume, you can look down at Pirate's Cove, two hundred yards of beach tucked away between two rocky outcroppings. In past years, this beach was the scene of much dispute between nude beach advocates, residents and the county sheriff.

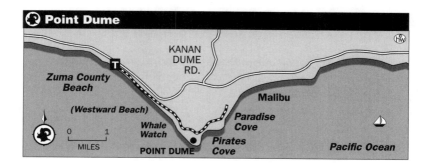

As you stand atop the rocky triangle projecting into the Pacific, observe the dense black Zuma volcanics and the much softer white sedimentary beds of the sea cliffs extending both east and west. The volcanics have resisted the crashing sea far better than the sedimentary rock and have protected the land behind from further erosion, thus forming the triangle shape of the point.

After enjoying the view and watching for whales, retrace your steps a short distance and continue on the main trail over the point, which has been set aside as a preserve under the protection of the California Department of Fish and Game. A staircase lets you descend to the beach.

A mile of beach-walking brings you to Paradise Cove, sometimes called Dume Cove. It's a secluded spot, and the scene of much television and motion picture filming. The Paradise Cove Restaurant and a private pier are located at the cove. The $25 parking fee tends to restrict the number of beach-goers.

Point Dume surf.

■ NICHOLAS FLAT
Nicholas Flat Trail
From Leo Carrillo State Beach to Nicholas Flat is 7 miles round trip with 1,600-foot elevation gain

Leo Carrillo State Beach has always been a popular surfing spot. Surfers tackle the well-shaped south swell, while battling the submerged rocks and kelp beds. In recent years, the state added a large chunk of Santa Monica Mountains parkland, prompting a name change to Leo Carrillo State Park.

The park is named after Angeline Leo Carrillo, famous for his TV role as Pancho, the Cisco Kid's sidekick. Carrillo, the son of Santa Monica's first mayor, was also quite active in recreation and civic affairs.

The park's Nicholas Flat area is one of the best spots in the Santa Monica Mountains for spring wildflowers because it's a meeting place for four different plant communities. Chaparral, grassland, coastal scrub and oak woodland all converge near the flat. Another reason for the remarkable plant diversity is Leo Carrillo's elevation, which varies from sea level to nearly 2,000 feet.

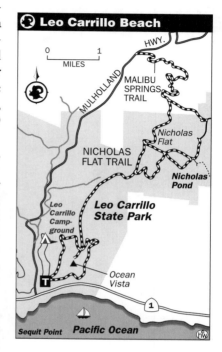

Along park trails, look for shooting star, hedge nettle, sugar bush, hollyleaf redberry, purple sage, chamise, blue dick, deer weed, burr clover, bush lupine, golden yarrow, fuschia-flowered gooseberry and many more flowering plants. Around Nicholas Pond, keep an eye out for wishbone bush, encelia, chia, Parry's phacelia, ground-pink, California poppy, scarlet bugler and goldfields.

Even when the wildflowers fade away, Nicholas Flat is worth a visit. Its charms include a big meadow and a pond patrolled by coots. Atop grand boulders you can enjoy a picnic and savor Malibu coast views.

Nicholas Flat Trail can also be savored for one more reason: In Southern California, very few trails connect the mountains with the sea. Get an early start. Until you arrive at oak-dotted Nicholas Flat itself, there's not much shade en route.

DIRECTIONS TO TRAILHEAD From the west end of the Santa Monica Freeway in Santa Monica, head up-coast on Pacific Coast Highway about 25 miles to Leo Carrillo State Beach. There's free parking along Coast Highway, and fee parking in the park's day-use area.

THE HIKE Signed Nicholas Flat trailhead is located a short distance past the park entry kiosk, opposite the day-use parking area. Soon the trail splits. The right branch circles the hill, climbs above Willow Creek, and after a mile, rejoins the main Nicholas Flat Trail. Enjoy this interesting option on your return from Nicholas Flat.

Take the left branch, which immediately begins a moderate to steep ascent of the grassy slopes above the park campground. The trail switchbacks through a coastal scrub community up to a saddle on the ridgeline. Here you'll meet the alternate branch of Nicholas Flat Trail. From the saddle, a short side trail leads south to a hilltop, where there's a fine coastal view. From the viewpoint, you can see Pt. Dume and the Malibu coastline. During the winter, it's a good place to bring your binoculars and scout the Pacific horizon for migrating whales.

A hiker enjoys the Nicholas Flat Trail.

Following the ridgeline, Nicholas Flat Trail climbs inland over chaparral-covered slope. Keep glancing over your right shoulder at the increasingly grand coastal views, and over your left at the open slopes browsed by the park's nimble deer.

After a good deal of climbing, the trail levels atop the ridgeline and you get your first glimpse of grassy, inviting Nicholas Flat. The trail descends past a line of fire-blackened, but unbowed, old oaks and joins an old ranch road that skirts the Nicholas Flat meadows. Picnickers may unpack lunch beneath the shady oaks or out in the sunny meadow. The trail angles southeast across the meadow to a small pond. The human-made pond, used by cattle during the region's ranching days, is backed by some handsome boulders.

Return the way you came until you reach the junction located 0.75 mile from the trailhead. Bear left at the fork and enjoy this alternate trail as it descends into the canyon cut by Willow Creek, contours around an ocean-facing slope, and returns you to the trailhead.

See Map on Page 69

■ LEO CARRILLO BEACH
Leo Carrillo Beach Trail
Leo Carrillo State Park to Ventura County line is 3 miles round trip

Angeline Leo Carrillo is best remembered for his movie role, then 1950's TV part as the Cisco Kid's sidekick. He and his prominent family were quite active in recreation and civic matters and it's altogether fitting he is remembered by this beach on the Ventura/Los Angeles county line.

Leo Carrillo Beach is stabilized to some extent by minor rocky breaks in the shoreline and by extensive kelp beds offshore. Seals sometimes come ashore (don't disturb). The beach is a popular locale for moviemakers, and after the propertymaster installs palm trees the beach doubles for a South Seas locale.

The beach trail follows an interesting and fairly natural length of coastline. At Sequit Point you'll find good surfing, swimming, skin diving and a cluster of caves and coves.

DIRECTIONS TO TRAILHEAD Leo Carrillo State Park is located on Pacific Coast Highway just down-coast from its junction with Mulholland Highway near the Ventura/Los Angeles county line. Park along PCH (free) or the state park (fee).

THE HIKE Head up-coast toward Sequit Point. The point bisects the beach, forming a bay to the south. Surfers tackle the well-shaped south swell, battling the submerged rocks and kelp beds.

Nearing the point, you'll pass a path which leads under the highway and connects the beach with the sycamore-shaded campground. Scramble around the rocks of Sequit Point to several rock formations, caves, coves, a rock arch and some nice tidepools.

Many a movie is filmed at Leo Carrillo Beach.

North of the point, Leo Carrillo Beach offers good swimming with a sandy bottom. The unspoiled coast here contrasts with development in the county line area. When the beach narrows and the houses multiply, return the way you came.

■ POINT MUGU STATE PARK
Sycamore Canyon Trail
From Big Sycamore Canyon to Deer Camp Junction is 6.5 miles round trip with 200-foot elevation gain; return via Overlook Trail is 10 miles round trip with 700-foot gain

Every fall, millions of monarch butterflies migrate south to the forests of Mexico's Transvolcanic Range and to the damp coastal woodlands of Central and Southern California. The monarch's awe-inspiring migration and formation of what entomologists call over-wintering colonies are two of nature's most colorful autumn events.

All monarch butterflies west of the Rockies head for California in the fall; one of the best places in Southern California to observe the arriving monarchs is the campground in Big Sycamore Canyon at Point Mugu State Park.

The monarch's evolutionary success lies not only in its unique ability to migrate to warmer climes, but in its mastery of chemical warfare. The butterfly feeds on milkweed—the favored poison of assassins during the Roman Empire. This milkweed diet makes the monarch toxic to birds; after munching a monarch or two and becoming sick, they learn to leave the butterflies alone.

The butterflies advertise their poisonous nature with their conspicuous coloring. They have brownish-red wings with black veins. The outer edge of the wings is dark brown with white and yellow spots. While one might assume the monarch's startling coloration would make them easy prey for predators, just the opposite is true; bright colors in nature are often a warning that a creature is toxic or distasteful.

Sycamore Canyon Trail takes you through a peaceful wooded canyon, where a multitude of monarchs dwell, and past some magnificent sycamores. The sycamores that shade the canyon bearing their name are incomparable. The lower branches, stout and crooked, are a delight for tree-climbers. Hawks and owls roost in the upper branches.

The trail follows the canyon on a gentle northern traverse across Point Mugu State Park, the largest preserved area in the Santa Monica Mountains. This trail, combined with Overlook Trail, gives the hiker quite a tour of the park.

During October and November, Sycamore Canyon offers the twin delights of falling autumn leaves and fluttering butterflies. (Ask park rangers where the monarchs cluster in large numbers.)

Sycamore and La Jolla Beach

La Jolla

Deer
Camp
Junction

BACKBONE
TRAIL

GUADALASCA
TRAIL

OVER-
LOOK
TRAIL

SYCAMORE
CYN. TRAIL

SERRANO
CYN. TRAIL

LA JOLLA
CYN.
TRAIL

La Jolla Beach

Pacific
Ocean

The Great
Sand Dune

Sycamore Cove Beach

0   1

MILES

1

DIRECTIONS TO TRAILHEAD Drive up-coast on Highway 1, 32 miles from Santa Monica, to Big Sycamore Canyon Campground in Point Mugu State Park. Outside the campground entrance is an area where you may park.

THE HIKE Hike past the campground entrance through the campground to a locked gate. The trail begins on the other side of the gate. Take the trail up-canyon, following the creek. Winter rains cause the creek to rise, and sometimes keeping your feet dry while crossing is difficult. Underground water keeps much of the creekside vegetation green year-round—so this is fine hike in any season.

One half mile from the campground you'll spot Overlook Trail, which switchbacks to the west up a ridge and then heads north toward the native tall grass prairie in La Jolla Valley. Make note of this trail, an optional return route. A second half mile of nearly level canyon walking brings you to another major hiking trail that branches right—Serrano Canyon Trail, an absolute gem.

Another easy mile of walking beneath the sycamores brings you to a picnic table shaded by a grove of large oak trees. The oaks might be a good turn-around spot for a family with small children. The total round trip distance is a little over 4 miles.

Continuing up the canyon you'll pass beneath more of the giant sycamores and soon arrive at Wood Canyon Junction, the hub of six trails which lead to all corners of the park. Bear left on signed Wood Canyon Trail and in a short while you'll reach Deer Camp Junction. Drinking water and picnic tables suggest a lunch stop. Oak trees predominate over the sycamores along Wood

Canyon Creek; however, the romantic prefer the sycamores, some of which have large clumps of mistletoe in the upper branches.

You can call it a day here and return the way you came. As you hike down the canyon back to the campground, the large and cranky blue jay population will scold you, but don't let the squawking birds stop you from enjoying one of California's finest sycamore savannas.

To return via Overlook Trail: Continue past the junction with Wood Canyon Trail and Deer Camp Junction on the Wood Canyon Trail, which becomes Pumphouse Road. You'll climb over the divide between Sycamore Canyon and La Jolla Valley. Upon reaching a junction, you'll head south on the Overlook Trail, staying on the La Jolla Canyon side of the ridge. True to its name, Overlook Trail offers good views of grassy mountainsides, Boney Peak and Big Sycamore Canyon.

You'll pass an intersection with Scenic Trail, a rough path that hugs the ridge separating La Jolla and Big Sycamore Canyon, where you'll bear right and follow the fire road a half mile back to the trailhead.

See Map
on Page
73

■ LA JOLLA VALLEY
La Jolla Valley Loop Trail
From Ray Miller Trailhead to La Jolla Valley is 7 miles round trip with 700-foot elevation gain; return via Overlook Trail, Ray Miller Trail is 7 miles round trip with 800-foot gain

Ringed by ridges, the native grassland of La Jolla Valley welcomes the walker with its drifts of oak and peaceful pond. This pastoral upland in the heart of Point Mugu State Park is unique: it has resisted the invasion of non-native vegetation. It's rare to find native grassland in Southern California because the Spanish introduced oats and a host of other foreign grasses for pasture for their cattle. In most cases, the imported grasses squeezed out the natives, but not in La Jolla Valley.

La Jolla Valley Loop Trail passes a small waterfall and tours the beautiful grasslands of the valley. This is a fine pathway to follow during the spring when wildflowers and numerous coastal shrubs are in bloom; this is a trail that smells as good as it looks.

Another way to loop through the park is to make use of Ray Miller Trail. Sometimes called La Jolla Ridge Trail, this trail is the beginning (or the end, depending on how you view the mountains) of the Backbone Trail. The path offers terrific coastal views and nicely complements the park's interior trails.

The trailhead in 1986 was named the Ray Miller Trailhead, a tribute to volunteer ranger Ray Miller. The first official camp host in the state park system, Miller spent his retirement years, from 1972 until his death in 1989, welcoming visitors to Pt. Mugu State Park. The trail was named for Miller in 1989.

DIRECTIONS TO TRAILHEAD Drive about 30 miles up the coast on Pacific Coast Highway from Santa Monica (21 miles up from Malibu Canyon Road if you're coming from the Ventura Freeway and the San Fernando Valley). The turnoff is 1.5 miles north of Big Sycamore Canyon Trailhead, which is also part of Point Mugu State Park. From the turnoff, bear right to the parking area. The signed trailhead, near an interpretive display, is at a fire road that leads into the canyon. La Jolla Ridge Trail begins on the right (east) side of the parking lot.

THE HIKE The fire road leads north up the canyon along the stream bed. As the canyon narrows, some tiny waterfalls come into view. Past the falls, the trail passes some giant coreopsis plants. In early spring the coreopsis, also known as the tree sunflower, sprouts large blossoms. Springtime travel on this trail takes the hiker past the dainty blue and white blossoms of the ceanothus and the snowy white blossoms of the chamise. Pause to take in the sight (and pungent smell!) of the black sage with its light blue flowers and hummingbird sage with its crimson flowers.

At the first trail junction, bear right on the La Jolla Valley Loop Trail. In a little less than a half mile, you'll arrive at another junction. Leave the main trail and you will descend the short distance to a lovely cattail pond. The pond is a nesting place for a variety of birds including the redwing blackbird. Ducks and coots paddle the perimeter.

Returning to the main trail, you'll skirt the east end of La Jolla Valley, enjoy an overview of waving grasses and intersect a T-junction. To the right 0.7 mile away is Deer Camp Junction, which provides access to trails leading to Sycamore Canyon and numerous other destinations in the state park. (To return via Overlook and Ray Miller Trails, bear right toward Deer Camp Junction. See instructions below.)

To continue with La Jolla Valley Loop Trail, bear left and in half a mile you'll arrive at La Jolla Valley Camp. The camp, sheltered by oaks and equipped with piped water and tables, is an ideal picnic spot. The valley is a nice place to spend a day. You can snooze in the sun, watch for deer, or perhaps stalk the rare and elusive chocolate lily, known as the Cleopatra of the lily family—the darkest and the loveliest.

After leaving the camp, you could turn left on a short connector trail that skirts the pond and takes you back to La Jolla Valley Loop Trail, where you retrace your steps on that trail and La Jolla Canyon Trail.

To complete the circle on La Jolla Valley Loop Trail, however, continue a half mile past the campground to the signed junction where you'll bear left and follow a connector trail back to La Jolla Canyon Trail.

Those returning via Overlook and Ray Miller Trails will find that bearing right (west) and the above described junction will soon bring you to Overlook Trail, a dirt road. Bear right (south) here, descending south along the ridge that separates Big Sycamore Canyon to the east from La Jolla Canyon to the west.

At a fork, bear right, continuing your descent to a junction with Ray Miller Trail. Join this trail, which descends over some red rock, then parallels the coast and coast highway for a time.

Listen carefully and you can hear the distant booming of the surf. Enjoy the stunning ocean views. The Channel Islands—particularly Anacapa and Santa Cruz—are prominent to the northwest. Farther south is Catalina Island. During the winter months, you might catch sight of a migrating California gray whale on the horizon.

The path works its way west, squeezing through a draw dotted with prickly pear cactus. The path marches down a brushy hill past a group camp and returns you to the trailhead.

■ PORT HUENEME BEACH
Port Hueneme Beach Trail
From Port Hueneme Beach Park to end of Ormond Beach is 6 miles round trip

Long, sandy Port Hueneme Beach comes complete with lifeguard towers, segregated areas for swimming and surfing, a snack bar and a fishing pier. In many ways, this Ventura County beach is your typical fun-in-the-sun Southland strand; Hueneme also mixes a lot of business along with its obvious pleasures.

The Port of Hueneme, located at the north end of the beach, is the only deepwater port between San Francisco and San Pedro. Offshore oil drilling equipment, oil, autos, fruit and lumber are among the diverse cargo shipped to and from Hueneme. The Seabees and their U.S. Naval Construction Batallion Center occupy the harbor and a big chunk of town.

(Note for the uncertain: pronounce Hueneme *why-nee´-mee*.) This curious name comes from a native Chumash village, *Wene´me,* ("Resting Place") once located near what is now the city of Port Hueneme. But Hueneme's history has not been a restful one.

A wharf was completed here in 1871, the first built between San Pedro and Santa Cruz. For years, Hueneme was one of the Pacific Coast's largest grain-shipping ports. Cattle, potatoes, beans and fruit were loaded onto horse-drawn flat cars and pulled to waiting steamers. Alas for Hueneme, the town's fortunes declined precipitously in 1896 when the railroad bypassed it in favor of nearby Oxnard.

In his 1913 travel narrative, *California Coast Trails,* nature writer Joseph Smeaton Chase observed: "Hueneme is the ghost of a once flourishing town. On its one business street the vacant stores, with their hopeless signs of TO RENT, stand ranked in shabby idleness, like a row of blind beggars."

In the late 1930s, a port was dredged into the original Hueneme Lagoon and after the outbreak of World War II, the Navy took over the entire harbor.

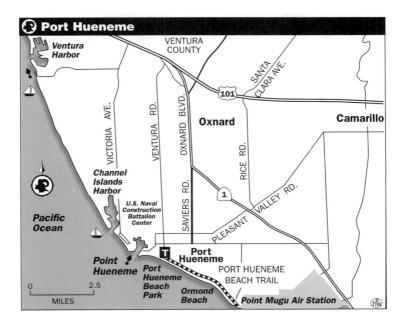

The term "bustling" might be understatement when describing Hueneme during the war when more than 200,000 military personnel and 2 million tons of supplies were dispatched to the Pacific theater. After the war, the local harbor district gradually reacquired parts of the port from the Navy.

To learn more about city and port, stop by the Port Hueneme Historical Museum at 220 N. Market Street, located in the chamber of commerce building.

More recently the beach area has been re-developed. Condos and a cultural center were built across from Point Hueneme Beach Park. A pedestrian walkway meanders through a mile-long greenbelt—Bubbling Springs Linear Park—connecting the city's residential area with the beach. The walkway could be a pleasant addition to your beach hike.

The old Hueneme wharf was replaced by a quarter-mile-long recreational pier constructed in 1978. Walk out on the pier and get great views of the Ventura coast, the Santa Monica Mountains to the east and the Channel Islands floating on the horizon.

From Port Hueneme Beach Park, you can walk up-beach a short distance, then out along the wave-battered jetty toward the harbor entrance, but it's not a particularly attractive stroll. Far more enjoyable is the walk down-coast along wide and sandy Ormond Beach.

The 3-mile-long beach is backed by some dunes that hide most signs of civilization with the major exception of the towering stacks of the Edison Company's Ormond Beach Generating Station. Power lines extend across the Oxnard Plain, borne by giant towers.

DIRECTIONS TO TRAILHEAD From Highway 101 in Oxnard, exit on Ventura Road and drive 6.5 miles south to Port Hueneme Beach Park. There is a fee for parking in the lot. Some free one-hour street parking is available near the beach; farther away, there's two-hour street parking.

THE HIKE Head south along the beach. Seashell admirers will note the abundance of sand dollars usually found along this shore; there's a dense bed of the echinoderms offshore. Pismo clams are also found along this beach. Heed all posted regulations if you plan to collect them.

From Port Hueneme Beach you'll travel onto wide Ormond Beach. Low dunes offer nesting sites for the endangered California least tern. Also back of the beach is a pickleweed- and saltgrass-dotted wetland, which provides habitat for many birds.

A bit more than halfway down Ormond Beach, you'll look up at the two giant 750-megawatt oil/gas fired generating units of Edison's power plant. Trail's end is the fenced boundary of Pt. Mugu Naval Air Station.

■ SILVER STRAND
Silver Strand Trail
From Channel Islands Beach Park to La Janelle Park is 2 miles round trip

Mile-long Silver Strand Beach is book-ended by two harbors—Channel Islands Harbor to the north and Port Hueneme to the south. With plenty of pleasure craft passing in and out of Channel Islands Harbor along with commercial and military vessels arriving and departing from Port Hueneme, boat-watching opportunities are many on this enjoyable stroll along the Silver Strand.

In 1960, the U.S. Army Corps of Engineers scooped up sand dunes and wetlands to create Channel Islands Harbor. Some of the surplus sand went to replenish Port Hueneme beaches. Today more than 2,500 boats call the harbor home, including sport-fishing and whale-watching boats.

Pedestrians can explore the harbor via waterfront paths. One path meanders along the south side of Channel Islands Beach Park. You may begin your walk at this harbor park or start right from Silver Strand County Beach.

DIRECTIONS TO TRAILHEAD From Highway 101 in Ventura, exit on Victoria Avenue and head south 7 miles to Channel Islands Harbor. Leave your vehicle in the lot along Victoria Avenue or turn right on Nicholas Avenue to the Silver Strand County Beach lot.

THE HIKE From the park's small, protected, sandy beach, leave the lifeguard station behind and saunter south on the Silver Strand.

Here's a question to ponder on the beach walk: What do Glendale, Ojai, Burbank, San Fernando and Santa Monica have in common?

Answer: They're all avenues perpendicular to Silver Strand Beach.

As you near the Silver Strand's south end, you'll likely spot surfers catching the waves breaking off the jetty. This jetty thrusting from the tip of Point Hueneme is a unique one. A severe storm drove the long, luxury liner *La Janelle* aground on April 13, 1970. Various state agencies combined resources to reposition the wrecked ship, fill it with rocks, and convert it to a fishing jetty.

The Silver Strand stroll ends at the jetty and unimproved La Janelle Park. Check out the dozen or so Ventura-themed murals painted on the park fence then return the way you came.

See Map on Page 79

■ MCGRATH STATE BEACH
McGrath Beach Trail
From State Beach to McGrath Lake is 4 miles round trip; to Oxnard Shores is 8 miles round trip; to Channel Islands Harbor is 12 miles round trip

McGrath State Beach and McGrath Lake were named for the McGrath family which had extensive coastal land holdings in the Ventura coastal area dating from 1874. Located on the western city limits of Oxnard, the two-mile-long state beach extends south from the Santa Clara River.

A small lake in the southern portion of the park helps to attract more than two hundred species of birds, including black-shouldered kites, northern harriers, owls and herons. Such rare birds as ospreys, white wagtails, black skimmers and peregrine falcons have been sighted here. The lake, which is partially on private property, was damaged by a 1993 oil spill caused by a ruptured pipeline.

The Santa Clara Estuary Natural Preserve on the northern boundary of the park offers a haven for birds and habitat for weasels, skunks, jackrabbits, opossum, squirrels and mice, plus tortoises and gopher snakes.

Near the state beach entry kiosk, a small visitor center features exhibits about the area's plants and wildlife.

This walk takes you on a nature trail through the Santa Clara River Estuary, visits McGrath Lake and travels miles of sandy beach to Channel Islands Harbor.

DIRECTIONS TO TRAILHEAD To reach McGrath State Beach, visitors southbound on Highway 101 take the Seaward Avenue offramp to Harbor Boulevard, turn south on Harbor and travel 4 miles to the park. Northbound visitors exit Highway 101 on Victoria Avenue, turn left at the light to Olivas Park Drive, then right to Harbor Boulevard. Turn left on Harbor and proceed 0.75 mile to the park. The signed nature trail leaves from the day-use parking lot. Signposts along the nature trail are keyed to a pamphlet, available at the entry kiosk.

THE HIKE Those hikers looking for the fastest way (10-minute walk) to the beach will join the wide path leading from the park campground to the shore.

A more scenic, but potentially mucky way to go is to head out on the 0.2-mile long River View Trail, the park nature trail, which meanders through the estuary to the banks of the Santa Clara River.

The river bank is a mass of lush vegetation: willow, silverweed and yerba mansa. In 1980, the Santa Clara River area was declared a natural preserve, primarily to protect the habitat of two endangered birds—the California least tern and Belding's Savannah sparrow.

Head toward the coast by following the muddy bank alongside the river. Intermittent trails weave along the banks above—and alongside—the river.

The heavy winter rains of 2005 altered the formerly fairly straight course of the river mouth; it now hooks a half mile down-coast between the beach and low dunes. Hike down-coast along the edge of what may be, depending on nature's moods over the years to come, a temporary or more permanent estuary. Upon reaching the southern end of this freshwater intrusion, head over the low dunes and walk along the shoreline.

Along the beach, visitors enjoy sunbathing or surf fishing for bass, corbina or perch. In 2 miles, if you head inland a short ways, you'll spot McGrath Lake, tucked away behind some dunes.

As you continue south, more sandy beach and dunes follow. You pass a huge old Edison power plant, and arrive at Oxnard Shores, a development famous for getting clobbered by heavy surf at high tide. The beach is flat and at one time was eroding at the phenomenal rate of ten feet a year. Homes were built right on the shoreline, and many have been heavily damaged. New homes are built on pilings, so the waves crash under rather than through them.

Past Oxnard Shores, a mile of beach walking brings you to historic Hollywood Beach. *The Sheik,* starring that great silent movie idol Rudolph Valentino, was filmed on the desert-like sands here. Real estate promoters of the time attempted to capitalize on Oxnard Beach's instant fame and renamed it Hollywood Beach. They laid out subdivisions called Hollywood-by-the-Sea and Silver Strand, suggesting to their customers that the area was really a movie colony and might become a future Hollywood, but it never became a mecca for the stars or their fans.

This walk ends another mile down-coast at the entrance to Channel Islands Harbor.

■ SAN BUENAVENTURA STATE BEACH

Buenaventura Trail
From Marina Park to the Ventura Pier is 4 miles round trip

When you walk San Buenaventura State Beach, you realize that this park didn't simply happen, it was designed—obviously during the state park system's pre-poverty era. Instead of the grungy tables stuck in the sand found at many beaches, San Buenaventura features wide green picnic areas. It boasts volleyball nets, a fitness trail and even a pier.

The state beach offers plenty of room for all the popular beach activities: swimming, surfing, cycling, fishing and picnicking. It's one of Ventura County's safest spots for a swim because the sand slopes very gradually into the ocean.

Although San Buenaventura's sands are easily accessible (Harbor Boulevard extends along its inland border), the low sand dunes fringing the state beach give it a feeling of isolation from freeway traffic and sounds of the nearby city.

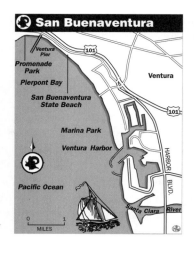

This San Buenaventura stroll begins at Marina Park, a family-friendly enclave perched just up-coast of Ventura Harbor's west channel. A little sandy beach, grassy hillocks and wooden windbreaks encourage spreading out the beach blanket and relaxing awhile. Children enjoy playing on the sand-locked two-masted *San Salvador,* a boatload of fun, with plenty of places to climb.

DIRECTIONS TO TRAILHEAD From Highway 101 in Ventura, exit on Seaward Avenue. Head briefly coastward and turn left (south) on Pierpoint Boulevard. Drive 0.7 mile to the boulevard's end and Marina Park.

THE HIKE From Marina Park, walk out to the end of the jetty, observe the many boats entering and leaving Ventura Harbor, then head up-coast. You can look across the harbor channel at an inviting sand strand, the southernmost segment of San Buenaventura State Beach.

The first mile of beach is fairly narrow and stabilized by a series of rock groins extending offshore. Houses line this length of shore. The second mile of beach, which sweeps toward Pierpont Bay and the Ventura Pier, is wider.

Stairs lead from the sand up to the Ventura Pier. The original pier was built way back in 1872. Today's recreational pier has a restaurant and a gift shop. Stroll past the anglers and enjoy great views of the coast and islands, as well Ventura and its mountain backdrop.

If you want to extend your outing, promenade Promenade Park, which begins near the foot of the pier. You can continue to the Ventura County Fairgrounds or even the Ventura River.

■ EMMA WOOD STATE BEACH
Ocean's Edge Trail
Emma Wood State Beach to Seaside Wilderness Park is 1.3 miles round trip

Several ecological communities converge near the mouth of the Ventura River: sand dunes, a floodplain, cobblestone beach, riparian woodland and wetlands. Botanists have tallied some 300 plant species in the area; more than half of them are native.

This diversity of riverfront and oceanfront life is explored by Ocean's Edge Trail. The path is a 12-stop interpreted nature trail keyed to a descriptive pamphlet available at the trailhead.

In the early years of this century, local naturalist E.P. Foster envisioned a world-class park like San Francisco's Golden Gate. He donated land at the Ventura River mouth to the county to create such a park. Alas, by the time the county began landscaping the area with Monterey pine, eucalyptus and palms, the Great Depression struck and the money ran out.

Instead of "Ventura's Golden Gate," the park became known as Hobo Jungle because of the many vagabonds who camped in the wetlands here. In bad weather, the hobos slept under the railroad bridge. Hobo Jungle now belongs to the city of Ventura, which renamed it Seaside Wilderness Park.

Emma Wood acquired large land holdings on the coast and coastal slope of north Ventura County, land that was originally part of Rancho San Miguelito. She died in 1944 and in the late 1950s her husband and heir gave to the state the beach west of the railroad overpass, a stretch of coast long popular with the public.

Ocean's Edge Trail takes you along Emma Wood's mixed rock and sand beach to Seaside Wilderness Park, where pine and palm trees rise above low sand dunes. The nature trail explores wetlands, including a second mouth of the Ventura River, a lagoon and sand bars.

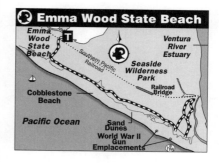

DIRECTIONS TO TRAILHEAD Emma Wood State Beach is located at the south end of old Pacific Coast Highway, north of West Main Street in Ventura. The turnoff for the Ventura River Group Camp area is just before the onramp to northbound Highway 101.

There's a fee for parking at the state beach. You can also park for free just outside the park and walk under the highway overpass to the group campground at the south end of the park. Signed Ocean's Edge Trail begins at an information display on the ocean side of the campground.

■ ANACAPA ISLAND
Anacapa Island Loop Trail
2 miles round trip

Anacapa, 12 miles southwest of Port Hueneme, is the most accessible Channel Island. It offers the hiker a sampling of the charms of the larger islands to the west. Below the tall wind-and-wave-cut cliffs, sea lions bark at the crashing breakers. Gulls, owls and pelicans call the cliffs home.

Anacapa is really three islets chained together with reefs that rise above the surface during low tide. West Anacapa is the largest segment, featuring great caves where the Chumash Indians are said to have collected water dripping from the ceiling. The middle isle hosts a wind-battered eucalyptus grove.

It's a romantic approach to East Anacapa as you sail past Arch Rock. As you come closer, however, the island looks forsaken—there's not a tree in sight. But as you near the mooring at the east end of the isle, the honeycomb of caves and coves is intriguing. A skiff brings you to the pier where you climb a ten-foot ladder go the dock. From the dock you climb 154 steps to the top of the island.

What you find on top depends on the time of year. In February and March, you may enjoy the sight of thirty-ton gray whales passing south on their way to

Anacapa's trails trace a figure-eight around this lovely isle.

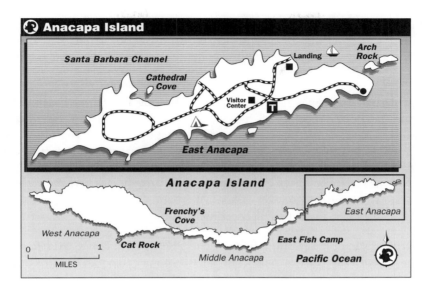

calving and mating waters off Baja California. In early spring, the giant coreopsis, one of the island's featured attractions, is something to behold. It is called the tree sunflower, an awkward thick-trunked perennial that grows as tall as ten feet.

The east isle, where the National Park has a visitor center, is the light of the Channel Islands; a Coast Guard lighthouse and foghorn warn ships of the dangerous channel.

Anacapa is small, but perfect-sized for the usual visit (2 to 3 hours). By the time you tour the lighthouse and visitor center, hike the self-guided trail and have lunch, it's time to board the boat for home.

This hike tours East Anacapa Island. The island is barely a mile long and a quarter-mile wide, so even though you tour the whole island, it's a short hike.

DIRECTIONS TO TRAILHEAD For the most up-to-date information about boat departures to Anacapa and to the other islands, contact Channel Islands National Park at (805) 658-5730 or the park concessionaire, Island Packers in Ventura Harbor at (805) 642-1393. The Channel Islands are also accessible from Santa Barbara; contact Sea Landing at (805) 963-3564.

THE HIKE The nature trail leaves from the visitor center, where you can learn about island life, past and present. A helpful pamphlet is available describing the island's features. Remember to stay on the trail; the island's ground cover is easily damaged.

Along the trail, a campground and several inspiring cliff-edge nooks invite you to picnic. The trail loops in a figure-eight through the coreopsis and returns to the visitor center.

■ SANTA CRUZ ISLAND
Pelican Bay and Prisoners Harbor Trails
3 miles round trip around Pelican Bay; 6 miles round trip from
Prisoners Harbor

Santa Cruz Island may not be celebrated in song like Santa Catalina (Ever hear The Four Preps' 1958 hit tune "Twenty-six Miles"?), but there are similarities. Like Catalina, Santa Cruz Island was, until recent years, a working cattle ranch. It's now managed by the Nature Conservancy and is part of Channel Island National Park.

Like Anacapa, Santa Cruz Island seems tantalizingly close to the mainland, dominating the seaward horizon of Santa Barbara. California's largest offshore island, it boasts the most varied coastline and topography, the highest peak, (2,434 feet) and safest harbors.

The island's anchorages hint at its history: Smugglers Cove, Prisoners Harbor (the island was once a Mexican penal colony), Coches Prietos ("Black Pigs," for the Mexican-introduced hogs). Chumash Indians had both permanent and summer villages on Santa Cruz until the early 1800s when they were brought to the mainland and confined in Spanish missions.

In the 1800s, a colony of French and Italian immigrants led by Justinian Caire began a Mediterranean-style ranch, raising sheep and cattle, growing olives and almonds, even making wine. In 1937, Edwin Stanton of Los Angeles bought the western nine-tenths of the island from the Caire family. Edwin's son, Dr. Carey Stanton, ran the Santa Cruz Island Co. from 1957 until his death in 1987, when the era of family ownership of the island ended and the Nature Conservancy assumed management.

Two of the most popular and easily booked trips to Santa Cruz Island depart with Island Packers the park's boat concession, from Ventura Harbor at

The island's ranching heritage is still very much in evidence.

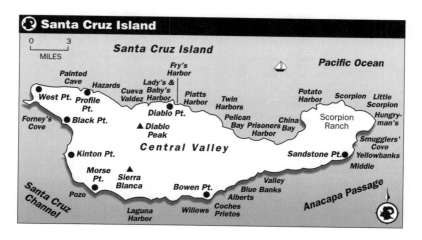

Santa Cruz Island

8 A.M. and return to the mainland between 5 and 6 P.M. Sometimes the boats pause to observe dolphins, whales, sea-lions and seals. Figure about a two-hour boat ride each way and about five hours on the island. You and three dozen others make up a good boatload. The Main Ranch's main emphasis is on human history, while the Pelican Bay Trip stresses natural history.

Main Ranch Day Trip: From the landing at Prisoners Harbor, it's a 3-mile hike under old oaks and through eucalyptus groves along an old fennel-lined ranch road. Your party will be accompanied by a Nature Conservancy employee who will point out some of the botanical and historical highlights encountered en route.

(See Anacapa walk for more visitor information)

Upon arrival at the ranch, visitors eat lunch around a pool. (Bring a swimsuit so you can take a dip.) After lunch you can take a tour of the ranch buildings, including a tiny cabin converted into an anthropology museum, the main ranch house and some dilapidated winery buildings. A restored stone Catholic church celebrated its 100th anniversary in 1991 with a visit by Archbishop (now Cardinal) Roger Mahony. Next to the old church is a cemetery where both humans and ranch dogs rest in peace.

Pelican Bay Day Trip: After arrival at Pelican Bay, landing is by a small skiff onto a rocky ledge. You'll have to climb up a somewhat precipitous cliff trail to reach the picnic spot overlooking the bay.

A Nature Conservancy naturalist leads your group on an educational hike along the north shore. Two special botanical delights are a bishop pine forest and a grove of Santa Cruz Island ironwood.

■ SANTA ROSA ISLAND
Lobo Canyon, East Point, Cherry Canyon Trails
5 miles round trip around Lobo Canyon; 1 mile around East
Point; 3 miles around Cherry Canyon

Rolling grasslands cover much of Santa Rosa Island, which is cut by rugged oak- and ironwood-filled canyons. Torrey pines are found at Beecher's Bay.

Santa Rosa had a considerable Chumash population when explorer Juan Rodríguez Cabrillo sailed by in 1542. Scientists who have examined the island's extensive archeological record believe the island was inhabited at least 10,000 years ago.

After the Chumash era, during Spain's rule over California, the island was land granted to Don Carlos and Don José Carrillo. For many years their families raised sheep on the island and were known on the mainland for hosting grand fiestas at shearing time.

In 1902, Walter Vail and J.W. Vickers bought the island and raised what many considered some of the finest cattle in California. The island became part of Channel Islands National Park in 1986.

The national park service offers a couple of ranger-guided walking tours of the island. Hikers are transported to the more remote trailheads by four-wheel drive vehicles.

DIRECTIONS TO TRAILHEAD
(See Anacapa Island walk for visitor information)

Lobo Canyon (5 miles round trip): Hikers descend the sandstone-walled Canada Lobos, pausing to admire such native flora as island monkeyflower, dudleya and coreopsis. At the mouth of the canyon, near the ocean, is a Chumash village site. The hike continues, as the trail ascends the east wall of the canyon, then drops into Cow Canyon. At the mouth of Cow Canyon is an excellent tidepool area.

East Point Trail (1 mile round trip): Here's an opportunity for hikers to visit a rare stand of Torrey pines, and a large freshwater marsh where

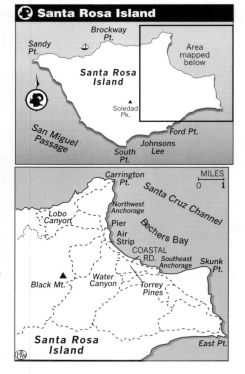

bird-watchers will enjoy viewing shorebirds and waterfowl. Trail's end is one of Santa Rosa's beautiful beaches.

The Torrey pines are an easy three-mile round trip walk from the campground; the stand is located on a hillside. From the top of this hill are spectacular views of Beecher's Bay.

Cherry Canyon Trail (3 miles round trip): Walking Cherry Canyon offers the opportunity to see some plants and animals that are found nowhere else. The trail heads 2 miles up the canyon to an oak grove. On the return trip, the trail offers far-reaching views of the interior, roaming deer and Roosevelt elk, and the dramatic sweep of Beecher's Bay. Trail's end is the island's historic ranch complex.

■ SAN MIGUEL ISLAND
San Miguel Island Trail
From Cuyler Harbor to Lester Ranch is 3 miles round trip with 700-foot elevation gain

San Miguel is the westernmost of the Channel Islands. Eight miles long, 4 miles wide, it rises as a plateau, 400 to 800 feet above the sea. Wind-driven sands cover many of the hills which were severely overgrazed by sheep during the island's ranching days. Owned by the U.S. Navy, which once used it as a bombing site and missile tracking station, San Miguel is now managed by the National Park Service.

Three species of cormorants, storm petrels, Cassin's auklets and pigeon guillemot nest on the island. San Miguel is home to six pinniped species: California sea lion, northern elephant seal, steller sea lion, harbor seal, northern fur seal and Guadalupe fur seal. The island may host the largest elephant seal population on earth. As many as 15,000 seals and sea lions can be seen basking on the rocks during mating season.

A trail runs most of the way from Cuyler Harbor to the west end of the island at Point Bennett, where the pinniped population is centered. The trail passes two round peaks, San Miguel and Green Mountain, and drops in and out of steep canyons to view the lunar landscape of the caliche forest. You must hike with the resident ranger and stay on established trails because the island's vegetation is fragile.

DIRECTIONS TO TRAILHEAD Plan a very long day—or better yet, an overnight trip to San Miguel. It's at least a five-hour boat trip from Ventura. (See Anacapa walk for more visitor information).

THE HIKE Follow the beach at Cuyler Harbor to the east. The harbor was named after the original government surveyor in the 1850s. The beach around

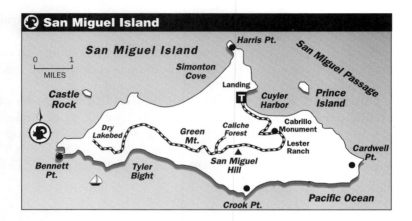

the anchorage was formed by a bight of volcanic cliffs that extend to bold and precipitous Harris Point, the most prominent landmark on San Miguel's coast.

At the east end of the beach, about 0.75 mile from anchoring waters, a small footpath winds its way up the bluffs. It's a relatively steep trail following along the edge of a stream-cut canyon. At the top of the canyon, the trail veers east and forks. The left fork leads a short distance to Cabrillo Monument.

You can anchor and come ashore at "The Palm Trees" during rough weather or under heavy swell conditions. In calm weather, however, come ashore at Gull Rock right in front of Nidever Canyon. You will be able to see the trail above the east side of the canyon. When you get to the top of the canyon the ranger station and pit toilet are straight ahead. Instead of going straight you can turn east. The trail ascends a short distance to the Cabrillo Monument. The Lester Ranch is a short distance beyond that.

Views to remember on a sojourn across San Miguel.

Juan Rodríguez Cabrillo, Portuguese explorer, visited and wrote about San Miguel in October 1542. While on the island he fell and broke either an arm or a leg (historians are unsure about this). As a result of this injury he contracted gangrene and died on the island in January 1543 and it's believed (historians disagree about this, too) he was buried here. In honor of Cabrillo, a monument was erected in 1937.

The right fork continues to the remains of a ranch house. Of the various ranchers and ranch managers to live on the island, the most well-known were the Lesters. They spent 12 years on the island and their adventures were occasionally chronicled by the local press. When the Navy evicted the Lesters from the island in 1942, Mr. Lester went to a hill overlooking Harris Point, in his view the prettiest part of the island, and shot himself. Within a month his family moved back to the mainland. Not much is left of the ranch now. The buildings burned down in the 1960s and only a rubble of brick and scattered household items remain.

For a longer 14-mile round trip the hiker can continue on the trail past the ranch to the top of San Miguel Hill (861 feet), down, and then up again to the top of Green Mountain (850 feet). Ask rangers to tell you about the caliche forest, composed of fossil sand casts of ancient plants. Calcium carbonate reacted with the plants' organic acid, creating a ghostly forest.

■ SANTA BARBARA ISLAND
Signal Peak Loop Trail
Loop around isle is 2 to 5 miles round trip with 500-foot elevation gain

Only one square mile in area, Santa Barbara is the smallest Channel Island. It's located some 38 miles west of San Pedro—or quite a bit south of the other islands in the national park.

Geologically speaking, Santa Barbara arose a bit differently from the other isles. The island is a volcano, leftover from Miocene times, some 25 million years ago, and shares characteristics with Mexico's Guadalupe Islands.

From a distance, the triangular-shaped island looks barren—not a tree in sight. The tallest plant is the coreopsis, the giant sunflowers that can grow ten feet high.

To bird-watchers, Santa Barbara means seabirds, lots of them—gulls, cormorants, pelicans and black oyster-catchers. And the island boasts some rare birds, too: the black storm-petrel and the Xantus murrelet. Land birds commonly sighted include burrowing and barn owls, hummingbirds, horned larks and finches.

Besides the birds, another reason to bring binoculars to the island is to view sea lions and elephant seals. Webster Point on the western end of the isle is a favorite haul-out area for the pinnipeds.

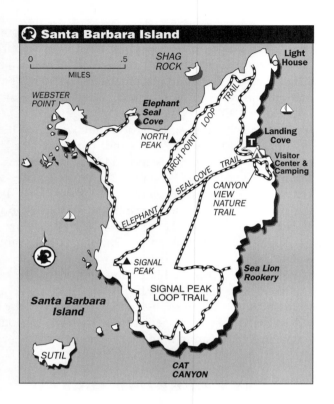

Santa Barbara Island

0   .5
MILES

SHAG ROCK

WEBSTER POINT

Elephant Seal Cove

NORTH PEAK

ARCH POINT LOOP TRAIL

SEAL COVE TRAIL

ELEPHANT

Light House

Landing Cove

T

Visitor Center & Camping

CANYON VIEW NATURE TRAIL

SIGNAL PEAK

SIGNAL PEAK LOOP TRAIL

Santa Barbara Island

Sea Lion Rookery

SUTIL

CAT CANYON

Sea lions come in all sizes on Santa Barbara Island.

Rich kelp beds surround the islands, habitat for a wide variety of fish. The subtidal waters harbor crabs, lobster, sea urchin and abalone, particularly the somewhat rare pink abalone.

Explorer Sebastian Vizcaíno sailed by on December 4, 1602. That day happened to be the day of remembrance for Saint Barbara, so the island was named for her. During the 1700s, the Spanish used the isle as a kind of navy base, from which they could set sail after the pirates plaguing their galleons.

Early in this century, the isle's native flora was all but destroyed by burning, clearing, and planting nonnative grasses, followed by sheep grazing. Besides the grasses, ice plant, a South African import, began to spread over the island. Even when the hardy ice plant dies, it hurts the native plant community because it releases its salt-laden tissues into the soil, thus worsening the odds for the natives.

Park service policy is to re-introduce native plants and eliminate non-natives.

Six miles of trail crisscross the island. A good place to start your exploration is Canyon View Nature Trail. Request an interpretive brochure from the resident ranger and enjoy learning about island ecology.

DIRECTIONS TO TRAILHEAD Santa Barbara Island is infrequently serviced by boat, but it is possible to join a trip. Contact park headquarters.

■ CARPINTERIA BEACH AND BLUFFS
Carpinteria Beach Trail
From Carpinteria State Beach to Harbor Seal Preserve is 2.5 miles round trip; to Carpinteria Bluffs is 4.5 miles round trip; to Rincon Beach County Park is 6 miles round trip

A long campaign to save the Carpinteria Bluffs, one of the last stretches of privately held, undeveloped coastline between Los Angeles and Santa Barbara, succeeded in 1998. Activists, local merchants, school children, and hundreds of Santa Barbara County citizens raised nearly $4 million to buy the bluffs from the property owner.

For more than two decades a battle raged between development interests with plans to build huge housing and hotel projects and local conservationists who wanted to preserve the bluffs. Surfers, hikers and bird-watchers have long enjoyed the bluffs, which rise about 100 feet above the beach and offer great views of Anacapa, Santa Cruz and Santa Rosa islands.

Now that the bluffs are in public domain, they are likely to add to Carpinteria's allure for coastal connoisseurs. Carpinteria residents boast they have "the safest beach in the world." Although the surf here can be large, it breaks far out

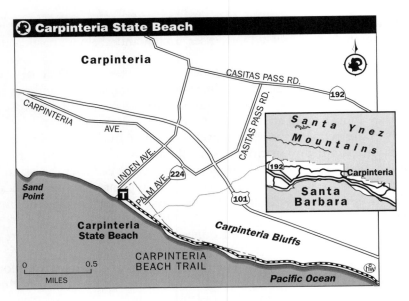

and there's no undertow. As early as 1920, visitors reported "the Hawaiian diversion of surfboard riding."

The Carpinteria Tar Pits once bubbled up near the state beach. Spanish explorers noted that the Chumash caulked their canoes and sealed their cookware with the asphaltum. Around 1915, crews mined the tar, which was used to pave the coast highway in Santa Barbara County. In order to dig the tar, workmen had to heat their shovels in a furnace; the smoking tar would slice like butter with the hot blade. Long ago, the tar pits trapped mastodons, saber-toothed tigers and other prehistoric animals, Unfortunately, the pits, which may have yielded amazing fossils like those of the La Brea Tar Pits in Los Angeles, became a municipal dump.

On August 17, 1769, the Portolá expedition observed the native Chumash building a canoe and dubbed the location *la carpinteria,* the Spanish name for carpenter shop.

Carpinteria is one of the state park system's more popular beachfront campgrounds. A broad beach, gentle waves, fishing and clamming are among the reasons for this popularity. A tiny visitor center offers displays of marine life and Chumash history, as well as a children-friendly tidepool tank.

This beach hike heads down-coast along the state beach to City Bluffs Park and the Chevron Oil Pier. A small pocket beach contains the Harbor Seal Preserve. From December through May this beach is seals-only. Humans may watch the boisterous colony, sometimes numbering as many as 150 seals, from a blufftop observation area above the beach.

After seal-watching, you can then sojourn over the Carpinteria Bluffs or continue down the beach to Rincon Point on the Santa Barbara/Ventura county line.

DIRECTIONS TO TRAILHEAD
From Highway 101 in Carpinteria, exit on Linden Avenue and head south (oceanward) 0.6 mile through town to the avenue's end at the beach. Park along Linden Avenue (free, but time restricted) or in the Carpinteria State Beach parking lot (fee).

"Safest Beach in the World," claim some Carpinteria boosters.

THE HIKE Follow "the world's safest beach" down-coast. After a half mile's travel over the wide sand strand you'll reach state beach-bisecting Carpinteria Creek. During the summer, a sand bar creates a lagoon at the mouth of the creek. Continue over the sand bar or, if Carpinteria Creek is high, retreat inland through the campground and use the bridge over the creek.

Picnic at City Bluffs Park or keep walking a short distance farther along the bluffs past the Chevron Oil Pier to an excellent vista point above the Harbor Seal Preserve. Ambitious walkers may continue along the beach to Rincon Beach County Park, one of the area's top surfing spots on the Santa Barbara/Ventura county line.

■ SUMMERLAND BEACH
Summerland Beach Trail
From Lookout County Park to Biltmore Beach and Hotel is 5 miles round trip

One might guess Summerland was named for the weather, but the name was taken from Spiritualist literature—something to do with the Second Heaven of Spiritualism. A century ago, Spiritualists pitched their tents on the tiny lots in Summerland.

In the waters here, the first offshore oil platform in the Western hemisphere was erected in 1896. Soon, more than three hundred wells were pumping oil from Pleistocene rocks at depths of 100 to 800 feet, an insignificant depth by today's standards.

Oil attracted far more people to Summerland than Spiritualism and soon the air was heavy with the smell of gas and oil. It was said illumination came easy—one simply pounded a pipe in the ground until reaching natural gas, and lit a match. Liberty Hall, the Spiritualists' community center, glowed with divine light and for a time Summerland became known as the "White City."

This walk travels due west along sandy Summerland Beach, rounds some rocky points, and concludes at the narrow beach in front of the famed Biltmore Hotel.

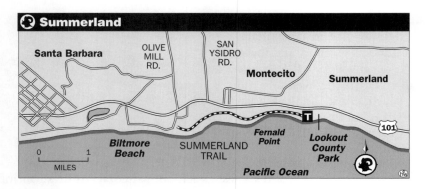

DIRECTIONS TO TRAILHEAD From Highway 101 in Summerland, take the Summerland exit and turn oceanward to Lookout County Park.

THE HIKE At Lookout County Park is a picnic area and a monument commemorating the first offshore oil rig. A well-marked ramp leads to the beach. From Lookout (Summerland) Beach, a sea wall extends 0.75 mile west to Fernald Point. At high tide, you may wish to walk atop it, but you might have to battle some brush. You soon pass a pretty little cove, bounded on the far side by Fernald Point, a fan delta deposited at the mouth of Romero Creek.

Around the point, as you approach Montecito, you'll see the higher parts of the Santa Ynez Mountains on the north skyline and the overturned beds of sandstone near the peaks. There are no official public beaches in Montecito, but most of the shoreline receives public use. Fernald-Sharks Cove is the first beach you travel, then Miramar Beach below the Miramar Hotel. "Miramar-by-the-Sea" has been a popular watering place since the completion of the Southern Pacific Railroad line in 1901. The hotel, with its finely landscaped grounds and blue-roofed bungalows, used to be a passenger stop.

Biltmore Beach: A favorite of locals and resort-goers for nearly a century.

In another quarter-mile, you'll begin hiking across Montecito's third beach, Hammonds, popular with surfers. Hammonds Meadows on the bluffs above the beach is a former Chumash habitation and listed on the National Register of Historic Places. The bluffs were developed in the 1980s and '90s.

Up-coast from Hammonds you'll pass a number of fine homes and arrive at narrow Biltmore Beach, frequented by the rich and beautiful. Opposite the beach is the magnificent Biltmore Hotel, built in 1927.

■ SANTA BARBARA'S EAST BEACH

East Beach Trail

From Stearns Wharf to Cabrillo Pavillion is 2.5 miles round trip; to Andree Clark Bird Refuge is 4 miles round trip

I t's the postcard view of Santa Barbara: a glistening sand strand, Chase Palm Park, white walls and red roofs, the Riviera and the Santa Ynez Mountains.

East Beach is the classic Southern California beach—long, sandy and rarely crowded. It's the place to play—beach volleyball, boogie boarding, sand sculpture contests—and the place to relax, with ample square footage of sand for the discriminating sunbather.

By the 1870s, wealthy health-seekers were flocking to Santa Barbara. And East Beach is where they flocked. Horse-drawn streetcars (electrified in 1896) traveled the length of East Beach, bringing bathers from the bathhouses to the beach.

Historians credit architect Peter Barber with the idea for a palm-lined shoreline drive along East Beach. Barber got his idea after visiting tree-lined avenues in Europe. As mayor of Santa Barbara in 1891, he helped win voter approval for the bond measure that beautified the beach area and made Cabrillo Boulevard (then East Beach Boulevard) the scenic drive it is today.

Another visionary, perhaps the quintessential Santa Barbara citizen of her era, Pearl Chase, also crusaded to preserve the coastline. Chase and her brother, Harold, were honored when the city renamed Palm Park, created in 1931, Chase Palm Park.

The walker has four ways to explore East Beach: the park along the mountainside of Cabrillo Boulevard, the sidewalk along Cabrillo Boulevard (the best option on Sundays when the weekly art sale takes place), along the beach itself, or my favorite, a stroll through the beachside of Chase Palm Park. The park is a bit more than a mile long. Near its east end is Cabrillo Pavillion, where you can break for refreshments, see an art show or rent a boogie board.

Santa Barbara's waterfront and Stearns Wharf attract visitors from around the world.

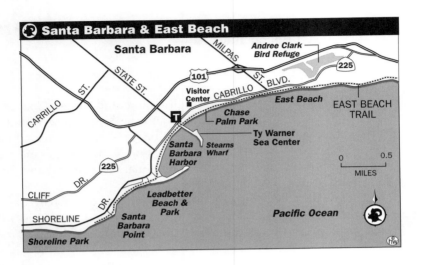

DIRECTIONS TO TRAILHEAD Begin at the foot of Stearns Wharf at the intersection of State Street and Cabrillo Boulevard.

THE HIKE Your path through *Washingtonia robusta* palms soon takes you over the mouth of Mission Creek.

At the foot of Santa Barbara Street, you'll find a plaque commemorating Pearl and Harold Chase for their civic and conservation efforts. At the corner of Santa Barbara Street and Cabrillo Boulevard is the Chamber of Commerce Visitor Center, one of the tiniest buildings in town. Built in 1911, and located around the corner on State Street, the sandstone structure formerly housed a fish market and restaurant. At Garden Street, the historic carousel opens the way to the mountainside of Chase Palm Park, a meandering walk that includes several water features, a playground called Shipwreck Park, and a number of whimsical sculptures.

After a bit more meandering through the palms you'll see Fess Parker's Doubletree Resort on the north side of Cabrillo Boulevard. The large round building is a recreation of a Southern Pacific Railway Roundhouse, which was used to handle steam locomotives from 1926 to 1961. After the 1925 earthquake damaged an earlier roundhouse, it was Pearl Chase who showed Southern Pacific officials a favorite postcard of a bullring in Seville and convinced them to build this most utilitarian of structures in the Spanish motif. The roundhouse was razed in 1982 and the "roundhouse" you see today is part of the hotel and convention center.

The Doubletree (formerly the Red Lion Resort) itself, successfully pushed through many layers of government regulation by actor-turned-developer Fess Parker (who portrayed both Davy Crockett and Daniel Boone), was a controversial project in the mid-1980s because of its size and scale. The Mission Revival buildings take the historic Spanish motif and offer beach and mountain views. You can't miss the Chromatic Gate, the geometric rainbow situated on the corner.

Another Santa Barbara luxury hotel in Spanish style, located a little farther along Cabrillo Boulevard, is the Santa Barbara Hotel. Formerly the Vista Mar Monte, the hotel was completed in 1930 at a then-astronomical cost of $5 million, attracted film industry executives and Hollywood stars in the 1930s, and is still popular with celebrities today. During President Ronald Reagan's two terms in office, 1981–89, when Santa Barbara was the Western White House, the national press corps headquartered at this hotel.

A block inland from the hotel is the Santa Barbara Zoological Gardens, a family-friendly zoo with more than 500 animals. At the end of Palm Park, skirt a small parking lot and proceed to Cabrillo Pavillion, where there's a café, as well as a bathhouse with changing rooms and beach equipment rentals, along with a small city playground.

Beyond Cabrillo Pavillion is another half-mile of East Beach with a turfed picnic area and very popular beach volleyballs courts. Those in the mood for beach-walking should head down to the shore; it's a bit more than a mile down-coast to the famed Biltmore Hotel and its narrow beach.

Otherwise, walk to the end of the picnic area and (carefully) cross Cabrillo Boulevard to Andree Clark Bird Refuge, where cormorants, egrets, herons and many species of ducks reside. Bird-watchers have sighted nearly 200 species in the 42-acre wildlife refuge.

You can follow the grass perimeter between the bike path and the lake shore about halfway around the lake. The path ends near a big bend in Cabrillo Boulevard.

■ ARROYO BURRO BEACH
Arroyo Burro Trail
From Arroyo Burro Beach County Park to Goleta Beach
County Park is 4.5 miles one way

At the turn of the century the Hendry family owned Arroyo Burro Beach and it was known as "Hendry's." Today some Santa Barbarans refer to it as "Henry's." The beach was officially rechristened Arroyo Burro in 1947 when the state purchased it for $15,000. The park, later given to the county, was named for the creek which empties into the ocean at this point. Arroyo Burro is popular for picnicking, boogie boarding, sunbathing and hang glider-watching.

On the bluffs above the beach is one of the most unique residential communities in America. "Sun-kissed, ocean-washed, mountain-girded, island-guarded" was the breathless description of Hope Ranch gushing forth from real estate brochures of the 1920s. In this case, the agents were offering more truth than hype. Hope Ranch was—and still is—one of the most naturally

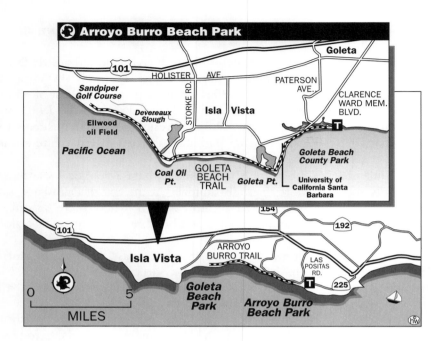

blessed residential areas on the West Coast. Residents often ride their horses along the surf line.

A cautionary note: Hendry's is a popular dog-walking beach, and not all pet owners are considerate about picking up what dogs do.

DIRECTIONS TO TRAILHEAD From Highway 101 in Santa Barbara, exit on Las Positas Road (225) and drive south to its intersection with Cliff Drive and turn right. Arroyo Burro Beach County Park is a short distance on your left.

You can use the MTD bus to return to the trailhead.

THE HIKE Head up-coast on Arroyo Burro Beach. The area was once the site of a major Chumash village. Archeological excavations have produced many tools and artifacts.

You'll round a minor point and after 2 miles or so of beach-walking, pass the red-tiled changing rooms of Hope Ranch Beach Club.

More Mesa Beach follows, one of the most peaceful beaches in the county. Only the buzzing of innumerable flies around the kelp disturbs the tranquility of the serious sun-worshippers who bake their hides here. The only public accessway is the dirt path and stairway leading up to More Mesa, an attractive blufftop preserve mixed with suburban developments.

Beyond More Mesa is another mile of sandy, kelp-strewn beach. The sea cliffs here and in other parts of Santa Barbara have receded three to ten inches per year or roughly 50 feet per century. While this erosion is less than other parts of the world—the White Cliffs of Dover, for example—it's still substantial enough to be a consideration for builders of bluff-top houses.

No, that's not a lighthouse you see in the distance. It's Storke Tower in the center of the University of California at Santa Barbara. As you walk Goleta Beach, you'll round the point and see Goleta Pier.

In 1981, five ancient cannons were found along Goleta Beach, a half-mile south of Goleta Slough. Pacific storms exhumed the circa-1700s cannons. Historians speculate the cannons are from British ships, which once lurked along the coast waiting for the treasure-laden galleons of the Spanish.

Beach hikers soon arrive at the mouth of Goleta Slough, large tidal mudflats that lie between the UCSB campus and the Santa Barbara Airport. Atascadero Creek empties into the slough, where a great variety of birds, crustaceans and native flora thrive.

Although the slough is smaller than it was before bulldozing and flood control projects, in the 1960s it was saved from a Santa Barbara mayor's pet plan: a speedboat lake surrounded by a racetrack for sports cars.

Wade the shallow, sandy-bottomed slough, resume walking on the sandy beach, and enter Goleta Beach County Park. Goleta Pier's 1,450-foot length is a nice walk in and of itself. It's a popular sport-fishing spot. A restaurant and picnic area are near the pier.

Unpack your picnic, unroll your beach towel and catch some rays, or walk up-coast to nearby UCSB.

See Map
on Page
100

■ ELLWOOD BEACH
Ellwood Beach Trail
From Goleta Beach to Coal Oil Point Preserve is 7 miles round trip; to Ellwood Beach Pier is 12 miles round trip

Around seven o'clock in the evening of February 23, 1942, while most Americans were listening to President Roosevelt's fireside chat on the radio, strange explosions were heard near Goleta. In the first attack on U.S. soil since the War of 1812, a Japanese submarine surfaced off the rich oil field on Ellwood Beach, twelve miles up-coast from Santa Barbara, and lobbed sixteen shells into the tidewater field.

"Their marksmanship was poor," asserted Lawrence Wheeler, proprietor of a roadside inn near the oil fields. Most observers agreed with Wheeler, who added there was no panic among his dinner patrons. "We immediately blacked out the place," he said. "One shell landed about a quarter-mile from here and the concussion shook the building, but nobody was scared much."

The unmolested, unhurried Japanese gunners were presumably aiming at the oil installations and the coast highway bridge over the Southern Pacific tracks. Tokyo claimed the raid "a great military success" though the incredibly bad marksmen managed to inflict only $500 worth of damage. The submarine disappeared into the night, leaving behind air raid sirens, a jumpy population and lower real estate values.

The walk along Goleta Beach to Ellwood Oil Field is interesting for more than historical reasons. On the way to the Oil Field/Battlefield, you'll pass tide-pools, shifting sand dunes, and the Devereux Slough. The slough is a unique intertidal ecosystem and is protected for teaching and research purposes by Coal Oil Point Preserve.

DIRECTIONS TO TRAILHEAD From Highway 101 in Goleta, head south on Ward Memorial Drive (Route 217) for 2 miles to Goleta Beach County Park. Park in the large beach lot.

THE HIKE Proceed up-coast and in 0.25-mile you'll reach a stretch of coast called the Main Campus Reserve Area, where you'll find the Goleta Slough. The same month the Japanese bombed Ellwood Beach, Santa Barbara voters approved a bond issue to buy land around Goleta Slough, and a modern airport was constructed on the site of the old cow pasture/airfield. The slough, host to native and migratory waterfowl, is a remnant of a wetland that was once more extensive.

Continue up-beach past the handsome sandstone cliffs. Occasionally a high tide may force you to detour atop the bluffs through the UCSB campus to avoid getting wet. A mile and a half from the county park, you'll round Goleta Point and head due west. You pass a nice tidepool area; judging from the number of college students, it is well studied.

Two more miles of beachcombing brings you to Coal Oil Point. You'll want to explore the nature reserve here. (Please observe all posted warnings; this is a very fragile area.)

Beautiful bluffs and beaches are part of UCSB's idyllic setting.

The dunes are the first component of the reserve encountered on the seaward side. Sandy hillocks are stabilized with grasses and rushes. Salty sand provides little nourishment yet the hardy seaside flora manage to survive, settling as close to the water as the restless Pacific will permit. The dunes keep the plants from blowing away and the plants return the favor for the dunes.

Pick up the trail over the dunes on the east side of the reserve. The fennel-lined trail passes under the cypress trees and climbs a bluff above the slough to a road on the reserve's perimeter. It's a good place to get "the big picture" of the slough, a unique ecosystem. Something like an estuary, a slough has a mixture of fresh and salt water, but an estuary has a more stable mixture. The water gets quite salty at Devereux Slough, with little freshwater flushing.

At the slough, bird-watchers rhapsodize over snowy egrets and great blue herons, black-bellied plovers and western sandpipers. Avid bird-watchers flock to the slough for bird-a-thons—marathon bird-sighting competitions.

Return to the beach and continue walking up-coast. Sometimes horses gallop over the dunes, suggesting Peter O'Toole and Omar Sharif's meeting in *Lawrence of Arabia*...except there's oil on the beach, as you'll readily notice when you look at your feet. In 2 miles you'll pass under an old barnacle-covered oil drilling platform and enter Ellwood Oil Field. Here the Japanese fired shots heard 'round the world...and missed.

■ EL CAPITAN STATE BEACH
El Capitan Beach Trail
From El Capitan to Refugio State Beach is 6 miles round trip

Monarch butterflies and mellow beaches are the highlights of this coast walk north of Santa Barbara. Autumn, when the crowds have thinned and the butterflies have arrived, is a particularly fine time to roam the coast from El Capitan State Beach to Refugio State Beach.

El Capitan is a narrow beach at the mouth of El Capitan Creek. Shading the creek is a woodland of coast live oak and sycamore. During autumn, monarch butterflies congregate and breed in the trees here. (Ask park rangers where the monarchs cluster.)

The butterflies have a distinctive coloring—brownish-red wings with black veins. The outer edges of their wings are dark brown with white and yellow spots. In October and November, the woodland of El Capitan Creek offers the twin delights of falling autumn leaves and fluttering butterflies.

"El Capitan" refers to Captain José Francisco de Ortega, a rotund Spanish Army officer who served as trail scout for the Portolá expedition. When he retired from service to the crown in 1795, he owed the army money and offered to square things by raising cattle. The government granted him his chosen land: a coastal strip, 2 miles wide and 25 miles long extending from just east of Pt. Concepción to Refugio Canyon. He called his land *Nuestra Señora del*

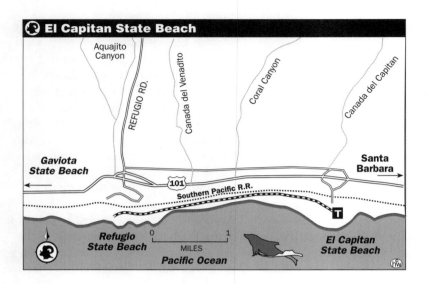

Refugio, "Our Lady of Refuge." Alas, Captain Ortega's retirement was short-lived; he died three years later and was buried at the Santa Barbara Mission.

After the death of El Capitán, the Ortega family continued living in Refugio Canyon for many years. The mouth of the canyon at the Pacific was the major contraband-loading point for Southern California during the early years of the nineteenth century when Spanish settlers were forbidden to trade with Americans. From the Ortega Ranch, hides, tallow, leather goods and wine were loaded onto Boston-bound sailing ships.

Smuggling activity came to an end in 1818 when French Captain (some would say pirate) Hippoloyte de Bouchard sailed by. Bouchard, a mercenary hired by the Argentines, then struggling for independence against Spain, put ashore and burned Ortega's ranch buildings to the ground.

Beach, bluff and bike trails link El Capitan and Refugio state beaches. Depending on the tide, you can usually travel up-coast along El Capitan Beach as far as Coral Canyon Beach. Then you can join the bluff trails or the bike path, which is also open to hikers, for the balance of the trip to Refugio Beach.

El Capitan and Refugio are popular beach campgrounds and nice places to spend a weekend.

DIRECTIONS TO TRAILHEAD From Highway 101, 19 miles up-coast from Santa Barbara, take the El Capitan State Beach exit. Park in one of the day-use areas; the park day-use fee is also honored at Refugio and Gaviota State Beaches.

THE HIKE Descend one of the paths or staircases to the shore, then head up-coast along the mixed sandy and rocky beach. Sea cliffs are steep here because they are constantly being cut back by wave erosion. You'll pass wide Coral Canyon, its walls covered with beds of highly deformed light-colored shales.

At Coral Beach, the tides often discourage beach-walking, so head up to the bluffs and follow the bike path.

Approaching Refugio State Beach, you'll see abundant kelp just offshore. If a breeze is blowing over the water, note how areas with kelp are smooth and kelpless areas are rippled.

Refugio State Beach, at the mouth of Refugio Canyon, is a rocky beach with tidepools. Turn around here, or continue beach-walking up-coast (it's 10 more miles to Gaviota State Beach) for as long as time and tides permit.

■ JALAMA BEACH
De Anza Trail
From Jalama County Park to just-short of Point Conception is 10 miles round trip

At Point Conception, the western-trending shoreline of Southern California turns sharply northward and heralds a number of changes: a colder Pacific, foggier days, cooler air. Ecological differences between the north and south coasts are illustrated by the differing marine life occupying the two sections. Point Conception serves as a line of demarcation between differing species of polyps, abalone, crabs and limpets. Climatically, geographically and sociologically, it can be argued that Southern California ends at Point Conception.

This hike takes you along a pristine section of beach and retraces the route of the De Anza Trail, a trail lost on most hikers for more than 200 years. The De Anza Trail was the route of the Juan Bautista De Anza Expedition of 1775–76, which brought 240 colonists from Mexico across the Colorado Desert and up the coast to found the city of San Francisco.

Historically, the Anza Trail is much better documented than the Lewis and Clark or other trails that opened up the west. This is due to the meticulous diary-keeping of Anza and the expedition's chaplain, Father Font.

On February 26, 1776, the Anza Expedition reached a Chumash village called Ranchéria Nueva, just east of Point Conception. Father Font noted the generosity of the Chumash, praised their well-crafted baskets and stone cups, and concluded that the local inhabitants would be good recruits for future missions.

This beach hike leaves from Jalama County Park, the only genuinely public access point anywhere near Point Conception. If the tide is right (be sure to consult a tide table), you can walk to within about a half mile of the point.

Cross the dunes to the inviting beach.

Travel writer Frank Riley facetiously remarked that "Anza, Father Font, Father Junípero Serra and Jesus himself would have to carry bail money to round Point Conception by land today." Riley is right; public outrage will ultimately see to it that some sort of trail or bike path gives the public access to the coast, but in the meantime be warned that the Bixby Ranch and Hollister Ranch are among the most aggressively anti-coastal access private property holders in the state.

Remember to keep to the beach and don't walk the inland trails onto ranch land.

DIRECTIONS TO TRAILHEAD Jalama County Park is located 20 miles southwest of Lompoc off Highway 1. From Highway 101, near Gaviota, exit on Highway 1 north and proceed 14 miles to Jalama Road. Turn left and go 14 miles through some beautiful ranch country to the county park.

THE HIKE Before heading south over the splendid sand dunes, check the tide table at the park store or at the entry kiosk. As you walk down-coast, you'll soon realize that although Jalama County Park is not on the main Los Angeles-San Francisco thoroughfare, two groups have found it and claimed it as their own—surfers and surf fishermen.

Jalama County Park includes only about 0.5 mile of shoreline, so you soon walk beyond the park boundary. The sandy beach narrows and gives way to rockier shore. Offshore, on the rocky reefs, seals linger. Depending on the tide,

Jalama Creek.

you'll encounter a number of sea walls. The smooth tops of the sea walls make a good trail. "1934" is the date imbedded in the concrete walls.

Occasionally, Southern Pacific railroad tracks come into view, though with the crashing of the breakers, you can barely hear the passing trains. Since there are no public roads along this section of coast, walking or looking out a train window are the only ways to see this special country. Halfway through your walk, after some lazy bends, the coastline heads almost due south, and the Pt. Conception Coast Guard Reservation comes into view.

A bit more than 0.5 mile from the lighthouse, you'll run out of beach to walk; passage is blocked by waves crashing against the point. Stay away from the lighthouse and Coast Guard Reservation; visitors are not welcome. A blufftop road and a number of cow trails lead toward the lighthouse, established by the federal government in 1855, however, these routes cross private ranch land and may not be used.

■ OCEAN BEACH

Ocean Beach Trail
From Ocean Beach County Park to Pt. Pedernales is 7 miles round trip

Pssssst! Want to know a secret? A military secret?

There's a 5-mile long beach in the middle of Vandenberg Air Force Base no one knows, where no one goes.

Vandenberg Air Force Base occupies more Southern California coastline than any other private landholder or government agency. The base encompasses some 35 miles of coastline—about the same amount of shore that belongs to Orange County—and public access is severely restricted.

Happily, Santa Barbara County's Ocean Beach County Park puts a small part of Vandenberg's beach within reach. This wild and windy beach offers a coast walk to remember.

Next to the county park is a large, shallow lagoon at the mouth of the Santa Ynez River. Most of this river's flow is captured high in the Santa Ynez Mountains by a series of dams and Cachuma Lake. By the time Santa Barbara and Lompoc Valley farmers take their allotted river water, not much of the Santa Ynez makes it to the Pacific. Today, looking at the river mouth, it's hard to imagine that the Santa Ynez River once supported the largest run of spawning steelhead trout in Southern California before Cachuma Lake Dam was built in the 1950s.

Still, there's enough freshwater, mixed with some Pacific saltwater, to form a 400-acre marsh back of the river mouth. Bird-watchers will especially enjoy spending some time exploring the wetlands. Near the sandbar at the river mouth, birders will spot gulls and sandpipers and perhaps even a nesting colony of the endangered least tern, Patrolling the estuary's cattail-lined tidal channels

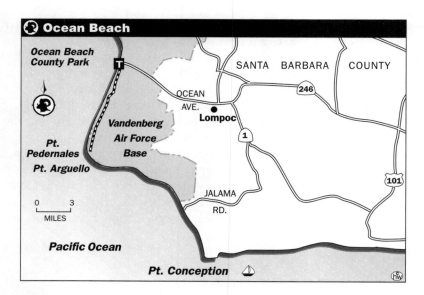

are mallards, canvas back and ruddy ducks. On the mudflat areas are such migrating shorebirds as willets and long-billed curlews.

After you've visited the estuary, it's time to hit the beach. This day hike heads south along windswept Ocean Beach toward Point Arguello. However, before you reach the point, you'll be stopped by another—Point Pedernales— named by the 1769 Portolá expedition when flints, or *pedernales,* were found here. Point Pedernales is about the end of the public beach; besides, the surf crashing against the point is nature's way of telling you to turn around.

DIRECTIONS TO TRAILHEAD North of Santa Barbara, just past the Gaviota Pass tunnel, exit Highway 101 onto Highway 1 and proceed toward Lompoc. Join Highway 246 heading west toward Vandenberg and drive about 8 miles out of Lompoc to reach signed Ocean Park Road on your right. Another sign reads: Ocean Park/Coastal Access. Turn right onto Ocean Park Road and drive a mile (don't be discouraged by the ugly approach) past some railroad sidings and freight cars to Ocean Beach County Park parking lot.

THE HIKE Walk over the low dunes, dotted with clumps of European beach grass, ice plant and hottentot fig, toward the ocean. You'll pass a couple of pilings sticking out of the sand—the remains of an old fishing pier. Continue over the sands, sprinkled with sea rocket and sand verbena, to shore. You could walk a mile north on public beach (though sometimes the Santa Ynez River mouth is difficult to ford), but this hike heads south.

After a mile of walking down-coast, the cliffs rise above you and add to a splendid feeling of isolation. Vandenberg Air Force Base, occupying the cliffs above, used to be the Army's Camp Cooke until the Army turned it over to the Air Force in 1957 and it was renamed for Air Force General Hoyt S. Vandenberg. Atlas ICBMs, Discoverer I, the first polar-orbited satellite and missiles of all kinds have been launched from the base during the last four decades.

Because this stretch of coast bends so far westward, it's ideal for launches into a polar orbit. Look on the world map and you can see there's nothing but empty ocean between here and the South Pole; if a launch fails, the debris will fall on water, not land.

You can see some of the launch pads and towers as you continue downcoast. You'll also sight dramatic Point Arguello, overlooking the treacherous waters that have doomed many a ship. One of the worst accidents in U.S. Naval history occurred in 1923 when seven destroyers ran aground just north of the point. In the dense fog of the Santa Barbara Channel, the ships got off-course. Officers refused to heed the new-fangled radio equipment or Radio Directional Finder (RDF) stations onshore and instead plotted their course by "dead reckoning" which proved to be dead wrong.

One of the minor reefs of Point Pedernales will no doubt stop your forward progress. If you have a pair of binoculars, you might be able to spot some harbor seals sunning themselves on the rocks below the point.

■ GUADALUPE DUNES
Guadalupe Dunes Trail
From Rancho Guadalupe Dunes County Park to Mussel Rock
is 5.5 miles round trip

If the Southern California coast "ends" at the Santa Barbara County/San Luis Obispo county line—as many geographers and demographers have determined—the finale is something to behold. Bold cliffs, towering sand dunes and isolated beaches combine to offer a tableau—and a coastal trek—to remember.

The Santa Maria River forms the Santa Barbara/San Luis Obispo county line. At the river's mouth is a wetland area where several endangered species reside, including the California least tern and brown pelican. Bald eagles and peregrine falcons have been spotted hunting for prey along the riverbanks.

Three miles south of the river is the highest sand dune on the West Coast, 450-foot tall Mussel Rock. It's not really all sand; most of it is a rock formation, though there's an ancient sand dune deposited atop it. It's an impressive landmark.

The Mussel Rock Dunes and Guadalupe Dunes south of the Santa Maria River (now part of The Nature Conservancy's Nipomo Dunes Preserve), along with the Oceano Dunes, Pismo Dunes and Callender Dunes to the north, are known collectively as the Nipomo Dunes, the highest and whitest sand dunes in California. These dunes evolved many thousands of years ago, between ice ages, through deposition by the Santa Maria River, and the sculpting of land

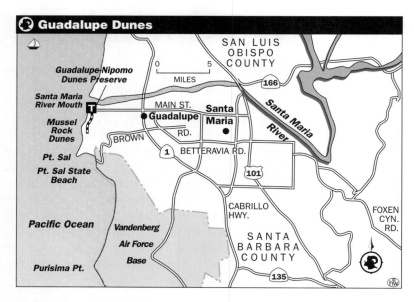

and sea. The cliffs of Pt. Sal act as a sand trap to keep the dunes from straying south.

Conservationists have worked for a decade to create a large park that would preserve the so-called Mussel Rock Dunes and dramatic beaches and bluffs of the Pt. Sal area.

Challenges to the Santa Barbara Land Trust, The Nature Conservancy, and other preservationists include purchasing some private land and getting the region's three public landowners—state parks, county parks and the U.S. Bureau of Land Management—to agree on a single park plan.

The beach walk from Rancho Guadalupe Dunes County Park to Mussel Rock is a fine one for the whole family. The beach route, for all intents and purposes, ends at Mussel Rock; hardy hikers will scamper up Mussel Rock and join a rugged unmaintained trail that contours around it, while the less intrepid, and those parties with children, will likely prefer to head inland over the sand dunes or retrace their steps back along the beach.

Safest and easiest access to, or exit from, the dunes is by way of one of the gulches located a few hundred yards north of Mussel Rock.

DIRECTIONS TO TRAILHEAD From Highway 101 in Santa Maria (some 75 miles up-coast from downtown Santa Barbara), exit on Main Street and head west 9 miles to the small town of Guadalupe and a junction with Highway 1. Continue 5 more miles on Main Street to road's end at a beach parking area for Rancho Guadalupe Dunes County Park.

THE HIKE Walk south. A series of tall signposts proclaim the upper (inland) part of the beach as a bird nesting area and instruct you to stay away.

In the first mile of your walk, you'll likely encounter the two dominant species of beach-goers in these parts—the surfer trying to catch a big wave and the surf fisherman trying to catch a surf perch or halibut.

After a mile, you'll leave most humans behind, and encounter great numbers of shorebirds. Keep an eye out for some intriguing sea shells, particularly sand dollars. A bit more than 2 miles out, you can look inland for a route up into the dunes.

Experienced hikers can continue right up to the base of Mussel Rock, scamper up the rock about 30 feet, and join a sandy trail that contours around the rock. The trail passes above a narrow cove, looks down on a small, wave-battered rock arch, and continues south.

Eventually (Mussel Rock is a big rock!), you'll emerge above what locals call Paradise Beach, a sand strand that extends from Mussel Rock to Pt. Sal.

The Guadalupe Dunes rank among the West Coast's highest.

Dune hikers will enjoy the return sojourn through this Sahara-by-the-Sea. The lower, shifting sand dunes are dotted with sea rocket, sand verbena and morning glory, while the more stable inland dunes are bedecked with lupine, mock heather and the endangered soft-leaved paintbrush.

The highest dunes are closest to Mussel Rock. Savor the fine coastal views south to Pt. Sal and the 35 miles of pristine coast monopolized by Vandenberg Air Force Base. Northern vistas take in the Nipomo Dunes, Pismo Beach and the sweep of San Luis Obispo Bay.

CHAPTER TWO

CENTRAL COAST

Between the Bay Area and the Southland are four coastal counties—San Mateo, Santa Cruz, Monterey and San Luis Obispo—that offer some of the most inspiring walking on the West Coast.

California is often divided into just two sections—Northern California and Southern California—though no two people agree about the dividing line. But the Central Coast is a land, a people, and an outlook all its own. As a walking province, it's second to none.

California's Central Coast shares some of the north's weather—generous rains, frequent fogs—as well some of the South Coast's sunshine and temperate breezes. The area combines the solemn redwood groves and precipitous coastline associated with the coast north of San Francisco with long crescents of sand and beach culture associated with the Southland.

But the beauty of the Central Coast lies not in comparisons with other places, but in the coast itself. Hiking California's Central Coast explores that beauty.

For the writer—and for the walker—the Central California Coast is defined as the shoreline that extends from a bit south of San Francisco Bay to a bit south of Morro Bay. It is a land that surprises. I say this with some authority, having walked the entire California coast and written a narrative of my journey, *A Walk Along Land's End: Discovering California Living Coast* [HarperCollins-West, 1995]. On my walk I found the north coast's beauty to be inspiring, but not surprising. And I found the south coast's beach culture to be intriguing, but not surprising.

The Central Coast, however, surprises: wildflower-covered bluffs, silver crescents of sand, tall dunes, rich estuaries and two long coastal ranges—the Santa Cruz Mountains and Santa Lucia Mountains, both of which offer the hiker excellent trails and fabulous coastal vistas.

The Santa Cruz Mountains extend some 80 miles along the coast from a bit south of San Francisco to the Pájaro River on the Santa Cruz/Monterey county border. Lower and narrower in the northern reaches, the range is higher, wider and wilder in the south. The young, geologically active mountains support impressive redwood groves. The delights of hiking the Santa Cruz Mountains include deep, Douglas fir- and redwood-lined canyons, view-filled ridges and tranquil canyons.

What is popularly known as Big Sur is really the Santa Lucia Mountains, a range extending 90 miles from the Carmel Valley in the north to San Simeon in San Luis Obispo. Trails probe the headwaters of the Arroyo Seco, Little Sur and Big Sur Rivers, which originate in the Ventana Wilderness.

In these mountains also is the southernmost limit of the natural range of the magnificent coastal redwood. Fern-lined canyons, oak-studded potreros and meadows smothered with colorful Douglas iris, pink owl's clover and California poppies greet the backcountry traveler.

A series of nine peaks between San Luis Obispo and Morro Bay originated as volcanoes beneath the sea that covered this area some 15 million years ago. These volcanic rocks or *morros* include Morro Rock, the famed Gibraltar of the Pacific, as well as several more that are fun to climb, including Black Mountain in Morro Bay State Park.

Along with its sandy beaches and dramatic rocky shoreline, the Central Coast boasts several sand dune complexes. Providing a dramatic backdrop to Monterey Bay's northern beaches are some of the Central Coast's tallest dunes, handsomely shaped mounds that are habitat for a number of rare native plants and animals. In the southern part of San Luis Obispo County are the Nipomo Dunes, one of California's largest dune systems. Here great heaps of wind-swept sand are held in place by ice plant, verbena, grasses and silver lupine.

Often overlooked areas of the Central Coast are its wetlands: fresh and salt-water marshes, estuaries, sloughs and lagoons. Scientists say that a very high percentage of all sea life along the Central Coast originates in Morro Bay Estuary. The triangular-shaped marsh, lined with eel grass and pickleweed, is an important spawning and nursery habitat for fish. A walk along the Morro Bay Sand Spit that separates Morro Bay from the ocean is one to remember.

Elkhorn Slough, largest wetland between Morro Bay and San Francisco Bay, is a critical rest stop and feeding ground for tens of thousands of migratory birds. Bird-watchers flock to Elkhorn Slough, where the record was established for the most bird species sighted in a single day—116, no less!

California's Central Coast, once considered a land simply situated between North and South has become a destination in itself—ready to be explored, discovered and enjoyed by the hiker who appreciates natural beauty, small-town life, and one of the world's great meetings of land and sea.

■ GUADALUPE DUNES NORTH
Oso Flaco Beach Trail
To the beach is 2 miles round trip; to Santa Maria River mouth is 8 miles round trip

The Guadalupe Dunes form a dynamic ecosystem; they've been building up—shifting in response to prevailing northwest winds—for the last 18,000 years or so. Some dunes continue to be formed today. The active, moving ones are those with little or no vegetation.

Flowers, plants and grasses are vital to the dune ecosystem because they stabilize the drifting sands. Brightening the dunes in springtime are yellow and magenta sand verbena, coreopsis, daisies and white-fringed aster.

During the Great Depression of the 1930s, the dunes were home to the "Dunites" a motley collection of writers, hermits, artists, nudists and astrologers, who lived in driftwood shacks and published their own magazine called *The Dune Forum*.

Shifting sands buried the Dunite community, as they had earlier buried more elaborate developments. In 1904, Oceano boasted beach cottages, a wharf and mammoth La Grande Beach Pavilion. The developer's grandiose plans of turning Oceano into a tourist mecca did not materialize and the pavilion, wharf and cottages were buried beneath advancing dunes.

This walk passes between Oso Flaco and Lower Oso Flaco lakes to the dunes, then travels down to the beach. The trail and lakes area of the dunes are operated by The Nature Conservancy.

The magnificent complex of dunes spanning 18 miles of California's Central Coast have a new name and a new center. A portion of the dunes is now part of the Guadalupe–Nipomo Dunes National Wildlife Refuge, so designated to conserve and protect a couple of endangered species and habitats.

The Dunes Center, a conservation organization dedicated to preserving

A long wooden boardwalk leads from the lakes to the dunes.

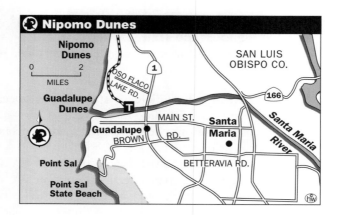

the great sandscape, scientific research and visitor education, has opened an upgraded interpretive facility a few miles inland from the dunes.

Located downtown in the drowsy farming hamlet of Guadalupe, the center is well worth a stop before continuing to the dunes for a hike. Kids will enjoy the hands-on interactive computer exhibits that offer an entertaining and educational tour of the dunes and its denizens, a unique gathering of birds, amphibians and reptiles.

Other exhibits give insights into the colorful history of the dunes, which have been known by a number of names: Pismo, Callender, Oceano, Guadalupe and Nipomo. The dunes are the burial ground of the massive set constructed for the 1923 epic motion picture, *The Ten Commandments*, directed by Cecil B. DeMille. Learn details about this milestone of film history and plans to unearth huge statues of Pharaohs and the rest of what was probably the largest set ever made for a silent film.

The center itself is a piece of local history, a lovingly restored 1910 Craftsman house. Arts and Crafts-era aficionados will appreciate a restoration job well done, the home's handsome interior and period furnishings.

The Dunes Center sponsors an ambitious hike schedule that includes the Oso Flaco Sunset Hike, Cecil B. DeMille Birthday Hike, The Fascinating World of the Snowy Plover, A Scavenger Hunt for the Senses and Evening Hike to Mussel Rock. Other docent-led interpretive walks focus on botanical and zoological life, bird-watching and dune photography.

To get to the Dunes Center, from Highway 101 in Santa Maria, exit on Main Street (Highway 166) and drive 9 miles west to an intersection with Highway 1. Turn right (north) on Highway 1 (Guadalupe Street) and drive a mile to the north end of town and the Dunes Center located on the west side of the street.

DIRECTIONS TO TRAILHEAD From Highway 1, some 9.5 miles south of Oceano and 3 miles north of State Highway 166, turn west on Oso Flaco Road and follow it 3.5 miles to road's end at the dunes. A state park parking fee is collected from a kiosk at the entrance to the dirt parking lot.

THE HIKE Follow the narrow, cottonwood-shaded paved road as it passes between the "big" and "little" Oso Flaco lakes. Rails and grebes nest at water's edge, and sandpipers and a rather raucous duck population winter here.

The Portolá Expedition camped at the lake in September 1769. The soldiers killed a bear and feasted on it. Although Father Crespi, diarist and spiritual counselor for the expedition, wanted to call the lake "Lake of the Martyrs San Juan de Perucia and San Pedro de Sacro Terrato," the soldiers' more humble name of Oso Flaco or "lean bear" stuck.

You'll cross a bridge over the placid lake waters, then follow a long wooden boardwalk toward the dunes. The trail tops a dune crest and offers fines coastal views from the bold headland above Avila Beach south to Point Sal.

Walk down the dunes to water's edge and head south. Three miles of beach-walking brings you to the Santa Maria River. Among the many native and migratory waterfowl residing at the river mouth are the California least tern and the California brown pelican. Across the river is Rancho Guadalupe County Park and the highest sand dune on the west coast, 450-foot tall Mussel Rock.

■ PISMO BEACH
Oceano Dunes Trail
2 or more miles round trip

Pismo Beach has a little something for everyone. Digging for the famed Pismo clam (now scarce) has long been a popular pastime. Two campgrounds at the state beach are favorites of families looking for weekend getaways. Oceano Dunes State Vehicular Recreation Area is a sandy playground for street vehicles and off-highway vehicles.

For walkers, the attraction is Oceano Dunes Preserve, a region of tall sand hills where vehicles are prohibited, and you can wander for miles. Often referred to as the Nipomo Dunes these days, they extend 18 miles from the northern end of Pismo State Beach to Point Sal State Beach.

This walk explores the dune preserve inland from Oceano Dunes State Vehicular Recreation Area. The shoreline itself is often a traffic jam of cars, trucks and off-highway vehicles, filled with families, low-riders, and what seems to be half the population of Bakersfield.

A few hundred yards inland from this shoreline Sigalert, it's quiet, even lonely. Virtually no one bothers to walk into the dune preserve to see Nature's handiwork.

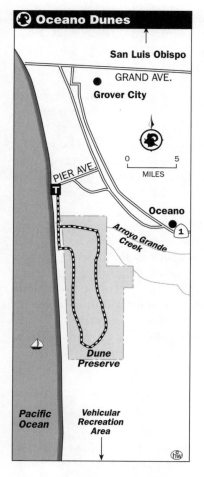

Oceano Dunes

San Luis Obispo

GRAND AVE.
Grover City

0   5
MILES

PIER AVE.

Oceano
1

Arroyo Grande
Creek

Dune
Preserve

Pacific
Ocean

Vehicular
Recreation
Area

DIRECTIONS TO TRAILHEAD From Highway 101 in Arroyo Grande, exit on Grand Avenue and follow it westward to Highway 1. Head south a mile to the community of Oceano, just south of Grover Beach, and turn west on Pier Avenue. Oceano Dunes State Vehicular Recreation Area entrance station is a short distance ahead. If you have a four-wheel drive or high-clearance vehicle, you can pay a fee here and drive onto the beach. (Pismo boosters claim their beach is the only one in California where the sand is firm enough to support travel by standard automobiles, even low-slung family cars, but I have my doubts; I've seen a lot of cars stuck in the sand.)

If you're driving, head south about a half mile. The beach is signed with numbered markers. Park near the first marker you see—Marker #1.

If you're not keen on driving the beach, park along Pier Avenue short of the entrance kiosk. You may then (1) walk a half-mile south along water's edge (not as treacherous as it looks from the distance with all those vehicles on the beach) to the dune entrance; or (2) walk a quarter-mile or so along Strand Way, a residential street paralleling the beach,

Clamming was a popular Pismo activity in generations past.

then continue south along the banks of Arroyo Grande Creek, which near its mouth also parallels the beach, to the dune preserve entrance.

(If you park on Pier Avenue, add about another mile to your walk.)

THE HIKE Head inland to the fence that marks the boundary of the Oceano Dunes Natural Preserve. Take any of the meandering southbound trails that cross the dunes. A ridgeline of sand shields walkers from the sights and sounds of the busy beach below.

Continue southward along the shrub-dotted base of the dunes for a mile or so, then ascend out of the foredunes toward the crest of the great dunes to the east. You can then return north via the crest of the large dunes.

When you reach Arroyo Grande Creek, the northern boundary of the preserve, return to the beach. At this point, you're a couple hundred yards north of Marker #1, so head south back to the trailhead.

■ POINT SAN LUIS LIGHTHOUSE
Pecho Coast Trail
7.25 miles round trip with 400-foot elevation gain

Between Montaña de Oro State Park and Avila Beach is 10 miles of California coast that nobody knows, where nobody goes.

The reason for the area's obscurity is that this land has been privately held since Spanish Mission days. For the last several decades, public access has been strictly forbidden because of a very security-conscious landowner: Pacific Gas & Electric, whose Diablo Canyon Nuclear Power Plant is in the middle of this pristine stretch of coast.

Pecho Coast Trail allows limited access to this coast. The pathway climbs the steep bluffs above Avila Beach to the historic Point San Luis Lighthouse, then crosses a coastal terrace to an oak woodland. The lighthouse is being restored by the dedicated and hard-working volunteers associated with the Point San Luis Lighthouse Keepers. One room, the parlor, has been restored with period furniture.

Naturalists lead hiking tours along Pecho Coast Trail, which can be traveled only on a guided walk. A 3.5-mile round trip tour, known as the half-day hike, ventures to the lighthouse and back. A 7.4-mile round trip tour, known as the full-day hike, continues past the lighthouse to Rattlesnake Canyon.

Reservations are required. To learn more about the guided hikes, as well as to make reservations, call (805) 541-TREK.

Diablo and other coastal canyons were the hunting grounds of the native Chumash and their predecessors, who inhabited this region more than 9,000 years ago. In 1968, PG&E began construction of the controversial Diablo Canyon Nuclear Power Plant. Engineering difficulties and court challenges, as

well as mass demonstrations over the building of reactors close to an active earthquake fault, slowed but did not stop the plant, which opened in 1986.

The $300,000 pathway project was funded by PG&E; the trail was a concession negotiated by the California Coastal Commission when it granted the utility permission for a 1983 construction project. The California Conservation Corps built and engineered Pecho Coast Trail.

A trail highlight is a tour of the old Point San Luis Obispo Lighthouse, built in 1890. The "Victorian Lady," as it's known to locals, warned ships off the rocky coast until 1975, when the facility was deactivated and replaced by an automated beacon.

The docents who lead the hikes are enthusiastic folks who share lots of nature lore and local history. Be aware that these are interpretive walks, not workouts, and are geared to the slowest hikers.

DIRECTIONS TO TRAILHEAD From U.S. 101, a little north of Pismo Beach, and a little south of San Luis Obispo, exit on Avila Beach Drive and follow it 4 miles to the gated entrance road of the Diablo Canyon Nuclear Power Plant. Park along Avila Beach Drive and join one of the docents who will guide you along the trail.

Point San Luis Lighthouse.

THE HIKE Don't judge a trail by its trailhead. At first, Pecho Coast Trail appears like the route to a minimum-security prison. However, it soon leaves the gates and barbed wire behind and begins ascending the dramatic bluffs above San Luis Obispo Bay via a narrow asphalt road.

Veering from the road, you'll join signed Pecho Coast Trail and get great over-the-shoulder views of the bay's three piers (from north to south: Harford, Unocal, Avila), as well as Avila Beach. Pacific currents carry sand past mostly rocky San Luis Obispo Bay, but deposit sand mass en masse at Pismo Beach and its southern neighbors, Grover Beach and Oceano. Forming a dramatic backdrop to these beaches are the sparkling Nipomo Dunes.

The path rejoins the asphalt road for a short distance and soon reaches the lighthouse. After learning about the lonely lives of the lighthouse keepers and their families, you'll hit the trail again, traveling north atop the coastal bluffs.

Pecho Coast Trail dips down to the coastal terrace, where you'll pass among grazing cattle. Advancing very quietly, you'll sneak a peek at the harbor seals and sea otters that sometimes haul out at low tide on shore.

The path loops through an oak grove, where you'll take a lunch break. After lunch, you'll return the way you came. The panorama of San Luis Obispo Bay is even better on the way back.

■ MONTAÑA DE ORO STATE PARK BLUFFS
Bluff Trail
4 miles round trip

Atop the Montaña de Oro State Park bluffs grow fields of mustard and pop-pies, which give the park its "Mountain of Gold" name.

In the early 1900s, the greater portion of what is now the state park was part of the Spooner Ranch. The most popular beach in the park is Spooner's Cove; its isolation made it an ideal landing spot for contrabandistas during the Span-ish era, and for bootleggers during Prohibition.

While walking the bluffs, you may see harbor seals venturing ashore or otters diving for food beyond the surf line. Bird-watchers delight at the peli-cans, albatross, cormorants and crimson-billed black oyster-catchers.

Inland areas of the park include Valencia Peak, which offers great Central Coast panoramas and Coon Canyon, where a stand of Bishop pine thrives. The park's campground occupies the bluffs above a small creek; the visitor center is the old Spooner ranch house.

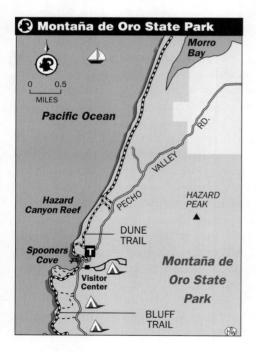

DIRECTIONS TO TRAILHEAD From Highway 101, exit on Los Osos Road, continuing northwest for 12 miles until the road turns south to become Pecho Valley Road, which leads to Montaña de Oro State Park. There's parking at Spooner's Cove. The trail begins a hundred yard south of the turnoff for the campground on the west side of Pecho Valley Road.

THE HIKE The path crosses a dry creek on a footbridge and leads up to the bluffs overlooking Spooner's Cove.

A half mile from the trailhead, a short fork to the right leads to Coralina Cove, bedecked with sea-polished broken shells and beautiful beach pebbles. The crystal-clear tide-pools are full of anemones, starfish, mussels and colorful snails.

Continuing on Bluffs Trail, you'll cross a wooden bridge. A mile from

the trailhead is Quarry Cove, a fine tidepool site. The wide trail, lined with this-
tle and New Zealand spinach, eventually brings you to an overlook above some
sea caves. Beyond is Grotto Rock.

You may return the same way, or cross Pecho Valley Road to the trailhead
for Coon Creek Trail.

See Map
on Page
122

■ MONTAÑA DE ORO DUNES
Dune Trail
To Hazard Canyon Reef is 2.5 miles round trip; to Shark Inlet
is 6.5 miles round trip

Most park visitors head for the well known bluffs south of Spooners Cove;
however another attraction north of the cove awaits the adventuresome
explorer—a magnificent coastline of reefs, ravines and dunes extending all the
way to Morro Bay.

Trails travel the bluffs just north of Spooners Cove, dipping in and out of
ravines on a series of horse and surfer trails. Your improvised route provides fine
overlooks of handsome (and accessible) pocket beaches and rocky coves. If it's
low tide, you might want to hike for stretches along the beach.

Blufftop trails bring you to narrow Hazard Canyon, where you join a
canyon trail, following it through aromatic eucalyptus. In the autumn this area
comes alive with congregations of monarch butterflies.

The mighty cliffs and dunes here were the site of practice invasions launched
by America's troops-in-training during World War II. In 1995, the shores were
again disturbed by explosions, this time by a bomb squad who located—and
detonated—the last of the "unexploded ordnance" left behind from these war
games of a half century ago. (The author had walked these shores since scout
days in the 1960s, blissfully unaware of any potentially disturbing ordnance.)

For a shorter ramble you can walk as far as Hazard Canyon. To partake of
more of the majesty of this coast, you can follow either bluff or beach to the
southernmost tip of Morro Bay.

The walk lends itself to improvisation. Spring wildflower bloom? Enjoy the
bluffs. Low tide? Walk the beach.

DIRECTIONS TO TRAILHEAD Look for a small grassy parking area off
Pecho Valley Road, just north of Spooners Cove. It's just opposite the start of
the Ridge Trail on the opposite side of the road. Alternative parking, if this
small lot is full, is available at horse trailer parking area a short distance north
on Pecho Valley Road.

THE HIKE Signed Dune trail has two branches: a left branch that makes a half-
circle above Spooners Cove and a more direct right branch that heads north.
The two join in a quarter-mile.

Marching across a "Mountain of Gold."

Dune Trail stays behind (on the inland side) of the dunes. Several sandy side trails invite you to climb to the top of the dunes for a look at what's below. After 1.75 miles of sandy trail, you'll reach Hazard Canyon Trail and descend 0.25 mile to the beach.

Along the shore of Hazard Canyon Beach are tidepools, flat rocks for pic-nicking and superb surfing. Also at the beach are thousands of wave-polished sandstone rocks with Swiss cheese-like holes in them. These holes are bored by the piddock, an industrious member of the mollusk family.

Dune Trail continues north, but perhaps a more enjoyable walk is along the beach. You can beachcomb all the way to Sharks Inlet at the southern tip of Morro Bay. Extend your walk even farther by walking the sand spit. (See the Morro Bay Sand Spit Walk in this guide.)

■ MORRO BAY SAND SPIT
Sand Spit Trail
4 miles one-way

Dominating the seascape of Morro Bay is the "Gibraltar of the Pacific," 576-foot-high Morro Rock, first sighted by Juan Cabrillo in 1542. The fifty-million-year-old volcanic peak was used as a rock quarry as late as 1969, but is now a wildlife preserve and part of the state park system.

On the inland side of Morro Bay is the state park, which includes a golf course, marina and superb nature museum.

Morro Bay is made possible by a long, narrow sand spit—one of Central California's special environments. Walkers stride the sand dunes and ridges that separate Morro Bay from the inland side and Estero Bay on the ocean side. Atop some of the higher dunes (about eighty feet above sea level), you'll be treated to good vistas of the bay, Morro Rock, and nearby mountains.

Heather, salt grass and coyote bush are among the hardy plants surviving in the harsh wind-lashed environment of the three-mile-long sand spit. Silver lupine, sea rocket and evening primrose add some seasonal color.

Bird-watchers may spot the snowy plover, which lays its eggs in the sand. On the muddy flats of the spit's bay side, willets, curlews and sandpipers feed.

Scientists say that a very high percentage of all sea life along the Central Coast originates in Morro Bay Estuary. The triangular-shaped marsh, lined with eel grass and pickleweed, is an important spawning and nursery habitat for such fish as the California halibut and sand perch. Beneath the surface of the bay are oysters, clams, worms, snails, crabs and shrimp.

To learn more about the bay's ecology, animal and plant life, visit the Morro Bay Museum of Natural History, which is located in Morro Bay State Park. Exhibits are well done and the panoramic view of the bay is superb.

I particularly enjoy renting a kayak from one of the waterfront establishments and paddling across the bay to the sand spit.

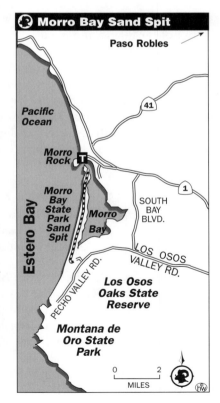

DIRECTIONS TO TRAILHEAD If you want to arrange a car shuttle or begin the hike at the south end of the sand spit, here's how to reach the south trailhead: From Highway 101 in San Luis Obispo, exit on Los Osos Valley Road and head west through the town of Los Osos. One block after the road curves left to become Pecho Road, turn right on Monarch Lane. Drive to the end of this road and park.

THE HIKE From the end of the sand spit, walk south along the bay. The shoreline is silty, salty and quite a contrast to the sandy dunes you'll be crossing further south.

A mile of bay-side walking brings you to Houseboat Cove. Across the bay from the cove is the Morro Bay Museum of Natural History. Continue another few hundred yards past the cove, then climb over the dunes to the ocean side of the sand spit. Walk south along surf's edge, which is littered with clam shells and sand dollars. After about 2.5 miles of travel, as the dunes on your left begin to recede, walk up a valley toward the top of the dunes.

You'll see a large shell mound in the center of the valley, a massive artifact left by the Chumash Indians. They piled clams, cockles, snails and even land game in these kitchen middens. (Inspect this shell mound and the others on the spit with care; they are protected archaeological sites.) The bountiful marsh is so full of bird, land and aquatic life that it's easy to imagine a large population of Chumash here; the men hunting rabbits in the dunes, the beautiful baskets of the women overflowing with shellfish.

From the top of the dunes, you'll get a good view for Morro Bay and spit's end at Shark's Inlet. Across the bay are the Morros, a series of extinct volcanoes that includes the famous Morro Rock. Rising behind the Morros are the Santa Lucia Mountains that stretch to Big Sur and beyond. This viewpoint is a good place to turn around and return to the trailhead at the north end of the spit.

■ MORRO BAY STATE PARK
Black Hill Trail
To Black Hill summit is 3 miles round trip with
600-foot elevation gain

A series of nine peaks between San Luis Obispo and Morro Bay originated as volcanoes beneath the sea that covered this area some fifteen million years ago. After the sea and volcanic explosions subsided, erosion began dissolving the softer mountain material around the volcanic rock and left nine volcanic peaks standing high above the surrounding landscape. These volcanic plugs include Hollister Peak and famed Morro Rock.

Black Hill, the last peak in the volcanic series before Morro Rock, has a trail that tours a little of everything—chaparral, eucalyptus, oaks, pines and coastal

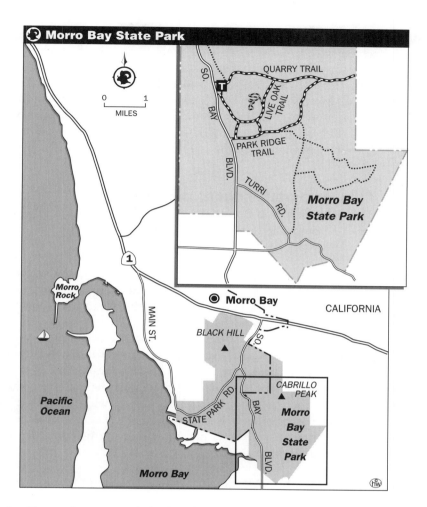

shrubs. From the mountain's 640-foot summit, you can view the Morro Bay Estuary, the sand spit, and the hills of nearby Montaña de Oro State Park.

DIRECTIONS TO TRAILHEAD Follow Coast Highway for 12 miles north of San Luis Obispo to the Los Osos-Baywood Park exit just before Morro Bay. Turn south on South Bay Boulevard and go 0.75 mile to Morro Bay State Park entrance. Bear left on the first fork beyond the entrance, heading 1 mile to the campground entrance directly across from the state park marina lot, where you should park. Park along the first crossroads inside the campground. Walk up the campground road to join the trail.

THE HIKE Walk up the group camp access road, past the group camp restroom. Follow the trail under the power lines between the golf course on the left and Chorro Group Camp on the right, cross a paved road and begin ascending the mountain. A mile from the trailhead, there's a junction. Bear left. The route becomes steeper, passing first through coastal shrubs then conifers. The trail passes a water tank, then switchbacks to the summit.

After enjoying the fine view, you may return the same way or return via the east fork of the old exercise trail by backtracking 0.5 mile to the trail junction, then heading straight (east). You'll discover a eucalyptus grove, where monarch butterflies cluster. Cross a golf course road and rejoin the eastern section of the Exercise Trail, which returns you to the trailhead.

■ MOONSTONE BEACH
Moonstone Beach Trail
From Santa Rosa Creek to Leffingwell Landing is 2.5 miles round trip

Named for its moonstones (milky translucent agates), gravely shored Moonstone Beach is a great place for rockhounds. Moonstones and jaspers—types of quartz—were carried here by streams from the nearby coastal range and then polished by surf and sand.

From the bluffs above Moonstone Beach—part of San Simeon State Beach—the hiker may observe sea otters; the beach marks the southern boundary of the California Sea Otter Game Refuge. During January and February, gray whale-watching is excellent here because the giants swim close to shore.

This hike begins at the mouth of Santa Rosa Creek, where there's a small freshwater lagoon. The path winds atop the bluffs above Moonstone Beach and visits Leffingwell Landing, the site of a pier once figuring prominently in the nineteenth-century coastal trade and now a fine picnic area.

DIRECTIONS TO TRAILHEAD From Highway 1, just north of Cambria, turn west on Moonstone Beach Drive. Park at the Santa Rosa Creek day-use area. (Moonstone Beach Drive intersects Coast Highway both north and south of Moonstone Beach.)

THE HIKE Follow the bluff trail north from the parking area. The rugged headlands are undeveloped, in contrast to "Motel Row" on the east side of Moonstone Beach Drive.

A mile of hiking along this beach of colored rocks brings you to the old highway bridge that spans Leffingwell Creek. Just above the creek is a state park day-use area at Leffingwell Landing, where picnic tables are nestled in a sheltered

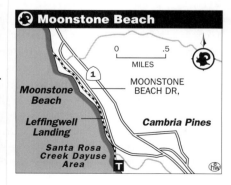

cypress grove. During the 1870s and 1880s, ships unloaded lumber and other goods here for the pioneer settlers who lived in the San Simeon Creek area.

The path picks up again at the bluff edge past the picnic area and winds through Monterey pine and cypress. Soon you'll be treated to views of Piedras Blancas Lighthouse to the north and Hearst Castle inland. Native American mortar holes are ground into the sandstone bluffs.

You can either descend the bluffs to the beach or angle over to a vista point located close to where Moonstone Beach Drive intersects the Coast Highway.

■ SAN SIMEON STATE PARK
San Simeon Creek Trail
3.5 miles round trip

What's there to see in San Simeon besides the castle? It's a common question asked by thousands of travelers on their way to Hearst Castle.

The answer is found at San Simeon State Park, which boasts a diversity of scenery from shoreline to Monterey pine forest: a new trail, complete with interpretive displays, a boardwalk that crosses a wetland, and numerous benches that offer a place to rest and observe the tranquil surroundings. The pathway circles the park's San Simeon Creek and Washburn campgrounds. About 0.25 mile of the path is wheelchair accessible.

Back in the 1880s, the park's 500 acres of backcountry were part of Ira Whittaker's ranch and dairy operation. Eucalyptus was planted, both as a windbreak and for firewood to fuel the dairy's boiler to make cheese.

Botanical highlight is a stand of Monterey pine, part of the famed Cambria pines, and one of only four native groves left on earth. In winter, monarch butterflies, more often seen on the Central Coast in eucalyptus trees and other nonnative flora, cluster in the park's Monterey pines.

San Simeon Creek is habitat for the endangered red-legged frog and Western pond turtle. Many migratory birds can be counted at the park's seasonal wetland: cinnamon teal, mallards, egrets and herons.

DIRECTIONS TO TRAILHEAD From Highway 1, just south of the turnoff for San Simeon Creek Campground, turn inland and park at Washburn day-use area. Walk inland along the service road to the signed trailhead on your right. Campers can walk to the trailhead—just west of San Simeon Creek bridge—along the campground road.

THE HIKE The path tours the eastern fringe of the seasonal wetland and soon reaches a boardwalk that leads across it from one viewing area to another. Beyond the boardwalk the trail junctions. The right fork leads southwest 0.2 mile to the Moonstone Gardens restaurant and Highway 1. Along this side

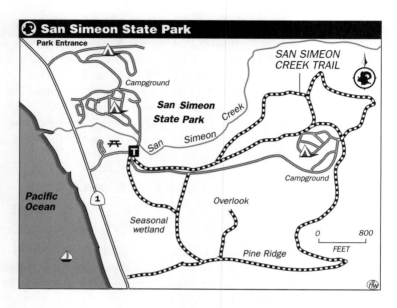

trail, Eagle-eyed hikers might get a glimpse of Hearst Castle located five miles north.

The main trail climbs onto a flat-topped, Monterey pine-dotted ridge. A sometimes overgrown path detours left (north) two hundred yards to a scenic overlook.

Our route descends from the pines into lush riparian area and turns north. A boardwalk crosses a boggy lowland filled with willow, cottonwood and a thick understory of wax myrtle and blackberry bushes.

The path next ascends grassy slopes along the eastern boundary of the park. From the former grazing land, you look out over a scene from the California of a century ago: a windmill, pastoral slopes dotted with cows, the unspoiled beauty of the southern Santa Lucia Mountains.

The trail skirts the edge of the campground, then leads west. Savor the mountain vistas as the path heads southwest on the bluffs above San Simeon Creek.

About a quarter mile from its end the trail splits. The path you've been following continues above San Simeon Creek back to the day use area. A second branch crosses the campground road and leads toward the wetland boardwalk, where you turn right and retrace the first five minutes of your hike back to the trailhead.

■ WILLIAM RANDOLPH HEARST STATE BEACH

San Simeon Bay Trail

To San Simeon Point is 2 miles round trip

Awalk along San Simeon Bay is a nice diversion before or after a tour of *La Cuesta Encantada,* the Enchanted Hill—the name of the famous castle built by newspaper publisher William Randolph Hearst.

In the mid-1860s a severe drought wrecked the Central Coast cattle business and forced many debt-ridden Spanish rancheros to sell their land. Senator George Hearst bought out the rancheros and began developing his family estate.

After the death of William Randolph Hearst in 1951, his heirs donated the beach south of Sebastian General Store for a park. It's a tranquil place; San Simeon Bay provides fairly good refuge from northwest and west winds. San Simeon Store was established in 1873 and is still in operation.

The Hearst Corp. drew up plans in the 1960s to develop what would have been a town of 65,000 people, floated various resort proposals during the 1990s, and finally agreed to sell a significant length of privately held coastline and interior ranchland to the state in 2005.

As a result of the $95 million deal, Hearst has turned over a 13-mile strip of shoreline west of Highway 1 for use as state parkland. The company also agreed to relinquish rights to develop most of the Hearst Ranch's 80,000 acres of rolling hills east of the highway.

Formerly part of the Hearst Ranch, this dramatic coast near Piedras Blancas Lighthouse is now state parkland.

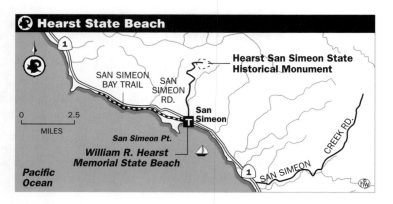

Coastal hikers cheered because the state received an easement to complete an 18-mile segment of the California Coastal Trail through the Hearst Ranch. Public access to, and trails through, the property will be phased in over the coming years as the state prepares and implements a management plan for the new parkland. Look for some exciting new hiking opportunities along this coast.

DIRECTIONS TO TRAILHEAD William R. Hearst Memorial State Beach is located on San Simeon Road west of Highway 1. Park in the state beach day use lot or along San Simeon Road south of Sebastian General Store. Park in designated areas and please respect private property signs.

THE HIKE Proceed through the picnic ground located in the eucalyptus grove just north of the fishing pier. When you reach the beach, turn up-coast. (Note that one of the development rights retained by the Hearst Corp. permits the company to build a 100-room hotel at San Simeon Point.)

When the beach begins to arc westward, ascend to a narrow dirt road leading atop the wooded bluffs. The road, which narrows to a trail, offers fine coastline and castle views as it curves toward San Simeon Point. From the point are additional breathtaking views to the south of the undeveloped San Luis Obispo County coast.

The path continues around the point on overgrown blufftop trails, then passes under the boughs of Monterey cypress on a dark tunnel-like trail for 0.25 mile before re-emerging back on the bluffs. The bluff trails grow more and more faint and erratic and you descend a low sand dune to the beach. You can follow the beach until tides and rocks prevent further progress and you meet the Coast Highway quite some distance north.

■ SILVER PEAK WILDERNESS
Salmon Creek Trail

From Highway 1 to Spruce Camp is 4 miles round trip with 800-foot elevation gain; to Estrella Camp is 6.5 miles round trip with 1,200-foot gain; return via Cruickshank-Buckeye trails is 14 miles round trip with 3,000-foot gain

Silver Peak Wilderness, situated in the far southwestern corner of Monterey County, near the border with San Luis Obispo County, is a rousing beginning to the Big Sur Backcountry. One highlight is an isolated grove of coastal redwoods along Villa Creek; it's the world's southernmost stand of these magnificent trees.

In addition to redwoods, there are other botanical highlights, including a grove of rare Sargent cypress at the head of Salmon Creek. The gray pine and Santa Lucia fir that bristle atop the peaks, and the files of oaks growing in the mountains' folds and hollows, are delights for photographers.

Other highlights of the little-visited wilderness at the far southern end of the Los Padres National Forest's Monterey District are three frisky creeks that flow from the mountains to the sea: Villa Creek, Salmon Creek and San Carpoforo Creek.

The area was geographically gerrymandered out of the Ventana Wilderness when it was established in 1984. The Sierra Club and other conservationists periodically mounted campaigns to add wilderness protection to the area and were successful in 1992 when Congress established the 14,500-acre Silver Peak Wilderness.

Hikers may see deer, squirrels, rabbits and raccoons, as well as those trail-side sunbathers—lizards. If you hear something gobble in the bushes, it's no doubt the call of a native wild turkey.

Salmon Creek Trail offers an engaging—but not easy—entryway into the southern Big Sur backcountry.

This hike, suitable for a strenuous day hike or more leisurely weekend backpack, offers a chance to sample the diversity of the south end of the Santa Lucia Mountains—lush fern canyons, fir forests, oak pasture lands—and sweeping views of the majestic coast and Salinas Valley.

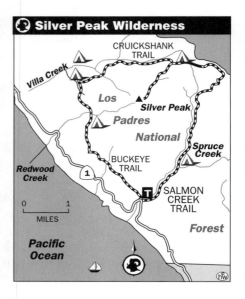

Silver Peak Wilderness

CRUICKSHANK TRAIL

Villa Creek

Los Padres National Forest

Silver Peak

Spruce Creek

BUCKEYE TRAIL

Redwood Creek

SALMON CREEK TRAIL

0   1
MILES

Pacific Ocean

DIRECTIONS TO TRAILHEAD

Salmon Creek Ranger Station (closed, but a good landmark) is located on Coast Highway, a few miles north of the San Luis Obispo/Monterey county line. The trailhead is a hundred yards south of the station.

Note the trailhead for Buckeye Trail located above the station. Buckeye Trail is your return path on your Silver Peak Wilderness loop.

Ample parking is available at the station. Signed Salmon Creek Trail begins on the east side of the highway on the south side of the creek. At the beginning of the trail, there's a great view of Salmon Creek Falls.

THE HIKE Salmon Creek Trail immediately begins climbing, first through lush stream-side vegetation, then across the exposed slopes of the canyon, covered with seasonal wildflowers. The often dense fog here guards the flower show late into spring.

A thousand feet above sea level, the trail crosses a stream and ascends into a forest of Douglas fir, often called spruce—which helps explain the forthcoming destinations of Spruce Creek and Spruce Camp.

Two miles from the trailhead is the Spruce Creek Trail junction. The trail to the right leads south toward Dutra Spring and San Carpojo Creek. The main trail continues straight ahead up the main canyon of Salmon Creek. A few hundred yards of hiking and you'll drop down to Spruce Creek Camp, located at the confluence of the waters of Salmon Creek and Spruce Creek. Spruce Creek Camp is in deep shade.

The trail resumes on the other side of Spruce Creek and continues along the south slope of Salmon Creek. You cross a meadow, then continue ascending moderately to Estrella Camp, a grassy, shady area along Salmon Creek.

The trail soon rises above the last trees and ventures out onto hot, brushy canyon slopes. You climb 1,800 feet in the next 2.5 miles; this is a very hot stretch of trail in summer.

You reach the high point of the trail (3,120 feet) at Coast Ridge Road, which marks the boundary between Ft. Hunter Liggett Military Reservation and Los Padres National Forest. Bear left on the road. On clear days you'll be able to see the ocean to the west, the Salinas Valley to the east. In 0.1 mile, you'll reach the junction with Cruickshank Trail. Descend 0.5 mile on rough eroded road to Lion's Den Camp—two small, flat areas, often situated just above the coastal clouds. Water supply is from a small creek.

Leaving Lion's Den, you follow Silver Peak Road 0.5 mile to a junction. (Peak baggers won't overlook Silver Peak—3,950 feet—on the left.) Cross the road and follow the Cruickshank Trail. The trail descends, crossing a creek, and drops 1,000 feet in the next 2.5 miles. You'll get fine views of the Villa Creek drainage. In spring, waterfalls can be seen cascading down the canyon. Silver Camp, not shown on forest service maps, is a stream-side camp with plenty of flat tenting sites.

About 0.75 mile from Silver Camp, veer south on the Buckeye Trail at Cruickshank Camp. The path begins ascending through heavy timber, climbing the shady north slope. The trail descends to Redwood Creek, crossing it and proceeding south along the ridge separating Villa Creek and Redwood Creek canyons. The trail grows more tentative as it enters a meadow and reaches Buckeye Camp, which has a developed spring.

Leaving the meadowland, you contour around to the western slopes, receiving the twin pleasures of ocean breezes and coastal views. You descend a ridge, cross Soda Springs Creek, and arrive at a signed junction. Buckeye Trail (signed Soda Springs Trail) descends to Highway 1. This hike heads south, descending a mile through grassland and chaparral back to the trailhead (behind the Salmon Creek Ranger Station).

■ SAND DOLLAR BEACH
Pacific Valley Coast Trail
From Sand Dollar Picnic Area across bluffs
is 2.5 miles round trip

Near the hamlet of Pacific Valley, the Big Sur coast arcs deeply inland in a horseshoe shape that is fringed by a long sandy beach. Sand Dollar Beach, one of Big Sur's longest sand strands, is a favorite of sunbathers and surfers; the wide bluffs above attract hikers as well as hang gliders looking for a safe landing spot.

Geologists say Pacific Valley isn't really a valley at all but a wide, flat marine terrace. (So precipitous are the Santa Lucia Mountains, early place-namers can be forgiven for calling any flatland bigger-than-a-blanket a valley.)

By whatever name, Pacific Valley is a marked contrast from most of Big Sur's slopes which tumble steeply and directly into the ocean. The valley offers a rare bit of relatively level coast walking.

Crumbly schist and shale form the coastal terrace which stands 60 to 100 feet above the surging Pacific. The blufftop is mostly covered with grass, along with clumps of lizardtail, buckwheat and sagebrush.

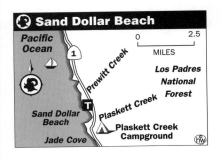

The bluffs offer dramatic coastal views as well as providing a good vantage point from which to spot sea otters and migrating California gray whales. Cows are by far the most common animal life here; Pacific Valley has been extensively grazed for decades.

You can join the trail from several hiker's stiles at Highway 1 turnouts located between Plaskett Creek Campground and the Pacific Valley store. Best place to start is at Sand Dollar Picnic Area, where you have a choice of three coastal trails.

The main trail descends directly to Sand Dollar Beach. Pause en route at the vista point, where interpretive panels help you identify the many shorebirds found here.

From the northwest end of the parking area, a footpath travels the cattle-grazed bluffs north of Sand Dollar Beach. The mile-long trail dips in and out of two ravines and crosses what has to be one of the prettiest pastures on the Pacific Coast. Shorter side trails lead to blufftop overlooks and hidden pocket beaches.

A third path leads south 0.5-mile from Sand Dollar Picnic Area toward Jade Cove.

DIRECTIONS TO TRAILHEAD The Forest Service's Sand Dollar Picnic Area is located west of Highway 1, some 4 miles south of Mill Creek Picnic Area, and about a mile south of the hamlet of Pacific Valley.

■ KIRK CREEK
Kirk Creek Trail
From Coast Highway to Espinosa Camp is 6.5 miles round trip with 1,400-foot gain; to Vicente Campground is 10 miles round trip with 2,000-foot gain

Kirk Creek Trail (often called Vicente Flat Trail) provides an ideal introduction to the charms of Big Sur, for in 5 miles the hiker experiences meadowland, coastal and canyon views, and a redwood forest.

Kirk Creek Trail climbs from the coastal scrub-covered slopes to redwood-shaded ravines to steep ridges offering dramatic vistas. Vicente Flat, which boasts campsites in both shady redwoods and sunny meadow, is a rewarding and relaxing destination.

You can make this a one-way hike if car shuttle arrangements are made. Join the upper trailhead for seven-mile long Kirk Creek Trail at Cone Peak Road (also called Coast Ridge Road) and hike 2 miles to Vicente Flat, then 5 miles down to Highway 1.

DIRECTIONS TO TRAILHEAD The signed trail is located opposite Kirk Creek Campground on Highway 1, just north of Nacimiento-Fergusson Road.

THE HIKE The trail immediately begins ascending on a series of well-graded switchbacks through brush and grassland. Sweeping views of the coast from Jade Cove to Gamboa Point are yours. One nice feature of this hike is the way it alternates from sunny exposed slopes to shady redwood ravines.

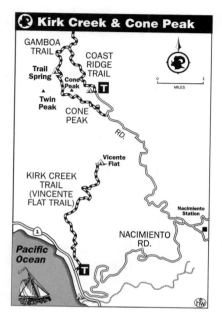

Three miles along, after topping a ridge, you'll reach the high point of Vicente Flat Trail and enjoy fine coastal views. Next you'll begin contouring above the watershed of Hare Canyon.

Tiny Espinosa Camp is 3.25 miles from the trailhead. Water is located 0.25 mile up-trail, where a tiny unnamed creek cascades down a redwood-line ravine to the trail.

The trail ascends briefly, then makes a short descent to Hare Creek and follows it. After crossing the creek, the walker encounters signed Stone Ridge Trail junction located on a low rise above the creek. To reach Vicente Flat Campground, hike upstream 150 yards.

Redwoods shade idyllic campsites. Water usually flows, even in summer and a lovely meadow beckons picnickers and sun-worshippers.

■ LIMEKILN STATE PARK
Limekiln Trail
To Limekilns is 1 mile round trip

Inspiring redwoods, a sandy beach, and a trail into Big Sur history are some of the attractions of Limekiln State Park. The park opened in September of 1995 after the state acquired a privately held campground and 716 acres of land in southernmost Big Sur.

The isolated coastal canyon was named for its 1870–80s lime-kiln operations. Quarried limestone was "kilned" (smelted) in four huge wood-fired kilns. The product—powdered lime—was packed into barrels which were then attached to cable that was strung from the canyon wall down to the beach and some 50 yards out into the Pacific Ocean. Schooners slipped into tiny Rockland Cove, as the landing was known, and loaded the lime. The lime, a primary ingredient in cement, was used to construct buildings in Monterey and San Francisco.

The backwoods industry was hard on the woods. Surrounding redwoods were chopped down to fuel the limekilns and to make barrels to store the lime.

Much of Limekiln Canyon, however, escaped harm from this early industry and, after a quiet century, nature has healed most of Limekiln Canyon's wounds. Today the canyon shelters some of the oldest, healthiest, largest and southernmost redwoods in Monterey County. Some scientists speculate that these redwoods, along with those in other nearby steep canyons, may prove to be a special subspecies or variety of redwood that differs slightly from more northerly stands.

Not everyone thinks these southern redwoods are so unique. In 1984, a private landowner wanted to log the redwoods along the west fork of Limekiln Creek. Thanks to conservationists from around the state and the local Big Sur Land Trust, the trees were spared, and their habitat preserved in the public domain.

Limekiln Canyon is one of the Pacific Coast's steepest coastal canyons; it rises from sea level to more than 5,000 feet in elevation in about 3.5 miles.

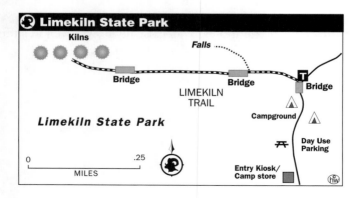

This abrupt gradient means a tremendous diversity of flora. Botanists have identified twelve different plant communities within the confines of the canyon.

When the California Department of Parks and Recreation acquired Limekiln Canyon, it made some facilities improvements, but not many. The park's plumbing system remains problematic. Campsites are Big Sur funky, definitely not of the quality of those grand northern redwood park campgrounds designed by landscape architects.

Still, the park is very much undiscovered, and its family atmosphere and tranquil redwoods more than make up for any lack of facilities. The state park's campground and small camp store is managed by California Land Management, a private concessionaire.

Hiking is limited to the half-mile long trail leading to the lime kilns. It's possible that one day trail links will be developed to connect to the extensive trail system higher on Cone Peak.

DIRECTIONS TO TRAILHEAD From San Luis Obispo, follow Highway 1 some 90 miles north to the signed turnoff for Limekiln State Park. The park is about 40 miles north of Hearst Castle, some 55 miles south of Carmel.

The turnoff is on the inland side of the highway, just south of the south end of the Limekiln Canyon bridge. Day-use parking is located just past the entry kiosk.

THE HIKE Walk through the campground to the first of three bridges and join the signed trail. Amble creekside to the next bridge where you'll spot a signed, right-forking side trail that leads one-eighth mile to a pretty little waterfall.

The path continues among the tall redwoods and within sight of some lovely pools and cascades. After crossing a third bridge, the path ends at the limekilns. Four towering kilns, partially engulfed by the recovering redwood forest, stand as peculiar monuments to a long-gone industry.

See Map on Page 137

■ **CONE PEAK**
Cone Peak Trail
To Cone Peak summit is 4.5 miles round trip with 1,400-foot elevation gain

Cone Peak, a geographical landmark to coast travelers for more than a hundred years, is the most abrupt pitch of country along the Pacific Coast. It rises to 5,155 feet in about 3.5 miles from sea level. On a clear day in winter, as you stand on Sand Dollar Beach, the snow-covered peak is a stirring sight.

Botanically, Cone Peak is a very important mountain. On its steep slopes Thomas Coulter and David Douglas discovered the Santa Lucia fir, considered the rarest and most unique fir in North America. (Tree-lovers know that when

A ranger inspects the Cone Peak Trail, 1920.

names were attached to western cone-bearing trees, Coulter's went to a pine, Douglas' to a fir.)

The spire-like Santa Lucia fir, or bristlecone fir, is found only in scattered stands in northern San Luis Obispo, and southern Monterey counties in the Santa Lucia Mountains. Typically, this fir occurs above the highest coast redwoods (about 2,000 feet) within evergreen mixed forest. Santa Lucia fir concentrates in steep, rocky, fire-resistant spots at elevations from 2,000 to 5,000 feet.

The steep trail to the top of Cone Peak rewards the hiker with great Big Sur views. Cone Peak's steepness—the sudden change in elevation—contributes to its habitat diversity and is apparent to toiling hikers who work their way slowly up the mountain's pine- and fir-dotted slopes.

DIRECTIONS TO TRAILHEAD From Highway 1, 4 miles south of Lucia and just south of Kirk Creek Campground, or about 9 miles north of Gorda, turn east on Nacimiento-Fergusson Road. This road provides dramatic coastal views as it ascends sharply 7 miles to Nacimiento Summit. At the signed junction at the summit, turn left on graded Coast Ridge Road (Cone Peak Road) and follow it 5 miles north along the ridge to the signed trail junction on the west side of the road. Parking is adequate for a few cars. (Warning: During rainy season, Cone Peak Road may be closed.)

THE HIKE The well-graded trail crosses brush-covered slopes. Soon the trail begins a series of steep switchbacks. You'll enjoy views of Santa Lucia fir and Coulter pine. As the trail gains elevation, sugar pine predominates.

After gaining more than two thousand feet in 2 miles, hikers reach a signed junction. (A trail leads west 1.25 miles down to steep, deeply shaded Trail Springs Camp. For an interesting loop around Cone Peak, you can join Gamboa Trail and ascend another 1.25 miles to the Coast Ridge Trail. You can then follow Coast Ridge Trail to its junction with Coast Ridge Road and follow the road a mile back to your vehicle.

From this junction, the Cone Peak summit trail ascends a final quarter-mile eastward to the fire lookout atop Cone Peak summit. The lookout is staffed during fire season.

Enjoy fine views of the valleys to the east and coastline to the west. Spreading before you is a panorama of peaks: Pinyon Peak, Ventana Double Cone, Junipero Serra Peak, Uncle Sam Mountain.

Return the same way, or hike the optional loop through Trail Springs Camp and around the great peak.

■ MCWAY FALLS
Waterfall, Overlook Trails
0.5 to 0.75 miles each

For most visitors, "Big Sur" is synonymous with popular Pfeiffer Big Sur State Park. Often overlooked is a smaller slice of Big Sur located 10 miles south—Julia Pfeiffer Burns State Park. It's a shame to overlook it. A redwood grove, dramatic coastal vistas and the only major California waterfall to tumble into the Pacific are some of the park's attractions.

The park is a tribute to hardy pioneer Julia Pfeiffer Burns, remembered for her deep love of the Big Sur backcountry. Her father, Michael Pfeiffer, started a ranch in the Santa Lucia Mountains in 1869. In 1915, Julia Pfeiffer married John Burns, and the two ran a cattle ranch while living at their home located south of the present park.

You can easily sample the coastal charms of four-square-mile Julia Pfeiffer Burns State Park by following the short Waterfall and Partington Cove trails. The park's coastal trails are great "leg-stretcher" jaunts to break up the coastal drive. In winter, the paths provide fine observation points from which to sight migrating California gray whales.

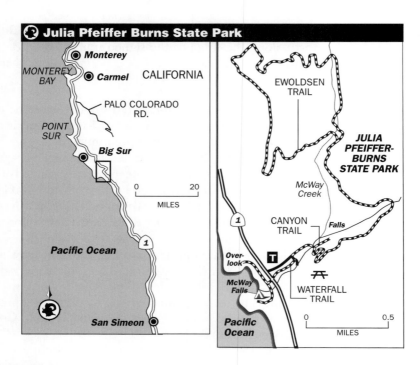

DIRECTIONS TO TRAILHEAD Julia Pfeiffer Burns State Park straddles Highway 1, about 36 miles south of Carmel and some 10 miles south of Pfeiffer Big Sur State Park. Turn inland into the park and proceed to the day-use lot.

THE HIKE From the Julia Pfeiffer Burns State Park lot, take the signed trail toward Scenic Overlook. Along McWay Creek you'll spot some eucalyptus, quite a botanical contrast to the redwoods growing up-creek. (During spring, ceanothus and dogwood splash color along the trail). The path leads through a tunnel under Coast Highway and emerges to offer the hiker grand panoramas of the Big Sur coast.

You'll soon reach the overlook, where you can observe slender but dramatic McWay Falls tumbling a hundred feet from the granite cliffs into McWay Cove. On your return, you can take a side trail and meander over to the park's cypress-shaded environmental campsites, which are perched on the former site of Waterfall House.

McWay Falls on the Big Sur Coast.

See Map on Page 142

■ JULIA PFEIFFER BURNS STATE PARK
Ewoldsen Trail
4.3 mile loop with 1,600-foot elevation gain

Sometimes visitors to Julia Pfeiffer Burns State Park are so enchanted by the spectacle of McWay Falls tumbling into the Pacific, they overlook the park's considerable backcountry—more than 3,600 acres of dramatic ridges, oak-dotted meadows and rugged, redwood-filled canyons.

Ewoldsen Trail, named for the former ranch foreman who fashioned this path from a one-time logging route back in 1933, tours McWay Canyon and surrounding slopes. The trail was closed after the 1985 Rat Creek Fire burned most of the state park but the lower portion has subsequently been repaired. Pre-fire Ewoldsen Trail connected to the Tanbark Trail; however this upper length has not been reconstructed.

For the hiker, Ewoldsen Trail offers an intriguing contrast between the cool, quiet redwood groves in McWay Canyon and the exposed grassy coastal ridge. Fogless days mean splendid views from Lopez Point north to Pfeiffer Point.

DIRECTIONS TO TRAILHEAD Julia Pfeiffer Burns State park is located just off Highway 1, some 36 miles south of Carmel and 10 miles south of Pfeiffer Big Sur State Park. Turn east into the park and proceed to the day-use lot.

THE HIKE Canyon Trail follows redwood-lined McWay Creek, passing the park's picnic area and crossing a bridge near an old barn. After a quarter-mile, the path reaches a junction. Canyon Trail continues a short distance up McWay Creek to reach a small waterfall.

Ewoldsen Trail switchbacks up the canyon wall amidst a mixed forest of tanoak, bay laurel and redwood. A bit more than a mile out, the trail reaches a junction. Fork right, taking the east leg of the Ewoldsen loop.

The path continues climbing along the cascading creek past fire-scarred redwoods. After a half-mile, the trail leaves McWay Canyon for scrubbier slopes, climbing 0.75-mile to the ridgetop crest of the trail. Some day you'll be able to hike to Tin House and connect with Tanbark Trail, but for now, you'll continue your loop, following the path to a Pacific-facing grassland, then beginning a somewhat steep descent.

Coastal vistas are inspiring. This part of the trail is a good lookout perch for California gray whales during their winter migration. Less inspiring is the rather close-up view of the Great Slide of 1983—or rather the scar from its repair—a terraced wasteland that is still ugly despite extensive replanting efforts.

The trail departs the ridge, descending back into McWay Canyon and the tranquillity of its redwoods. You'll cross McWay Creek and close the loop, retracing your initial steps a mile back to the trailhead.

■ PARTINGTON COVE
Partington Cove Trail
From Highway 1 to Partington Cove is 0.5-mile round trip

Partington Cove, part of Julia Pfeiffer Burns State Park, was once the site of a dock where tanbark was loaded onto waiting ships. During the 1880s, homesteader John Partington operated a landing here.

Woodsmen stripped the tanbark oak, a kind of cross between an oak and a chestnut. Before synthetic chemicals were invented to tan leather, gathering and shipping of the bark was a considerable industry along the Big Sur coast.

This short leg-stretcher of a walk drops down to Partington Creek and over to the deep blue waters of the cove.

DIRECTIONS TO TRAILHEAD Partington Cove Trail begins 1.8 miles north of Julia Pfeiffer Burns State Park entrance at the point where Highway 1 crosses Partington Creek.

THE HIKE From an iron gate, follow the dirt road that drops down into the canyon cut by Partington Creek. (A steep side trail continues down to the tiniest of beaches at the creek mouth.) The main trail crosses the creek on a wooden footbridge and passes through a hundred-foot-long tunnel that was blasted through the rocky cliffs.

At Partington Cove are the remains of a dock. The not-so-placid waters of the cove stir the seaweed about as if in a soup, and you wonder how boats moored here actually managed to load their cargo of bark and lumber.

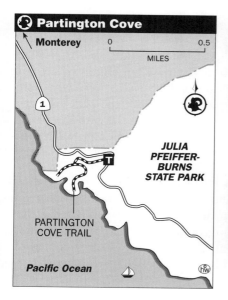

Partington Cove.

Offshore, between Partington Point and McWay Creek to the south, is Julia Pfeiffer Burns Underwater Area, placed under state protection in 1970. Kelp forests provide habitat for abalone, lingcod and many more sea creatures, as well as for otters, which you may glimpse if you follow the crumbling cliffside trail from the dock site to the end of Partington Point.

■ BIG SUR RIVER
Pine Ridge Trail
To Ventana Camp Junction is 4.25 miles one way with 1,100-foot elevation gain; to Barlow Flat is 7 miles; to Sykes Camp is 10 miles; to Redwood Creek Camp is 12 miles with 1,400-foot gain

Sykes Camp, on the banks of the Big Sur River, has a little bit of everything—morning sun, afternoon shade, a deep swimming hole and hot springs. The camp is a 10-mile journey from Pfeiffer Big Sur State Park, and one of California's classic weekend backpacking trips.

Sykes' charms are undeniable, but seekers of solitude should steer clear on weekends during the summer months. Rangers estimate that during some years, about 75 percent of the backcountry use in the Monterey District of Los Padres National Forest occurs along the 10 miles of trail from Pfeiffer Big Sur State Park to Sykes.

A rustic sign marks a rugged land.

If you like to swim, Ventana Camp has some excellent swimming holes. It's a 10-mile round trip day hike to reach the camp.

DIRECTIONS TO TRAILHEAD Pfeiffer Big Sur State Park is about 26 miles south of Carmel on Highway 1. The trailhead for Pine Ridge Trail is located about a mile south of the park entrance at a wide turnout on the east side of the highway. Close by is the Big Sur Multi-Agency Facility—an information center.

THE HIKE Leaving the highway behind, Pine Ridge Trail marches up redwood-shaded slopes above Big Sur Campground. Mt. Manuel dominates the northern skyline, while glimpses of the Pacific can be seen behind you.

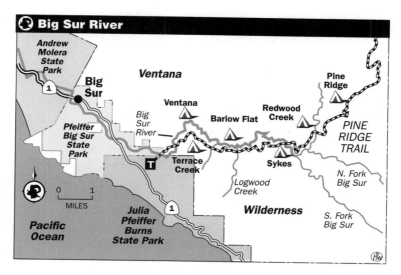

The trail passes thorough a tanbark oak forest, enters the Ventana Wilderness and offers westward views of the Big Sur River. After about 4 miles of dipping and climbing, the trail reaches a junction with a side trail leading to Ventana Camp, 1.25 miles north. For a walk of slightly more than 10 miles round trip, take the trail to Ventana Camp, located near the convergence of Ventana Creek and the Big Sur River. In 1968, the camp achieved national notoriety when the U.S. Forest Service closed it for a time due to the so-called "hippie problem." Near the camp is a great swimming hole. After lunch and a swim, return to the trailhead.

Pine Ridge Trail continues east for a mile to another side trail. This one leads a short distance to redwood-shaded Terrace Creek Camp, another destination that would make an ideal lunch stop/turnaround point for a day hike.

Pine Ridge Trail crosses Terrace Creek, ascends through woodland, descends a hill, crosses Logwood Creek and arrives at Barlow Flat. This flat, expansive camp is on the north side of the Big Sur River, in the shade of redwoods. Great swimming and sunbathing here. Leaving Barlow Flat, the trail stays below the river for another 3 miles until it reaches Sykes Camp.

A quarter-mile downriver, via some wading and a side trail, is Sykes Hot Springs, which includes a couple of hot seeps dammed to create small pools, as well as a big ten-foot-long, rock-lined pool. You'll enjoy basking in the 100-degree waters and gazing up at the night sky.

Two more miles of steep, uphill travel on Pine Ridge Trail will bring you to Redwood Creek Camp, which has several tent sites. It's a rarely visited alternative to Sykes Camp.

■ PFEIFFER BIG SUR STATE PARK

Valley View Trail

From Big Sur Lodge to Pfeiffer Falls, Valley View, is 2 miles round trip with 200-foot elevation gain

For most visitors, "Big Sur" means Pfeiffer Big Sur State Park. The state park—and its brief but popular trail system—is dominated by the Big Sur River, which meanders through redwood groves on its way to the Pacific Ocean, 5 miles away.

John Pfeiffer, for whom the park was named, homesteaded 160 acres of mountainous terrain between Sycamore Canyon and the Big Sur River. In 1884, he moved into a cabin perched above the Big Sur River Gorge. (You can see the reconstructed "Homestead Cabin," which is located on the park's Gorge Trail.) John Pfeiffer sold and donated some of his ranchland to the state in the 1930s, and it became the nucleus of the state park.

This walk, which follows the Pfeiffer Falls Trail and Valley View Trail, is an easy "leg stretcher" suitable for the whole family. It visits Pfeiffer Falls and offers a good introduction to the delights of the state park.

DIRECTIONS TO TRAILHEAD Pfeiffer Big Sur State Park is located off Highway 1, some 26 miles south of Carmel and 2 miles south of the hamlet of Big Sur. Beyond the entry booth, turn left at the stop sign, then veer right (uphill). Very soon, you'll find some day-use parking. A much larger parking area is located near the store and restaurant at the bottom of the hill.

THE HIKE From the signed trailhead, follow the trail to Pfeiffer Falls. Very shortly, on your left, you'll spot a trail heading left to Valley View; this will be

The Pfeiffer family's rustic resort welcomed forest visitors.

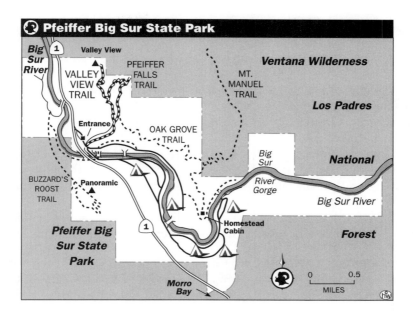

your return path. The walk continues under stately redwoods and meanders along with Pfeiffer-Redwood Creek.

You'll soon ascend a redwood stairway to a junction with Oak Grove Trail, which leads rightward 1.5 miles through oak and madrone woodland over to the Mt. Manuel Trail. Stay left at this junction and follow Pfeiffer Falls Trail through the forest and past a second branch of the Valley View Trail.

A stairway leads to an observation platform at the base of the falls. Pfeiffer-Redwood Creek cascades over a 40-foot precipice to a small grotto.

After enjoying the falls, descend the stairway and bear right on the Valley View Trail, which leaves behind the redwoods and ascends into a tanbark oak and coast live oak woodland.

At a signed junction, turn right and follow the pathway along a minor ridge to a lookout. The Pacific Ocean pounding the Point Sur headlands and the Big Sur River Valley are part of the fine view.

Backtrack along Valley View Trail and at the first junction stay right and descend on Pfeiffer Falls Trail back to Pfeiffer-Redwood Canyon. Another right at the canyon bottom brings you back to the trailhead.

■ PFEIFFER BEACH
Pfeiffer Beach Trail
To Pfeiffer Beach is 0.75-mile round trip

Los Padres is one of only three national forests in America with ocean frontage. Named for the pioneer Pfeiffer family, this secluded white sand beach faces the turbulent sea which sends awesome waves crashing through blowholes in the rocks.

Many scenes from the film *The Sandpiper*, with Elizabeth Taylor and Richard Burton, were shot here. The magic of motion pictures gave us a calm beach where small boats landed easily. Big Sur residents laugh every time this movie is shown on late-night television.

With its hazardous surf and gusty winds, Pfeiffer Beach cannot be said to be a comfortable stretch of coastline; it is, however, a magnificent one.

DIRECTIONS TO TRAILHEAD Driving south, a mile south of Big Sur State Park, take the second right-hand-turn off Highway 1 (west). Sycamore Canyon Road is a sharp downhill turn. Follow the 2-mile narrow, winding and sometimes washed-out road to the Forest Service parking area.

THE HIKE Follow the wide sandy path and boardwalk leading from the parking lot through the cypress trees. Sycamore Creek empties into a small lagoon near the beach.

Marvel at the sea stacks, blowholes and caves, and try to find a place out of the wind to eat your lunch. The more ambitious may pick their way over rocks northward for a mile around a point to a second crescent-shaped beach.

Early forest rangers inspect the Big Sur coastline.

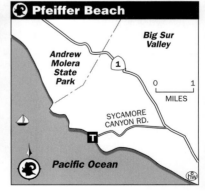

■ ANDREW MOLERA
STATE PARK'S BEACH
Beach, Headlands Trails
3 miles round trip

Mountains, meadows and the mouth of Big Sur River are some of the highlights of a walk through Andrew Molera State Park, largest state park along the Big Sur coast.

More than 20 miles of trail weave through the park, which has a diversity of ecosystems. You can hike along the bluffs overlooking 3 miles of beach, and climb through meadows and oak woodland. At the river mouth are a shallow lagoon and beautiful sandy beach.

In 1855, Yankee fur trader Juan Bautista Roger Cooper acquired this land, formerly part of the Mexican land grant Rancho El Sur. Acquaintances of his day—and historians of today—speculate that Cooper used his "Ranch of the South" as a landing spot, bringing cargo ashore at the Big Sur River mouth to avoid the high customs fees of Monterey Harbor.

Grandson Andrew Molera, who inherited the ranch, had a successful dairy operation. His Monterey Jack cheese was particularly prized. He was a hospitable fellow, popular with neighbors who camped along the river while awaiting shipments of supplies from San Francisco.

A good leg-stretcher walk is to take Beach Trail to the beach at the mouth of the Big Sur River, then return via Creamery Meadow Trail. Beach Trail and a number of other park roads are old dirt roads, which allow side-by-side walking, thus appealing to sociable hikers.

Molera's bold headlands offer a hike to remember.

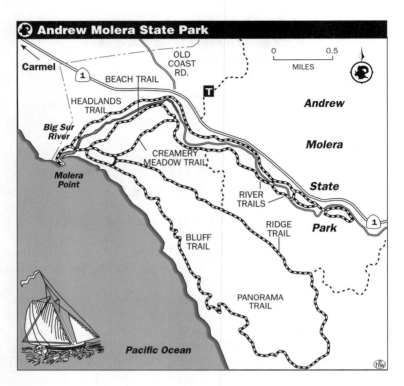

During summer, you'll see surfers heading for the beach. You may also hear a number of foreign languages en route. The state park's walk-in campground is very popular with European visitors.

A longer tour of the park can be made via the Bluff, Panorama and Ridge trails. The coastal views from these trails are magnificent.

Note that the round trip loop described below relies on seasonal (late spring to early fall) footbridges. At other times, you'll have to make this trip an out-and-back or get your feet (and possibly much more) wet by crossing the river.

DIRECTIONS TO TRAILHEAD Andrew Molera State Park is just off Highway 1, some 21 miles south of Carmel.

THE HIKE From the parking lot, cross the Big Sur River on the seasonal footbridge. Walk 100 yards of so along a broad path that soon splits. Bear right onto Beach Trail. (The left fork joins Creamery Meadow Trail, an ideal return route for those who like loop trails.) The trail stays near the river, whose banks are crowded with thimbleberry and blackberry, honeysuckle vines, willow and bay laurel.

At 0.3 mile, you pass through the park's campground. A side trail leads to Cooper Cabin, an 1861 redwood structure that's the oldest building on Big Sur's coast.

At the river mouth is a small beach and shallow lagoon, frequented by sanderlings, willets and many more shorebirds. A short path (Headlands Trail) leads above the beach to Molera Point, where you can watch for whales (January through April) or passing ships. The beach to the south is walkable at low tide.

Loop around the point and then either return the same way or via Creamery Meadow Trail on the south side of the Big Sur River.

■ ANDREW MOLERA STATE PARK'S BACKCOUNTRY
Beach, Bluff, Panorama, Ridge Trails
9.5-mile loop with 1,000-foot elevation gain

The largest state park (4,800 acres) on the Big Sur coast, Andrew Molera offers the hiker access to broad bluffs, redwood-shaded canyons and high ridgetops. Depending on time, inclination and creative route-planning, a short, medium-sized or lengthy loop can be made through the big park.

One of my favorite loops, a 9.5-mile jaunt, links a half-dozen paths and provides a memorable tour: the Big Sur River, the bluffs above Molera Beach, steep grassy ridgetops that afford vistas of the coast as well as Ventana Wilderness peaks.

Note that the round trip loop described below relies on seasonal (late spring to early fall) footbridges. At other times, you'll have to get your feet (and possibly much more) wet by crossing the Big Sur River.

DIRECTIONS TO TRAILHEAD Andrew Molera State Park is just off California 1, some 21 miles south of Carmel.

THE HIKE From the parking lot, cross the Big Sur River on the seasonal footbridge. Walk 100 yards of so along a broad path that soon splits. Bear right onto Beach Trail. (The left fork joins Creamery Meadow Trail, an ideal return route for those who like loop trails.) The trail stays near the river, whose banks are crowded with thimbleberry and blackberry, honeysuckle vines, willow and bay laurel.

At 0.3 mile, you pass through the park's campground. A side trail leads to Cooper Cabin, an 1861 redwood structure that's the oldest building on Big Sur's coast.

At the river mouth is a small beach and shallow lagoon, frequented by sanderlings, willets and many more shorebirds. A short path (Headlands Trail) leads above the beach to Molera Point, where you can watch for whales (January through April) or passing ships. The beach to the south is walkable at low tide.

Loop around the point and then cross the summer footbridge over the Big Sur River. You'll follow the upper part of the beach, climb the bluffs and head south to a junction with Bluff Trail and Ridge Trail.

Wide Bluff Trail, an old road, heads south over the almost level bluffs, a marine terrace cloaked in grasses and coastal scrub. Summer-blooming lizard-tail blankets the terrace in yellow. Bluff Trail reaches a junction with Spring Trail, which offers a quarter-mile route to Molera Beach. (A picnic on the beach and a return to the trailhead from here would add up to a 6-mile round trip hike.)

About 1.75 miles from the mouth of the Big Sur River, Bluff Trail gives way to Panorama Trail, a more rigorous path that soon drips into a deep gully, then climbs steeply up a ridge. Wind-stunted redwoods cling to life on the ridge, which climbs toward the southern boundary of the park and ascends to a junction with Ridge Trail at about 5.5 miles from the trailhead. A bench offers a place to take it easy and eat your lunch. Your rewards for gaining about 900 feet in elevation are great views of the state park, the coast to the south and triangular-shaped Cone Peak, one of the high points of the Santa Lucia Mountains.

Ridge Trail begins its long (nearly 4 miles) descent northwest along the park's main ridge. You'll pass through an oak grove, then a tanoak and redwood forest, soon emerging onto the trail's more characteristic open, grassy slopes. Hidden Trail offers something of a shortcut to River Trail and back to the trailhead.

Ridge Trail continues back toward the coast, whereupon you can retrace your steps by taking Beach Trail to the trailhead or return via River Trail on the south side of the Big Sur River.

■ POINT SUR LIGHT STATION STATE HISTORIC PARK
Point Sur Light Station Trail
0.5-mile guided walk

During the nineteenth century, when coastal roads were few and poor, most cargo was transported by ship. Ships traveled close to shore so that they could take advantage of the protection offered by bay and point. This heavy coastal trade—and its dangers—prompted the U.S. Lighthouse Service Board to establish a series of lighthouses along California's coast located about 60 miles apart.

Point Sur had been the death of many ships, and mariners had been petitioning for a beacon for many years when the government in 1885 appropriated $50,000 to construct a light station. The Point Sur light joined the one at Piedras Blancas situated 60 miles south and the one located 60 miles north at Pigeon Point.

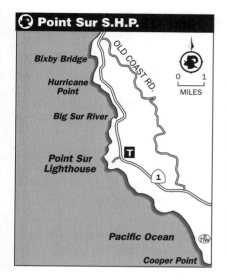

Point Sur S.H.P.

Bixby Bridge

OLD COAST RD.

Hurricane
Point

Big Sur River

Point Sur
Lighthouse

Pacific Ocean

Cooper Point

0   1
MILES

The first light, which became operational in 1889, utilized one of the famed Fresnel lenses designed by French physicist Augustin Jean Fresnel. A whale oil lantern was the first light source. In later years, kerosene fueled the operation. Soot problems from the not-very-clean burning kerosene kept the keepers busy polishing the glass and worrying about surprise visits from supervisors who conducted "white glove" inspections.

The lighthouse became fully automated in 1975. The original light, visible for 23 miles out to sea, is now on display in the Maritime Museum of Monterey.

Point Sur Lighthouse.

The old stone buildings, when viewed from Highway 1, are intriguing; they're even more so when viewed up close on one of the tours conducted by volunteer docents. While the station undergoes restoration, the only way to see the facility—the only intact light station with accompanying support buildings on the California coast—is by guided tour.

The tour includes the lighthouse itself, the keepers' houses, the blacksmith shop and the barn, where livestock was kept. You'll learn the fascinating story of the isolated life lived by the four keepers and their families.

Docent-led tours are currently offered on weekends and on some Wednesdays: Saturdays 10 A.M. and 2 P.M., Sundays 10 A.M. and Wednesdays 10 A.M., weather permitting. There's a fee for the tours, which have a limited number of slots—available on a first-come, first-served basis. Suggestion: Arrive early. For more information: (408) 625-4419.

The walk to the lighthouse is interesting for more than historical reasons. Geology buffs will call the path to the light the "Tombolo Trail;" a tombolo, rare on the California coast, is a sand bar connecting an island to the mainland.

The view from atop the 360-foot-high basaltic rock is superb. You're eyeball-to-eyeball with the gulls and cormorants. To the south is False Sur, named for its confusing resemblance to Point Sur, when viewed from sea.

In 1980, Point Sur Light Station was designated a state historic landmark, and in 1984 the U.S. Department of the Interior turned it over to the California Department of Parks and Recreation. The old Lighthouse Service Board was long-ago absorbed by the U.S. Coast Guard, and the kerosene lamp and steam-driven warning whistle have been replaced by a computer-directed electric beam and radio beacon, but Point Sur Light Station, as it has for a century, continues to warn ships of the treacherous Big Sur Coast.

DIRECTIONS TO TRAILHEAD Point Sur Light Station State Historic Park is located on the west side of Highway 1, some 19 miles south of Carmel and one quarter mile north of Point Sur Naval Facility.

■ SOBERANES POINT
Soberanes Point Trail
1.75 miles round trip

"Overlooked and underrated" would be one way to characterize the dramatic shoreline of Garrapata State Park. Neighbor to the north Point Lobos State Reserve, often billed as "the greatest meeting of land and sea in the world," deservedly gets a lot of attention. And Andrew Molera, Garrapata's sister state park to the south, boasts the Big Sur River and a walk-in campground that attracts visitors from around the world.

What Garrapata offers is some of the Central Coast's most striking coastline—hidden beaches, rocky coves and bluffs carpeted with native wildflowers

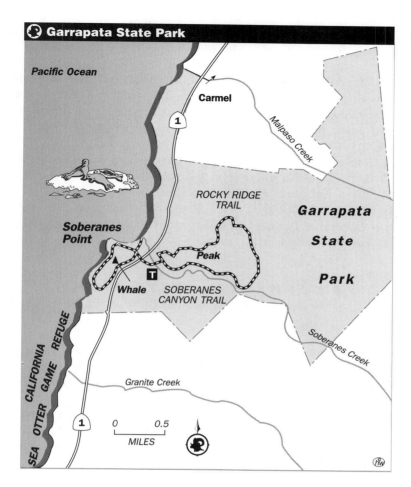

and introduced ice plant. Another lure is wonderful wildlife-watching: Sea otters and sea lions bask on Lobos Rocks just offshore. Sea birds, such as oyster catchers and cormorants glide over the waves. Garrapata's bluffs are excellent vantage points from which to observe California gray whales on their annual winter migration.

Garrapata Beach is a half-mile long sand strand accessible by a short quarter-mile long trail that begins at Gate 32 on the ocean side of Highway 1.

Be extra cautious on Garrapata's sandy shores and rocky points. The coast here is known for its "rogue" waves—ocean swells that have swept the unwary off their feet, and in some cases to their deaths.

Best marked paths in the park surround Soberanes Point, a bold headland that terminates in a roundish ridge known as Whale Peak.

DIRECTIONS TO TRAILHEAD From Highway 1, some 7 miles south of Carmel, look for GATE 13 on the west side of the highway. Park in a safe manner off the highway. Soberanes Point Trail shares a trailhead with Soberanes Canyon Trail located on the east side of Highway 1.

THE HIKE Head south, visiting some windswept cypress, then walking onto the bluffs to an unsigned junction. Head right toward Soberanes Point, passing along the coastal side of Whale Peak. Go right at the next junction, dropping toward a second point. You'll contour to the Coast Highway side of Whale Peak.

A mile from the trailhead, an inviting quarter-mile-long connector path leads to Whale Peak Saddle, where short footpaths lead in turn to the north and south summits of the peak. From both summits, hikers enjoy grand coastal views north to Carmel's Yankee Point and south to Point Sur.

Return to Soberanes Point Trail, which heads south, rejoining the first 0.1-mile of trail and returning to the trailhead.

See Map
on Page
157

■ GARRAPATA STATE PARK
Rocky Ridge, Soberanes Canyon Trails
7 miles round trip with 1,200-foot elevation gain

Undeveloped and usually overlooked, Garrapata State Park offers a lot of Big Sur in a compact area. The park features 2 miles (probably closer to 4 miles counting the twists and turns) of spectacular coastline and a steep sampling of the Santa Lucia Mountains.

Rocky Ridge Trail quickly leaves Highway 1 behind and offers far-reaching views of the Santa Lucia Mountains and the sea. A grand loop of the state park can be made by returning to the trailhead via redwood-lined Soberanes Canyon.

The name Soberanes is linked with the early Spanish exploration of California. Soldier José María Soberanes marched up the coast to Monterey with the Gaspar de Portolá expedition of 1769. Seven years later, Soberanes served as a guide for Juan Bautista De Anza, whose party pushed north to San Francisco Bay. Grandson José Antonio Ezequiel Soberanes acquired the coastal bluff and magnificent backcountry that became known as the Soberanes Ranch.

Rocky Ridge Trail will be more enjoyable for the gung-ho hiker than the novice. The trail ascends very steeply as it climbs Rocky Ridge. Then, after gaining the ridge, hikers must descend an extremely steep mile (we're talking about a 20 to 30 percent grade here) to connect to Soberanes Canyon Trail.

The leg-weary, or those looking for an easier walk, will simply stroll through the redwoods of Soberanes Canyon and not attempt Rocky Ridge Trail.

DIRECTIONS TO TRAILHEAD Garrapata State Park is 7 miles south of Carmel Valley Road, off Highway 1 in Carmel. There's a highway turnout at mileage marker 65.8.

THE HIKE From the gate on the east side of Highway 1, walk inland over a dirt road to a nearby barn, then a wee bit farther to cross Soberanes Creek and reach a trail junction. Soberanes Canyon heads east along the creek, but Rocky Ridge-bound hikers will keep with the closed road, heading north and dipping in and out of a gully.

Hikers rapidly leave the highway behind as the path climbs the rugged slopes, which are dotted with black sage, golden yarrow and bush lupine. The route uses few switchbacks as it ascends 1,435-foot Rocky Ridge. From atop the ridge are good views to the east of Soberanes Creek watershed, to the west of Soberanes Point, and to the north of Carmel and the Monterey Peninsula.

The route contours eastward around the ridge. To the north is the steep canyon cut by Malpaso Creek. After leveling out for a time, the grassy path reaches a small cow pond, then begins to descend over steep but pastoral terrain.

The trail is cut by cattle paths, a reminder of a century of grazing. The route plunges very steeply down the bald north wall of Soberanes Canyon. The mile-long killer descent finally ends when you intersect Soberanes Canyon Trail and begin descending, much more gently, to the west.

Soberanes Canyon Trail stays close to the creek and enters the redwoods. Western sword fern, redwood sorrel, blackberry bushes and Douglas iris decorate the path.

Near the mouth of the canyon, the trail becomes gentler. Willow, watercress and horsetail line the lower reaches of Soberanes Creek. Soon after passing some out-of-place mission cactus, brought north from Mexico by Spanish missionaries, hikers return to the trailhead.

■ POINT LOBOS STATE RESERVE'S CYPRESS GROVE
Cypress Grove Trail
0.75-mile round trip

Sometimes it's the tranquil moments at Point Lobos you remember: Black-tailed deer moving through the forest, the fog-wrapped cypress trees. And sometimes it's nature's more boisterous moments that you recall: the bark of sea lions at Sea Lion Point, the sea thundering against the cliffs.

A visit to Point Lobos State Reserve, in good weather and bad, is always memorable. Some of photographer Ansel Adams' greatest work was inspired by the wind-sculpted cypress, lonely sentinels perched at the edge of the continent. Landscape artist Francis McComas called Point Lobos "the greatest meeting of land and water in the world."

At Point Lobos, the Monterey cypress makes a last stand. Botanists believe that during Pleistocene times, some half-million years ago, when the climate was wetter and cooler than it is now, huge forests of cypress grew along the

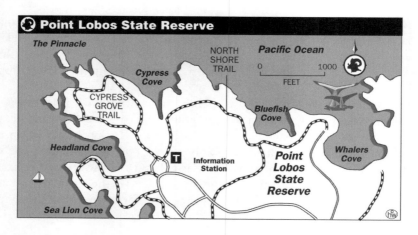

coast—indeed, throughout North America. When the world's climate warmed, the cypress retreated to a few damp spots. Nowadays, the grove at Point Lobos and another across Carmel Bay at Cypress Point are the only two native stands in existence.

The Monterey cypress, with the help of humans, can cross hot and dry regions and become established in cool areas elsewhere. In fact, this rare conifer is easily grown from seed and has been successfully distributed all over the world, so it's puzzling why the trees' natural range is so restricted.

Cypress Grove Trail, a 0.75-mile loop, visits Allan Memorial Grove, which honors A.M. Allan who, in the early years of this century, helped preserve Point Lobos from resort developers. When Point Lobos became a reserve in 1933, Allan's family gave the cypress grove to the state.

The trail passes near The Pinnacle, northernmost point in the reserve. Winds off the Pacific really batter this point and the exposed trees. To combat the wind, the trees adopt a survival response called buttressing: a narrow part of the trunk faces the wind while the trunk grows thicker on the other side in order to brace itself. The wind-sculpted trunks and wind-shaped foliage give the cypress their fantastic shapes.

Cypress Grove Trail offers great tree-framed views of Carmel Bay and Monterey peninsula. Offshore are the rocky islands off Sea Lion Point. The Spaniards called the domain of these creatures *Punto de los Lobos Marinos*— Point of the Sea Wolves. You'll probably hear the barking of the sea lions before you see them.

DIRECTIONS TO TRAILHEAD Point Lobos State Reserve is located 3 miles south of Carmel just off Highway 1. Both Cypress Grove Trail and North Shore Trail depart from the northwest end of Cypress Grove parking area.

See Map on Page 160

■ POINT LOBOS STATE RESERVE'S NORTH SHORE
North Shore Trail
3 miles or more

North Shore Trail meanders through groves of Monterey pine, less celebrated than the Monterey cypress, but nearly as rare. Native stands of the fog-loving, three-needled pine grow in only a few places in California.

North Shore Trail wanders through the pines and offers terrific coastal panoramas. Watchers of the late, late show and admirers of spooky beauty will enjoy the shrouds of pale green lichen hanging from the dead branches of the Monterey pines. Lichen, which conducts the business of life as a limited partnership of algae and fungi, is not a parasite and does not hurt the tree. It's believed that the presence of lichen is an indication of extremely good air quality.

The trail also gives a bird's-eye view of Guillemot Island. A variety of birds nest atop this large offshore rock and others. Pigeon guillemots, cormorants and gulls are some of the birds you might see.

As you hike by Whalers Cove, you'll probably see divers entering the Point Lobos Underwater Reserve, America's first such reserve set aside in 1960. Divers explore the 100-foot high kelp forests in Whalers and Bluefish coves. Mineral rich waters from the nearby 1,000-foot deep Carmel Submarine Canyon upwell to join the more shallow waters of the coves.

The reserve has an excellent interpretive program. Docent-led walks explore the trails and tidepools. Ask rangers or visit the park's information station for scheduled nature walks.

DIRECTIONS TO TRAILHEAD Point Lobos State Reserve is located 3 miles south of Carmel just off Highway 1. There is a state park day-use fee. Both Cypress Grove Trail and North Shore Trail depart from the northwest end of Cypress Grove parking area.

■ CARMEL RIVER STATE BEACH
Carmel River Beach Trail
2 miles round trip

Carmel River, which arises high on the eastern slopes of the Santa Lucia Mountains and empties into the sea just south of Carmel, is a river of many moods. Some of its forks, swollen by winter and spring rains, can be capricious, frothy waterways as they course through the Ventana Wilderness.

Tamed by Los Padres Dam on the northern boundary of the national forest, the river's descent through Carmel Valley is relatively peaceful. At its mouth, too, the Carmel River has differing moods and appearances. About

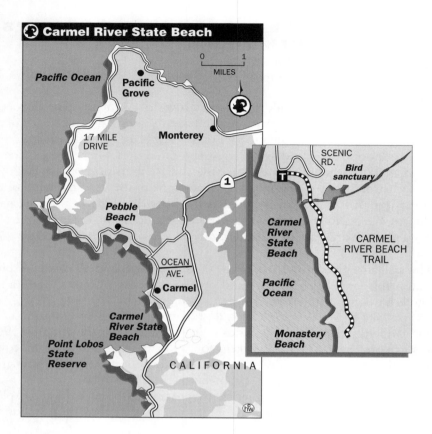

May, a sandbar forms, turning the river mouth into a tranquil lagoon. During winter, the river bursts through the berm and rushes to the sea. Steelhead trout swim upriver to spawn.

At the north end of Carmel River State Beach is a brackish lagoon, where shorebirds feed. Carmel River Lagoon and Wetlands Natural Reserve is here, and even the most casual bird-watcher will be impressed by the abundance of waterfowl. Ducks, mallards and coots patrol the lagoon. Egrets and herons stand amongst the reeds. Hawks hover overhead. Bring your binoculars.

This walk explores the river mouth, then travels the length of Carmel River State Beach to a point just north of Point Lobos named Monastery Beach, for the Carmelito Monastery located just across Highway 1 from the shore.

DIRECTIONS TO TRAILHEAD During the summer and autumn months, the sandy berm at the Carmel River mouth provides a fine path between river and sea. At this time of year, you can start this walk at the north end of Carmel River State Beach. From Highway 1, just south of the town of Carmel, turn west on Rio Road. When you reach Santa Lucia Street, turn left, then proceed five more blocks to Carmelo Street. Turn left and follow this road to the beach.

You can also start at the south end of Carmel River State Beach, easily accessible from Highway 1.

THE HIKE Follow the shoreline down coast over the sandy berm. In places, the route is rocky, the domain of nervous crabs, who scatter at your approach. You'll surely notice the ice plant-lined path above the beach; save this path for the return trip.

After rounding a minor point and passing some wind-bent Monterey cypress, you'll arrive at Monastery Beach—also known as San Jose Creek Beach, for the creek that empties onto the northern end of the beach. With the chimes from the nearby monastery ringing in your ears, you might be lulled into thinking that Monastery Beach is a tranquil place, but it's not; the surf is rough and the beach drops sharply off into the sea. Even the most experienced swimmers should be ultra-cautious.

For a little bit different return route, take the state beach service road, which farther north becomes a trail. This dirt road/trail, just before reaching the lagoon, climbs a small hill where a large cross is implanted. The cross was erected by the Carmel Mission in 1944, and is similar to the one put here by the 1769 Portolá expedition in order to signal the Spanish ship that was to resupply them. Unfortunately, the expedition did not realize how close it was to its intended destination—Monterey Bay—and turned back south.

From the cross, follow a path down slope and intersect another path that leads along the south bank of the Carmel River. Follow the berm and beach back to the trailhead.

■ JACKS PEAK COUNTY PARK
Skyline, Iris, Rhus Trails
Skyline Nature Trail is 0.8-mile loop; return via Iris and Rhus trails is 2.8 miles round trip

Monterey Peninsula high point Jacks Peak offers terrific vistas of Monterey Bay and Carmel Bay.

Jacks Peak is forested with the largest remaining native Monterey Pine grove in the world. Only three other native stands exist: near Cambria, Santa Cruz and on Guadalupe Island some 200 miles off the coast of Baja California. While the fast-growing Monterey pine has been successfully transplanted across California and around the world, there is something special about visiting the conifer in its native habitat.

Jacks Peak and Jacks Park honor Scottish immigrant David Jacks, successful nineteenth-century businessman, dairy owner and land speculator. Jacks is best remembered today, however, for his Monterey Jack cheese, the only native California cheese.

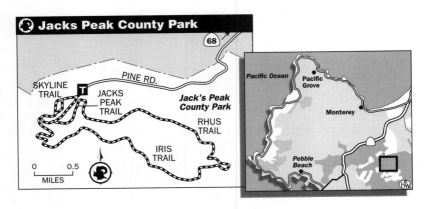

About 10 miles of trail meander through Jacks Peak Park. Paths visit the Monterey pines, as well as oak woodland- and wildflower-dotted meadows.

For a quick tour and a view, take the Skyline Nature Trail, a 0.8-mile loop keyed to an interpretive pamphlet. The quick route to the top is via 0.6-mile long Jacks Peak Trail. The summit of Jacks Peak offers glorious views of the Carmel Coast, Carmel Valley and the Santa Lucia Mountains of the Big Sur backcountry; it does not however offer good views of Monterey Bay, which is better observed from the lower slopes of the peak.

DIRECTIONS TO TRAILHEAD From Highway 1 in Monterey, take Highway 68 east 1.5 miles toward Salinas. Turn right on Olmsted Road and drive another 1.5 miles to Jacks Peak Drive, which travels a mile to the entrance of Jacks Peak County Park.

The park (entrance fee) is open daily from 10:30 A.M. to 7:30 P.M. Those hikers preferring an earlier start may park along Jacks Peak Drive below the gated park entry. It's about a 15-minute uphill walk on Jacks Peak Drive to the park entry kiosk.

From the park's entry kiosk, turn right on Pine Road and continue to road's end at Jacks Peak Parking Area.

THE HIKE Begin on Skyline Nature Trail, which makes a counterclockwise circle of the mountain. An interpretive pamphlet, available at the trailhead, points out birdlife, geology, and Monterey pine forest ecology.

Not far from the start, a vista point offers an excellent panorama (on fog-free days): Fisherman's Wharf, downtown Monterey, Cannery Row, Monterey Bay Aquarium, the Marina State Beach sand dunes and Moss Landing.

From the nature trail, Jacks Peak Trail branches the short distance to the top of Jacks Peak.

Continue on Skyline Nature Trail as it rounds the peak, descending and contouring south then east to intersect Iris Trail. Iris Trail descends Jacks' forested eastern slopes then turns north to meet Rhus Trail. Turn left and head west back to Skyline Nature Trail. Follow the nature trail back to the trailhead.

■ MONTEREY BAY

Monterey Bay Recreation Trail

From Fisherman's Wharf to Monterey Bay Aquarium is 2 miles round trip

Before the 1849 gold rush and overnight rise of the city and port of San Francisco, Monterey was the political and commercial center of California. A waterfront walk of Monterey offers a glimpse backwards at this time—and to other colorful periods of the city's history.

Monterey is probably most identified with its world-renowned sardine canning industry, but the city has hosted many other enterprises that reflect the diverse ethnic heritage of California. Monterey's storied shores have been the work site for Mexican custom officials, Yankee traders, Portuguese whalers, as well as Chinese and Italian fishermen.

As a supplement to this walk, which stays close to the waterfront, be sure to venture downtown along the self-guided "Monterey Path of History." This tour visits many of the buildings within Monterey State Historic Park. Of particular interest to central coast history buffs is the Old Whaling Station, a boarding house for whalers in the 1850s, and the Allen Knight Maritime Museum, which features exhibits of maritime and naval history. One museum highlight is the 1887 Fresnel lens from the Point Sur Light Station.

This walk's destination, the Monterey Bay Aquarium, is open daily from 10 A.M. to 6 P.M.

Bubble window brings visitors closer than ever to sharks and colorful fishes.

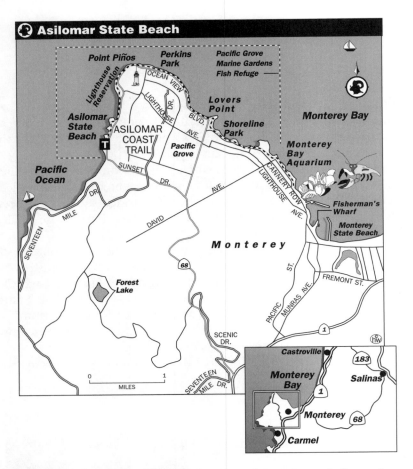

DIRECTIONS TO TRAILHEAD From Highway 1, and from downtown Monterey, signs direct you to FISHERMAN'S WHARF. There's parking in the municipal lot at the end of Alvarado Street.

THE HIKE Before heading for Fisherman's Wharf, also known as Wharf #1, check out Municipal Wharf, or Wharf #2. This utilitarian structure, built in 1926, serves Monterey's commercial fishing fleet. Cranes, hoists and forklifts unload the fleet's catch, which can include squid, shrimp, salmon, sole, anchovy and Pacific herring.

Built in 1870 by the Pacific Coast Steamship Company to serve cargo schooners, Fisherman's Wharf became a bustling adjunct to the canneries of Cannery Row during the 1930s. If you walk past the tourist shops, fish markets and seafood restaurants, you can see sea lions frolicking below the pier. Beware of sea gulls flying overhead; they compete for the fish that tourists throw to the sea lions and pelicans.

Before heading around the bay to Cannery Row, detour across the plaza adjacent the wharf and stop by Custom House, the oldest public building on the California coast. When Mexico ruled California, custom duties were collected from foreign ships. The building now houses a collection of clothing, leather goods and china—items typical of what was imported through the port of old Monterey.

Proceed through Shoreline Park on the Monterey Recreation Trail, a paved bicycle/pedestrian path. The level route follows the old railbed of the Del Monte Express, which from 1879 to 1972 carried passengers from San Francisco to Pebble Beach and Del Monte Lodge.

Stay on the pedestrian path along the waterfront to the Coast Guard Pier at the southeast end of Cannery Row. A rock jetty extending from the end of the pier is a favorite haul-out for sea lions.

Follow Cannery Row past a mix of abandoned canneries, luxury hotels, restaurants, tourist shops, and a bust of John Steinbeck. As Steinbeck, on a return visit many years after publication of his novel, *Cannery Row,* summed up the place: "They fish for tourists now."

The Monterey Bay Aquarium, which opened in 1984, is one of the world's finest. The state-of-the-art exhibits and display tanks are superb. Particularly noteworthy for admirers of California's Central Coast is the fact that almost all displays emphasize the rich underwater world of Monterey Bay.

One aquarium highlight is a mature kelp forest. A multitude of fish swim past tall stands of giant help, one of the world's fastest growing plants. Another absorbing exhibit is the Monterey Bay Tank, which recreates the world of a submarine canyon, complete with sharks and brightly colored fish.

Beyond the aquarium, the Monterey Recreation Trail leads past rows of Victorian houses to the wind-sculpted cypress trees atop Lover's Point. From the point's grassy picnic area, you can enjoy a great view of the southern sweep of Monterey Bay.

See Map on Page 166

■ ASILOMAR STATE BEACH
Asilomar Coast Trail
0.5 to 2 miles round trip

A silomar State Beach, located on the southwest shores of Pacific Grove, packs a lot of interest into a mile of coastline: a restored dune ecosystem, rocky coves, and a broad sand beach. Add a visit to the historic Asilomar Conference Center and you have a walk to remember.

Bordering the west side of the conference center are white sand dunes, vegetatively restored to original condition. A boardwalk provides close-up views of this living example of plant succession. Just inland from the water, "pioneer" species of sand verbena and beach sagewort have taken hold; these colonizers

Beach, bluff, and boardwalk trails offer tranquil hiking at this "refuge by the sea."

created soil conditions acceptable for larger plants such as coffeeberry and coyote bush to thrive; ultimately Monterey pine and coast live oak will succeed.

The conference center at Asilomar (pronounced Ah-*seel*-o-mar), derived from the Spanish to suggest "refuge by the sea" was originally founded by the YWCA for use as a summer retreat in 1913. Architect Julia Morgan, who would later gain worldwide fame as the designer of Hearst Castle, was commissioned to plan the original buildings.

Asilomar Conference Center now belongs to the state and is managed by a concessionaire. Trail advocates take note: Asilomar is the spring gathering place for the annual meeting of the California Recreational Trails Committee, a group that promotes trails statewide.

Asilomar Coast Trail extends a mile along the length of the state beach. From the trail, several side paths fork to tidepools and pocket beaches. Sea otters, sea lions and seals are sometimes seen from vantage points along the trail. In winter, scan the horizon for migrating California gray whales.

From the coast, walkers can follow the boardwalk across dunes to the Asilomar Conference Center, a national historic landmark set in the piney woods.

DIRECTIONS TO TRAILHEAD From Highway 1 between Carmel and Monterey, turn west on Highway 68 (which becomes Sunset Drive) and follow it to the beach. If you're in the Cannery Row area, follow Ocean View Boulevard west and south along the coast.

You can begin this walk opposite Asilomar Conference Center or at the north end of Asilomar State Beach just south of the Sunset Drive–Jewell Avenue intersection.

■ SALINAS RIVER STATE BEACH
Dune Trail
2 miles round trip

Mile-long Dune Trail explores some of Monterey Bay's intriguing sand dunes and links two coastal access points of Salinas River State Beach. The dunes back the state beach, a popular fishing spot.

East of the dunes are croplands and wetlands in the former Salinas River channel, which extends south from Moss Landing to the Salinas River Wildlife Area; in 1908, farmers diverted its course in order to create additional farmland.

Dune Trail begins south of the harbor of Moss Landing, often a surprisingly good place to watch for wildlife: sea otters paddle here and there, sea lions bask on a narrow finger of sand and pelicans are abundant on air and land and sea.

From the harbor, walkers can follow a 0.5-mile dirt road (closed to vehicles) south to the Salinas River State Beach access and parking area off Potrero Road, where Dune Trail officially begins.

The path is over soft sand, seasonally colored by lupine, Indian paintbrush and California poppy. Hikers get mostly inland views, though the path does crest a rise for a peek at the coast. A mile out, you have the choice of retracing your steps or returning via the beach.

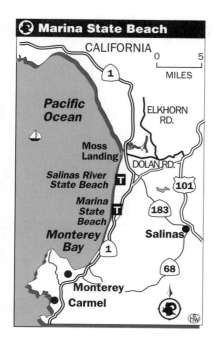

Please heed all posted warnings and don't walk over those areas of the dunes' complex undergoing environmental restoration.

DIRECTIONS TO TRAILHEAD From Highway 1 at Moss Landing, exit on Portero Road and follow it 0.5 mile to the parking lot at Salinas River State Beach.

The other trailhead is off Molera Road. Follow signed Monterey Dunes Way 0.5 mile to the beach.

Warning: Both trailheads have been the site of vehicle break-ins. Lock your car and take your valuables with you.

See Map on Page 169

■ MARINA STATE BEACH
Dune Nature Trail
Nature trail with return via beach is 0.6-mile round trip

Providing a dramatic backdrop to Marina State Beach are some of the central coast's tallest dunes, handsomely shaped sand mounds that are habitat for a number of plants and animals. Rare native flowers such as Monterey paintbrush and the coast wallflower brighten the dunes, where the black legless lizard and the ornate shrew skitter about. These dune creatures and their habitat are threatened by the encroachment of nonnative ice plant and, of course, human developments.

Marina State Beach is popular with hang glider enthusiasts and with locals who flock to the shore at day's end to watch the often colorful sunsets.

Dune Nature Trail, a 0.3-mile interpretive pathway, explores the dune ecosystem. The trail is mostly a wooden boardwalk linked with "sand ladders." Signs identifying the flora and a swell view of the Monterey Peninsula add to the walk's enjoyment.

Ambitious hikers can walk the shoreline 3.5 miles north to Salinas River Wildlife Refuge.

DIRECTIONS TO TRAILHEAD From Highway 1 in Marina, exit on Reservation Road and drive west 0.25 mile to the Marina State Beach parking lot.

■ ELKHORN SLOUGH
Long Valley, Five Fingers Loop Trails
Five Fingers Loop is 2 miles; South Marsh Loop is 3 miles

Three words to remember at Elkhorn Slough: birds, birds, birds. From a slough-side observation point in 1983, the record was established for the most bird species (116!) seen in a single day in North America.

The birds, from snowy egrets to great blue herons to the California clapper rail, are some of the slough showstoppers. More than 250 species have been sighted at the slough. Fat worms and fast crabs—bird food—are abundant on the mudflats and are often as fascinating as the birds to visiting children.

Elkhorn Slough, largest wetland between Morro Bay and San Francisco Bay, is a critical rest stop and feeding ground for tens of thousands of migratory birds. The slough, located halfway between Santa Cruz and Monterey, is believed to have received its name from the herds of tule elk that once roamed these coastal wetlands. Another guess is that the antler-like shape of the slough prompted its name.

The 1,400-acre slough, officially the Elkhorn Slough National Estuarine Research Reserve, is managed by the California Department of Fish and Wildlife in partnership with NOAA (National Oceanic and Atmospheric Administra-

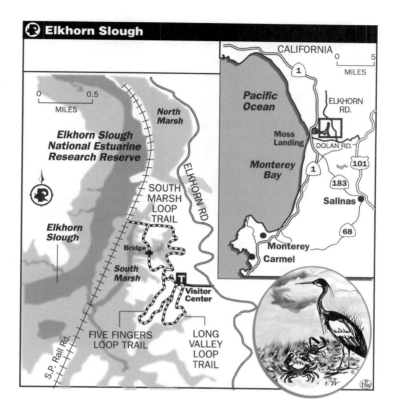

Elkhorn Slough

tion). A visitor center features interpretive displays and a book/gift shop. Elkhorn Slough and its visitor center is open only Wednesday through Sunday.

Three loop trails tour the slough, as well as adjacent oak woodland and grassland environments. From the visitor center, a paved path offers wheelchair access to a viewpoint.

The reserve's two west-side loop trails—Long Valley and Five Fingers—are primarily upland trails through oak-dotted grassland; they do, however, touch the slough in a couple of places. If you have time for only one walk, take the South Marsh Loop Trail, which stays closer to the slough's shores.

Long Valley Loop Trail forks left from the main path leading from the visitor center. A wooden dock provides a good viewpoint. Cresting a low rise, the trail junctions with Five Fingers Loop Trail: Fork left to make a second loop. (At Parsons Slough Overlook you'll probably figure out how Five Fingers Loop got its name.) When Five Fingers Loop Trail returns to the main preserve path, you can return to the visitor center or join South Marsh Loop Trail.

South Marsh Loop Trail briefly descends, approaching the abandoned barns of the old Elkhorn Dairy, then forks left, soon crossing a footbridge over the slough. Walking westward brings you to the primary channel of the slough. You can detour north across a dike bordering Whistle Stop Lagoon and view a couple "Art in Nature" projects at an overlook of Elkhorn Slough channel. The trail passes a heron rookery and a eucalyptus woodland before angling back toward the visitor center.

DIRECTIONS TO TRAILHEAD
From Highway 1 in Moss Landing, turn east on Doland Road and drive 3 miles. Turn left (north) and proceed 2 more miles to the entrance of Elkhorn Slough Reserve.

More than 250 species of birds have been sighted at the slough.

■ MOSS LANDING WILDLIFE AREA
Marsh Trail
To picnic area is 4.5 miles round trip

Elkhorn Slough, the Central California coast's second-largest salt marsh, preserves crucial habitat for waterfowl. The north bank of the slough is protected within the confines of the 700-acre Moss Landing Wildlife Area.

Salt is a word to remember around here. During the late 1800s, the Monterey Bay Salt Company constructed salt ponds, harvesting the salt and supplying the Monterey and Moss Landing canneries. Today these former saltwater evaporation ponds host thousands of California brown pelicans.

The Moss Landing Wildlife Area, managed by the California Department of Fish and Wildlife is managed differently than adjoining Elkhorn Slough National Estuarine Reserve. Waterfowl hunting is permitted. Trails wind through various habitats: coastal salt marsh, freshwater ponds, oak woodland and grassland.

DIRECTIONS TO TRAILHEAD From Highway 1 at the highway bridge in Moss Landing, drive 1.7 miles north to a somewhat inconspicuous dirt road on the right that leads a short distance to the Moss Landing Wildlife Area parking lot.

For safety reasons, southbound travelers should continue past the entrance to the wildlife area to Struve Road, then turn around and come back on Highway 1 northbound.

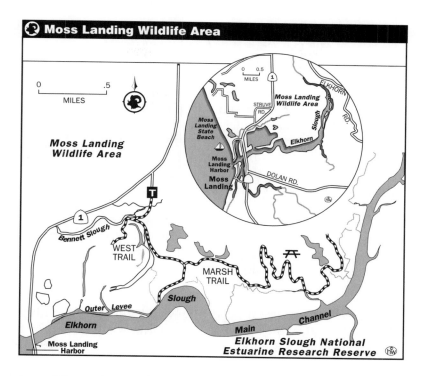

Moss Landing Wildlife Area

THE HIKE The path crosses a low dike and soon reaches a signed junction. A side path (sometimes called West Trail or West Blind Trail) leads to the early twentieth-century salt ponds where salt was harvested. Brown pelicans roost here in the summer. The salt flats, with the twin towers of the Moss Landing power plant in the background, and all those pelicans add up to a somewhat surreal scene.

Mostly level, Marsh Trail travels along the slough's northwest shoreline and brings you to another side trail—leading to an overlook of the main channel of Elkhorn Slough.

The path leads a bit away from the slough through a rolling grassland environment. Cows graze adjacent private property. A couple of oak-shaded tables on a bluff high above the slough make a fine picnic area.

If you want to extend your hike, Marsh Trail continues a few more miles, skirting a native oak woodland and bending north to follow the main channel of Elkhorn Slough.

■ BUTANO STATE PARK
Mill Ox, Goat Hill, Año Nuevo Trails
4 miles round trip with 700-foot elevation gain

According to Native American lore, *butano* means "a gathering place for friendly visits." Visitors who find out-of-the-way Butano State Park will no doubt agree with this assessment.

On the map, Butano State Park seems rather close to the bustling Santa Clara Valley, and to the Bay area. But this 2,800-acre park, tucked between sharp Santa Cruz Mountains ridges, has a remote feeling.

While most of the redwoods in the park are second-growth, some grand old first-growth specimens remain.

On lower slopes, just above Butano Creek, the walker encounters the forest primeval: redwoods, trillium and sword ferns. Moss-draped Douglas fir, tangles of blackberry bushes and meadowland are some of the environments visited by the park's diverse trail system. Año Nuevo Lookout offers fine views of the elephant seal reserve and of the San Mateo coastline.

DIRECTIONS TO TRAILHEAD From Highway 1, turn inland on Pescadero Road, and drive 2.5 miles to Cloverdale Road. Drive south 3 miles to Butano State Park Road and turn left into the park. Park near the entry kiosk.

THE HIKE Signed Jackson Flats Trail begins just across from the park entry kiosk. The path starts out in meadowland, but soon enters redwoods.

The trail follows the north slope of the canyon cut by Little Butano Creek, and junctions with Mill Ox Trail. Take Mill Ox Trail to the right, down to the

Waiting out the rain, a frequent occurrence in Butano State Park and elsewhere in the Santa Cruz Mountains.

Butano State Park

MILL OX
TRAIL

Butano Creek

Little

Entrance

ANO NUEVO
TRAIL

CLOVERDALE
RD.

Vista Point

canyon bottom. Cross Butano State Park Road, and join an unmarked (except for an AUTHORIZED VEHICLES ONLY sign) paved road. Ascend through redwoods on this access road. The route soon junctions with Goat Hill Trail, which you follow into a mixed forest of oak and madrone. Follow this trail to the next intersection: Goat Hill Trail heads left and melts into the woods, but you take the short connector path to Olmo Fire Trail. Turn right. Olmo Fire Trail leads to a junction with Año Nuevo Trail on your left. Take this path over fir- and blackberry bush-covered slopes to Año Nuevo Viewpoint, located in a clearing. On clear days, you can look south to Año Nuevo Island.

From the viewpoint, the trail descends—with enough switchbacks to make a snake dizzy—back to the park entrance.

■ FOREST OF NISENE MARKS STATE PARK

Loma Prieta Grade Trail

From Porter Picnic Area to Hoffman's Historic Site is 6 miles round trip with a 400-foot elevation gain; several longer hikes are possible

One of the largest state parks in Central California, The Forest of Nisene Marks has few facilities, but it is this very lack of development that makes it attractive to anyone looking for a quiet walk in the woods.

The woods, in this case, are second-growth redwoods. The park is on land near Santa Cruz that was clear-cut during a lumber boom lasting from 1883 to 1923.

Loma Prieta Lumber Co. had quite an operation. Using steam engines, oxen, skid roads and even a railway, loggers ventured into nearly every narrow canyon of the Aptos Creek watershed.

After the loggers left Aptos Canyon, the forest began to regenerate. Today a handsome second generation of redwoods is rising to cover the scarred slopes.

The Marks, a prominent Salinas Valley farm family, purchased the land in the 1950s. In 1963, the three Marks children donated the property to the state in the name of their mother, Nisene Marks. As specified in the deed, the forest must not be developed and the natural process of regeneration must be allowed to continue.

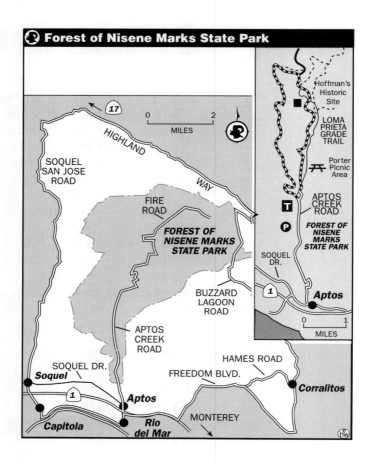

Ferocious winter storms in 1982 and 1983 battered the canyons and ruined part of the park's trail system, in particular the paths in the upper reaches of Aptos Canyon. Railroad grades and trestles that had withstood a century of storms were washed away. Volunteers and the California Conservation Corps repaired the damage.

Loma Prieta Grade Trail follows parts of an old railway bed. A narrow-gauge steam railway ran from a mill to China Camp. A few ramshackle wooden buildings are all that's left of this lumber camp that once housed 300 workers.

DIRECTIONS TO TRAILHEAD From Highway 1 in Aptos, take the Aptos–Seacliff exit to Soquel Drive. Turn right (east) and proceed 0.5 mile into Aptos. Turn left on Aptos Creek Road and drive 4 miles to a locked gate at The Forest of Nisene Marks' Porter Picnic Area.

THE HIKE From the picnic area, follow Aptos Creek 0.4 mile to the Loma Prieta Grade trailhead. (An old mill site is a short walk up the road.)

For a short stretch, the trail stays near Aptos Creek. This creek, which rises high on Santa Rosalia Ridge, is joined by the waters of Bridge Creek, then spills into Monterey Bay at Rio Del Mar Beach. Silver salmon and steelhead spawn in the creek.

The old railway bed makes a gentle trail except for a few places where the old bridges have collapsed into steep ravines. Your destination of China Camp, now called Hoffman's Historic Site, has a few wooden structures.

You can return the same way or take the Ridge Connector Trail over to West Ridge Trail. This latter trail runs south and connects with Aptos Creek near the trailhead. Be warned that Ridge Trail is sometimes crowded by large amounts of poison oak.

■ HENRY COWELL REDWOODS STATE PARK
River, Eagle, Pine, Ridge Trails
4 miles round trip with 500-foot elevation gain

Henry Cowell Redwoods State Park preserves first- and second-growth redwoods in a tranquil Santa Cruz Mountains setting.

Henry Cowell and Joseph Welch, who in the 1860s acquired the former Mexican land grant Rancho Cañada de Rincón, shared a similar commitment to protect the Big Trees Grove (now Redwood Grove). Welch's holdings were purchased by Santa Cruz County in 1930 and became parkland; in the 1950s this land was combined with 1,500 acres donated by Cowell's heirs to become a state park.

Thanks to the preservation efforts by these men, the "Big Trees" are as stirring a sight now as they were a century ago when railroad passengers bound for Santa Cruz from San Jose made a lunch stop amongst the tall trees.

The short Redwood Grove Nature Trail, which visits one of the finest first-growth groves south of

The "Big Trees" have inspired park-goers for more than a century.

San Francisco, is a good place to start your exploration of the Santa Cruz Mountains. This popular trail, complete with interpretive leaflet, loops along the San Lorenzo Riverbank among the redwoods, some of which have been given names. One of the larger commemorative redwoods honors President Theodore Roosevelt, who enjoyed his 1903 visit to the grove.

The state park is hilly, and with changes in elevation come changes in vegetation. Moisture-loving redwoods predominate on the lowlands while the park's upper ridges are cloaked with oak woodland and chaparral.

By connecting four of the park's trails, you can walk through all of the park's diverse ecosystems. You'll begin in the redwoods and ascend chaparral-covered slopes to an observation deck located in the middle of the Park. Great mountain and coastal views are your reward for the ascent.

Be sure to stop in at the park interpretive center, which has exhibits and sells maps and books. Redwood Grove Nature Trail begins near the center.

DIRECTIONS TO TRAILHEAD Henry Cowell Redwoods State Park is located just south of Felton on Highway 9. You can pick up River Trail near the park entrance at Highway 9, or from the picnic area.

THE HIKE River Trail meanders downriver along the east bank of the San Lorenzo. You may hear the whistle of the Roaring Camp & Big Trees Railroad, a popular tourist attraction located adjacent to the park. The steam-powered train takes passengers through the Santa Cruz Mountains on a narrow gauge track.

About 0.25 mile after River Trail passes beneath a railroad trestle, you'll intersect Eagle Creek Trail and begin ascending out of the redwood forest along Eagle Creek. Madrone and manzanita predominate on the exposed sunny slopes.

Bear right on Pine Trail (the pines you'll see en route are ponderosa pine) and climb steeply up to the observation deck. Enjoy the view of the Monterey and Santa Cruz coastline, the redwood forests and that tumbled-up range of mountains called Santa Cruz.

On the return trip, take Ridge Trail on a steep descent to River Trail. Both River Trail and its nearly parallel path—Pipeline Road—lead back to Redwood Grove and the picnic area.

■ BIG BASIN REDWOODS STATE PARK

Skyline to the Sea Trail

12 miles one way with 1,200-foot elevation loss

In 1902, the California State Park System was born with the establishment of the California Redwood Park at Big Basin Redwoods State Park in Santa Cruz County.

California preserved many more "redwood parks" during the twentieth century, but the redwoods at Big Basin are some of the gems of the park system.

And one of the gems of the state's trail system—Skyline to the Sea Trail—explores Big Basin Redwoods State Park. As its name suggests, the path drops from the crest of the Santa Cruz Mountains to the Pacific Ocean.

For the most part, it runs downhill on its scenic 35-mile journey from Castle Rock State Park to Big Basin Redwoods State Park to Waddell Beach. Views from the Skyline—redwood-forested slopes, fern-smothered canyons and the great blue Pacific—are superb.

Berry Creek Falls.

This gem of a trail has many friends. During one weekend in 1969, dedicated members of the Sempervirens Fund and the Santa Cruz Trails Association turned out more than 2,000 volunteers to dig, clear, prune and otherwise improve the trail. Area volunteers put together an annual Trails Day that is now a model for trails organizations throughout the state.

A fine backpacking trip for a three-day weekend would be to trek the 35 miles of Skyline from Castle Rock State Park to Big Basin, then on to the sea.

The wildest and most beautiful part of the Skyline stretches from park headquarters at Big Basin to Waddell Creek Beach and Marsh. It winds through deep woods and explores the moist environments of Waddell and Berry Creeks.

Springtime, when the creeks are frothy torrents and Berry Creek Falls cascades at full vigor, is a particularly dramatic time to walk the

Skyline to the Sea Trail. During summer, the cool redwood canyons are great places to beat the heat.

DIRECTIONS TO TRAILHEAD From Santa Cruz, drive 12 miles north on Highway 9. Turn west on Highway 236 and proceed 9 miles to Big Basin Redwoods State Park.

If you're hiking from Big Basin to the sea, you'll need to arrange a car shuttle. Waddell Beach, at trail's end, is 18 miles up-coast from Santa Cruz on Highway 1.

Better yet, take the bus, which stops at both the state park and Waddell Beach. One suggestion: Leave your car at the Santa Cruz bus station (920 Pacific Avenue) and take the 7:45 A.M. (weekends) bus bound for the state park. You'll arrive about 9 A.M.

Hit the trail and take the 5:15 P.M. bus from Waddell Beach back to Santa Cruz. Schedules are different on weekends and weekdays and change frequently. Call the Santa Cruz Metropolitan Transit District for the latest bus schedule.

THE HIKE The trail begins in the nucleus of the park on Opal Creek flatlands at the bottom of the basin. From park headquarters, join Redwood Trail, which crosses a bridge and travels a few hundred yards to a signed junction with Skyline to the Sea Trail. You'll turn toward the sea and begin a stiff climb out of the basin, passing junctions with other park trails.

After climbing, the trail descends through deep and dark woods, first with Kelly Creek, then along the west fork of Waddell Creek. Ferns, mushrooms, salamanders and banana slugs occupy the wet world of the trail.

Some 4 miles from the trailhead, just short of the confluence of Waddell Creek and Berry Creek, you'll intersect Berry Creek Falls Trail. The falls cascade over fern-covered cliffs into a frothy pool.

An ideal lunch stop, or turnaround spot is Sunset Trail Camp, located a mile up Berry Creek Falls Trail and near another falls—Golden Falls.

Skyline to the Sea Trail descends with Waddell Creek and passes through the heart of the beautiful Waddell Valley. Rancho del Oso, "Ranch of the Bears," as this region is known, has second-generation redwoods, Douglas fir and Monterey pine, as well as lush meadows.

A mile and a half from the ocean, you'll reach Twin Redwoods Camp. As you near the sea, the redwoods give way to laurel groves and meadow land. Near trail's end is a freshwater marsh, a favorite stopping place for migratory birds on the Pacific flyway.

A wildlife sanctuary, Theodore J. Hoover Natural Preserve has been established in the heart of the marsh area for more than 200 kinds of native and migratory birds.

The trail ends at Highway 1. West of the highway is a bus stop and windswept Waddell Beach.

■ POGONIP
Old Stables, Brayshaw, Spring Trails
4 miles round trip with 200-foot elevation gain

Few universities can boast the scenic surroundings of the University of California Santa Cruz. Set amidst stands of redwood and mountain meadows, the campus commands a grand view of Monterey Bay.

One way to visit the university is to walk the campus itself, which is divided into eight colleges, each constructed in a different architectural style. Another way to go is to hike the Pogonip, a wild city park adjacent to the campus. Pogonip, a 600-acre preserve of shady glens and sunny meadows, is a walker's delight.

Henry Cowell, who left his mark on Santa Cruz in so many ways, owned a limestone quarry and lime-making operation during the last decades of the 1800s and into this century as well. In 1961 a 2,000-acre parcel of the old Cowell Ranch was purchased by the state of California as the site of UC Santa Cruz. The 600-acre Pogonip was acquired from Cowell's heirs in 1989.

The native Ohlone, acute observers of the natural world, called this land *pogonip*, meaning "icy fog." Fog, both chilly and tepid, often enshrouds Pogonip's evergreen forest (oak, madrone, bay) and the park's second-growth redwood groves. One frequently seen denizen of the wet forest floor is the banana slug, the popular mascot of UC Santa Cruz.

A network of trails and service roads crosses Pogonip, a Santa Cruz city park. The trails are mostly unsigned, so first-time visitors need to pay heed where they're going. Some trails on the park map such as Pogonip Creek (overgrown, no footbridges) and Haunted Meadow (incomplete) are inviting, but difficult to negotiate for a newcomer to the area.

Two favorite loops explore the south and north areas of the park. My favorite southern loop (about 4 miles) travels Brayshaw Trail to Spring Trail to Lookout Trail to Pogonip Creek Trail. Redwoods, views and a feeling of really getting away from it all are highlights of this circuit.

Rangers recommend the walk described below as a good introduction to the Pogonip.

DIRECTIONS TO TRAILHEAD In Santa Cruz, from the junction of Highway 1 and Highway 9, head north on Highway 9 for 0.4 mile and turn left on Golf Club Drive. Park in the lot at the corner.

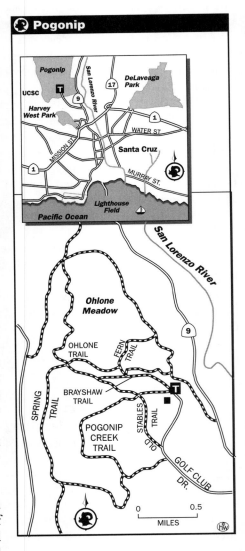

THE HIKE Head up Golf Club Drive 0.25 mile, passing under a railroad trestle, to the entrance to Pogonip. You'll walk along the back of Pogonip Club, once a premiere polo club of the 1930s and 1940s. After World War II, the facility became a social club. It's now closed.

Join Old Stables Trail, crossing a meadow and passing an unsigned junction with Pogonip Creek Trail. The trail joins Brayshaw Trail, a service road, and ascends to a junction with Spring Trail. Go right (north) to the handsome meadow at the junction with Ohlone Trail. From Haunted Meadow, those experienced with Pogonip pathways might improvise a return route via Haunted Meadow Trail or Lookout Trail, but first-timers will return the way they came.

■ NATURAL BRIDGES STATE BEACH
Monarch Trail
0.75 mile round trip

Until October 1989 when the devastating Loma Prieta Earthquake shook Santa Cruz, it was easy to see why the beach here was named Natural Bridges. Alas, this strong temblor doomed the last remaining natural bridge.

While its offshore bridges are but a memory, this park on the outskirts of Santa Cruz nevertheless offers plenty of other natural attractions. A eucalyptus grove in the center of the park hosts the largest concentration of monarch butterflies in America. The park has an extensive interpretive program from October through March, when the monarchs winter at the grove.

Another park highlight is a superb rocky tidepool area, habitat for mussels, limpets, barnacles and sea urchins. After you explore the park, visit nearby Long Marine Laboratory, located just up-coast at the end of Delaware Avenue. University of California Santa Cruz faculty and students use the research facility, which studies coastal ecology. The Lab's Marine Aquarium is open to the public by docent tours.

DIRECTIONS TO TRAILHEAD Natural Bridges State Beach is located off Highway 1 in Santa Cruz at 2531 W. Cliff Drive. Follow the signs from Highway 1.

The last Natural Bridge fell down in the great quake of 1989.

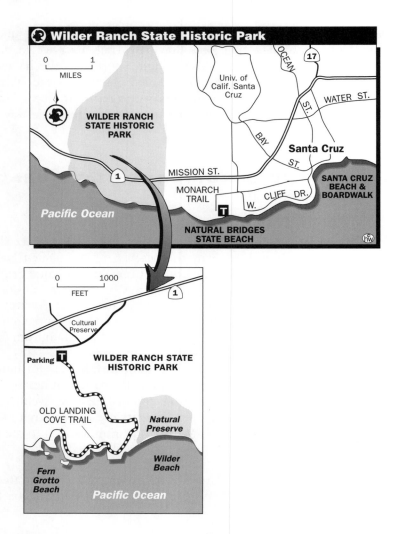

THE HIKE Signed Monarch Trail begins near the park's small interpretive center. Soon the trail splits; the leftward fork leads to a monarch observation platform. Sometimes on cold mornings, the butterflies look like small, brown, fluttering leaves. As the sun warms the tropical insects, the "leaves" come to life bobbing and darting. As many as 200,000 monarchs cluster in the state park on a "good" butterfly year. The other branch of the trail is a self-guided nature trail. It ends in a grove of Monterey pine.

When you head back to the visitor center, detour down to the beach. Just up the beach is Secret Lagoon, the domain of ducks and great blue herons. Farther up the beach is one of the Central Coast's truly superb tidepool areas.

See Map
on Page
184

■ WILDER RANCH
STATE HISTORIC PARK
Old Landing Cove Trail, Ohlone Bluff Trail

From Wilder Ranch to Old Landing Cove is 2 miles round trip;
to Four Mile Beach is 10.5 miles round trip

At Wilder Ranch State Historic Park, located on the coast just north of Santa Cruz, you get the feeling that not one stone has gone unpreserved.

The brussels sprouts fields are in an agricultural preserve, the former Wilder Ranch is in a cultural preserve, and Wilder Beach is now a natural preserve for the benefit of nesting snowy plovers. All these preserves are found within Wilder Ranch State Historic Park, which in turn preserves some 4,000 acres of beach, bluffs and inland canyons.

Rancho del Matadero was started here by Mission Santa Cruz in 1791. The Wilder family operated what was by all accounts a very successful and innovative dairy for nearly 100 years. The California Department of Parks and Recreation acquired the land in 1974.

The Wilder's ranch buildings, barn, gardens and Victorian house still stand, and are open to public tours. The parks department is slowly restoring the area to reflect its historic use as a dairy.

In addition to the guided historic walks, the park boasts Old Landing Cove Trail, a bluff-top path that as its name suggests, leads to a historic cove. From the 1850s to the 1890s, schooners dropped anchor in this cove to load lumber. Observant hikers can spot iron rings, which supported landing chutes, still embedded in the cliffs.

Fans of Brussels sprouts will see more of this vegetable than they ever dreamed possible; fully twelve percent of our nation's production is grown in the state park.

DIRECTIONS TO TRAILHEAD From Santa Cruz, head north on Coast Highway 4 miles to the signed turnoff for Wilder Ranch State Park on the ocean side of the highway. Follow the park road to its end at the large parking lot, where the signed trail begins.

THE HIKE The path, an old ranch road, heads coastward. Signs warn you not to head left to Wilder Beach (where the snowy plovers dwell) and discourage you from heading right, where pesticides are used on the fields of Brussels sprouts.

The trail offers a bird's-eye view of the surf surging into a sea cave, then turns north and follows the cliff edge.

Old Landing Cove is smaller than you imagine, and you wonder how the coastal schooners of old managed to maneuver into such small confines. If it's low tide, you might see harbor seals resting atop the flat rocks located offshore.

One more natural attraction at the cove: a fern-filled sea cave. The ferns are watered by an underground spring.

The trail continues another half mile along the bluffs, offering vistas at seals basking on the rocks below to sandy beach. This is a good turnaround point (for a 3.5-mile round trip).

Ambitious hikers will continue north another 3.5 miles along land's end, following footpaths and ranch roads past Strawberry Beach, and Three Mile Beach, retreating inland now and then to bypass deep gullies, and finally arriving at the park's north boundary at Four Mile Beach. A splendid coastal hike!

■ AÑO NUEVO STATE RESERVE
Año Nuevo Trail
3 miles round trip

O ne of the best New Year's resolutions a walker could make is to plan a winter trip to Año Nuevo State Reserve. Here you'll be treated to a wildlife drama that attracts visitors from all over the world—a close-up look at the largest mainland population of elephant seals.

From December through April, a colony of the huge creatures visits Año Nuevo Island and Point Año Nuevo in order to breed and bear young. To protect the elephant seals (and the humans who hike out to see them), the reserve is open only through naturalist-guided tours during these months.

Slaughtered for their oil-rich blubber, the elephant seal population numbered fewer than 100 by the early 1900s. Placed under government protection, the huge mammals rebounded rapidly from the brink of extinction. Año Nuevo State Reserve was created in 1958 to protect the seals.

Año Nuevo's elephant seals.

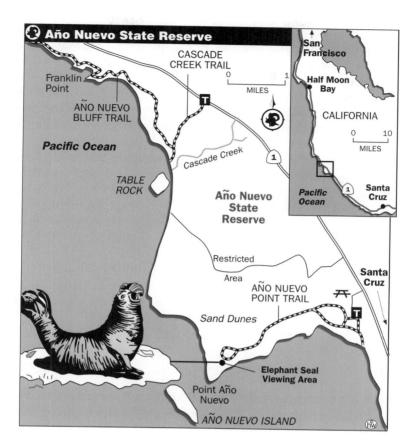

Male elephant seals, some reaching lengths of 16 feet and weighing three tons, arrive in December and begin battling for dominance. Only a very small percentage of males actually get to inseminate a female; most remain lifelong bachelors. The females, relatively svelte at 1,200 to 2,000 pounds, come ashore in January and join the harems of the dominant males.

La Punta de Año Nuevo (The Point of the New Year) was named by the Spanish explorer Sebastián Vizcaíno on January 3, 1603. It's one of the oldest place-names in California.

At the time of its discovery, the Point was occupied by the Ohlone, who lived off the bounty of sea. Judging from kitchen midden sites—shell mounds—found in the nearby dunes, it was a rich bounty indeed.

The Año Nuevo area later hosted a variety of enterprises. From the 1850s to 1920, redwood cut from the slopes of the nearby Santa Cruz Mountains was shipped from Año Nuevo Bay. A dairy industry flourished on the coastal bluffs. The reserve's visitor center is a restored century-old dairy barn.

While the elephant seals are clearly the main attraction when they come ashore during the winter to breed and during the spring and summer to molt, the reserve is even fascinating when the big creatures are not in residence; in fact, Año Nuevo is a year-round destination.

Bird-watchers may glimpse a cliff swallow, Western gull, red-tailed hawk and many other inland and shore birds. The beautiful sand dunes of the reserve are covered with beach grass, morning glory and extensive patches of beach strawberry.

Joining the elephant seals on Año Nuevo Island are Steller sea lions, California sea lions and harbor seals. Seals inhabit Año Nuevo year-round. Viewing is great in the spring and summer months—on the beaches. Autumn brings one- to-three year-old "yearling" seals ashore to rest on the beaches.

Reservations/information: Año Nuevo Point, where the elephant seals reside, is open only to visitors on guided walks, conducted by state park volunteer naturalists, from December through March.

Guided walks are conducted daily and consist of a 2.5-hour, 3-mile long walk. Advance reservations for the guided walks are strongly recommended. Reservations can be made through the state park system's reservation contractor.

From April through November, access to the Año Nuevo Point Wildlife Protection Area is by permit only. Permits are issued free of charge daily at the reserve, on a first-come–first-served basis.

DIRECTIONS TO TRAILHEAD Año Nuevo State Reserve is located just west of Highway 1, 22 miles north of Santa Cruz and 30 miles south of Half Moon Bay.

See Map on Page 187

■ CASCADE CREEK
Cascade Creek, Año Nuevo Bluff Trails
To Franklin Point is 3 miles round trip; to Gazos Coastal Access is 5 miles round trip

True, the elephant seals do steal the show, but there's more than bellowing pinnipeds to see at Año Nuevo State Reserve. North of the restricted access around Año Nuevo Point is a coastline of rocky coves, low dunes and wildflower-strewn meadowland.

The dunes north of Año Nuevo Point are colorfully dotted with yellow sand verbena, morning glory and beach strawberry. Archeologists have discovered evidence—chipped tools and mounds of seashells—of a lengthy occupation by native peoples.

This walk visits Franklin Point, named when the clipper ship John Franklin rammed into the rocks here in 1865. At low tide, the point's tidepools can be visited. Seals and sea otters can be glimpsed from Franklin Point.

The walk can be extended by traveling bluff trail north to Gazos Creek Coastal Access, a favorite of the surf fishing set; however, this path is irregularly maintained and often crowded with poison oak.

DIRECTIONS TO TRAILHEAD Proceed 2.2 miles north of the main Año Nuevo State Reserve entrance to a turnout on the west side of Highway 1.

THE HIKE Follow the dirt road a short 0.5 mile west across grassy bluffs to a small cypress and eucalyptus grove. Head north over low bluffs, perhaps detouring to visit the wild beach just below. A mile out, a right-forking path leads to Highway 1, but you take the left fork and descend toward a cove at the mouth of Whitehouse Creek.

You'll cross the creek and continue hiking north along the bluffs to Franklin Point. Watch the marine mammals, retrace your steps, or head north on a more tentative trail compromised by an overgrowth of poison oak.

■ BEAN HOLLOW BEACH
Arroyo de los Frijoles Trail
From Pebble Beach to Bean Hollow Beach
is 2 miles round trip

Pebble Beach—not to be confused with the Pebble Beach of 18-hole renown near Carmel, the Pebble Beach in Tomales Bay State Park, or the Pebble Beach near Crescent City—is one of those enchanting San Mateo County beaches that extend from Año Nuevo State Reserve to Thornton State Beach, a bit south of San Francisco. The pebbles on the beach are quartz chipped from an offshore reef, tumbled ashore, then wave-polished and rounded into beautifully hued small stones.

The one-mile walk between Pebble Beach and Bean Hollow Beach offers a close-up look at tidepools, wildflowers (in season), and colonies of harbor seals and shorebirds. Some walkers say that the San Mateo County beaches and bluffs remind them of the British coast near Cornwall. This comparison is reinforced at the beginning of the trail, which crosses a moor-like environment bedecked with iris and daisies.

The rocky intertidal area is habitat for sea slugs and snails, anenomes and urchins. Bird-watchers will sight cormorants, pelicans and red-billed oyster catchers flying over the water. The sandy beach is patrolled by gulls, sandpipers and sanderlings.

DIRECTIONS TO TRAILHEAD Pebble Beach is located some 40 miles south of San Francisco. The beach is off Highway 1, about 2.5 miles south of Pescadero. The trail begins at the south end of the parking lot.

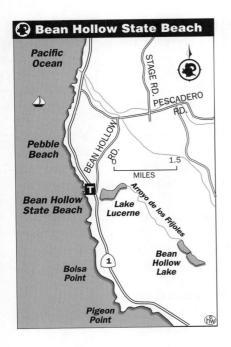

Bean Hollow State Beach

Pacific Ocean

STAGE RD.

PESCADERO RD.

Pebble Beach

BEAN HOLLOW RD.

1.5

MILES

Bean Hollow State Beach

Lake Lucerne

Arroyo de los Frijoles

Bean Hollow Lake

Bolsa Point

Pigeon Point

THE HIKE The first part of the walk is along a nature trail. Waves crashing over the offshore reef are a dramatic sight. Keep an eye out for harbor seals swimming just offshore.

A couple of small footbridges aid your crossing of rivulets that carve the coastal bluffs. To the south, you'll get a glimpse of Pigeon Point Lighthouse, now part of a hostel. If the tide is low when you approach Bean Hollow State Beach, head down to the sand.

The state beach originally had the Spanish name of *Arroyo de los Frijoles,* "Creek of the Beans," before being Americanized to Bean Hollow. Picnic tables at the beach suggest a lunch or rest stop.

■ PESCADERO MARSH
Sequoia Audubon Trail
From Pescadero State Beach to North Marsh is 2.5 miles round trip; to North Pond is 2.5 miles round trip; Precautions: North Pond area closed 3/15 to 9/1

Bring a pair of binoculars to Pescadero Marsh Natural Preserve, the largest marsh between Monterey Bay and San Francisco. Pescadero Creek and Butano Creek pool resources to form a lagoon and estuary that is a haven for birds and a heaven for bird-watchers.

Peer through willows, tules and cattails, and you might spot diving ducks, great egrets or yellow-throated warblers. More than 180 species of birds have been sighted in the preserve.

Best bird-watching is in late fall and early spring. To protect the birds during breeding season, the northernmost preserve trail is closed. You may take one of the walks described below, or simply wander the perimeter of the marsh to one of the wooden observation decks, and begin your bird-watching.

DIRECTIONS TO TRAILHEAD Pescadero State Beach and Pescadero Marsh Natural Preserve are located off Highway 1, some 15 miles south of Half Moon Bay. The state beach has three parking areas. The largest area is at the south end of the beach, where Pescadero Road junctions Highway 1.

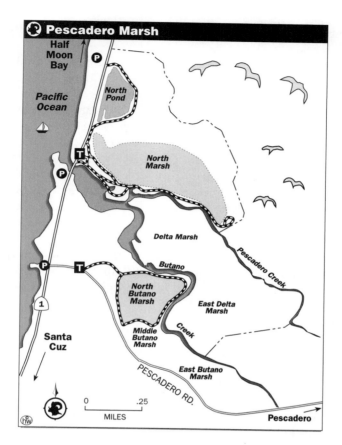

Pescadero Marsh

Half Moon Bay

Pacific Ocean

North Pond

North Marsh

Delta Marsh

Pescadero Creek

Butano

North Butano Marsh

East Delta Marsh

Santa Cuz

1

Middle Butano Marsh

Creek

East Butano Marsh

PESCADERO RD.

0 .25 MILES

Pescadero

THE HIKE From the southernmost beach parking area, follow the beach north. If it's low tide, you'll get a good look as some fascinating tidepools.

A half-mile of travel brings you to the mouth of Butano Creek. You may have to hike inland a bit to find a good place to ford the creek.

Turn inland and pass under the highway bridge. You'll join Sequoia Audubon Trail, which meanders between the south shore of North Marsh and the north bank of Butano Creek. Take the first fork to the left and loop toward North Marsh. A right turn, as you near the marsh, will allow you to loop back to the Sequoia Audubon Trail.

To North Pond: Walk north on Pescadero Beach. A half-mile beyond Butano Creek, you'll come to the massive cliff faces of San Mateo Coast State Beaches. (With a low tide, you could walk along the base of the cliffs to San Gregorio Beach.) Turn inland to the northern Pescadero State Beach parking area. Directly across the road from the entrance to the parking lot is the trailhead for North Marsh Trail.

Follow the half-mile path as it loops around North Pond. Cattle graze the slopes above the pond, and abundant birdlife populates the surrounding thickets.

The path climbs a small hill where a wooden observation deck affords a grand view of the large North Marsh.

You can return by taking the trail south and to the left. It leads to Sequoia Audubon Trail, which in turn takes you under the Butano Creek Bridge. You then follow the beach back to your starting point.

West Butano Loop: For another fine bird walk, transport yourself 0.5 mile up Pescadero Road. Entry to the small, dirt parking area is almost directly opposite the San Mateo County road maintenance station.

The unsigned trail leads north from the parking area, and winds through a wide, lush meadow. When you get to the creek, follow the trail east (rightward). As you follow Butano Creek, you'll be walking the tops of dikes which once allowed coastal farmers to use this rich bottom land for growing artichokes, brussels sprouts and beans. Adjacent lands are still carefully cultivated by local farmers.

Watch for blue herons and snowy egrets. Perhaps you'll even spot the San Francisco garter snake, an endangered species. After following Butano Creek through the marsh, you'll join the trail to the right to return to the starting point.

■ HALF MOON BAY
Coastside Trail
From Francis Beach to Roosevelt Beach is 6 miles round trip

From East Breakwater, Half Moon Bay arcs southward, backed by a long sandy beach. Forming a backdrop to the beach are eroded cliffs and low dunes.

Three miles of shoreline and four beaches—Roosevelt, Dunes, Venice and Francis—comprise Half Moon Bay State Park. Extending north of the park is more accessible—and walkable—shoreline.

Coastside Trail, extending along the park's eastern boundary, is a multi-use pathway open to cyclists and walkers. Depending on the tide, you can return via the beach. Coastside Trail is a better bike ride than walk; its function is to link the various state beaches and it does that quite well, but it isn't all that interesting of a saunter. It does, however, bring some marvelous beaches within reach, and for that reason is worth the walk.

DIRECTIONS TO TRAILHEAD From Highway 1 in the town of Half Moon Bay (0.25 mile north of the intersection with Highway 92) turn west on Kelly Avenue and drive to Francis Beach. There is a state park day-use fee.

THE HIKE The trail winds past low sandy hills, dotted by clumps of cordgrass. At trail's end you can extend your walk by beachcombing northward toward Pillar Harbor by way of Miramar Beach and El Granada Beach.

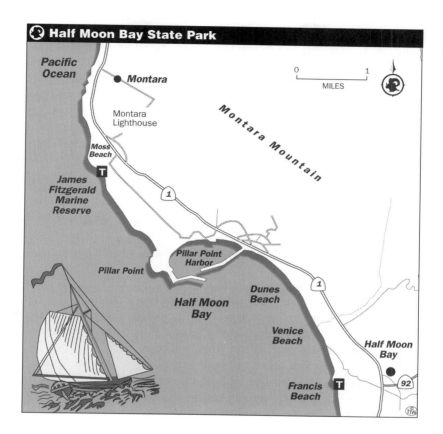

Half Moon Bay State Park

Pacific Ocean

● Montara

Montara Lighthouse

Montara Mountain

0   1
MILES

Moss Beach

James Fitzgerald Marine Reserve

Pillar Point

Pillar Point Harbor

Half Moon Bay

Dunes Beach

Venice Beach

Half Moon Bay

Francis Beach

92

See Map
ABOVE

■ FITZGERALD MARINE RESERVE
Reserve Trail
1 mile round trip

When the ocean retreats at low tide, hundreds of tidepools are exposed to view at James V. Fitzgerald Marine Reserve. Starfish, sea snails, sea anemones, rock crabs and hermit crabs are some of the many tidal creatures on display. Tidepool plants and creatures at the reserve have been studied since the 1920s; in fact, more than two dozen unique species have been discovered here.

The lower the tide, the better the look, but at least some tidepools are worth visiting when the reef is partially revealed.

Starfish.

A half-mile-long trail travels the bluffs, offering an alternative to the beach route. Most folks head right down to the shore, but to join the bluff trail angle left on the path that leads over a wooden bridge. Very soon the path leads to a lookout perch, then continues south along a fence to a cypress grove.

About 0.5 mile out, the path drops to the beach. Retrace your steps or visit the tidepools on the way back.

DIRECTIONS TO TRAILHEAD From Highway 1 in Moss Beach, 7 miles north of Half Moon Bay, turn west on California Street. A tiny visitor center is located at the edge of the parking lot.

■ MCNEE RANCH STATE PARK
Montara Mountain Trail
7.5 miles round trip with 2,000-foot elevation gain

Not even a sign welcomes you to McNee Ranch State Park, located on the San Mateo County coast 25 miles south of San Francisco.

But what the park lacks in signs and facilities, it makes up in grand views and wide open spaces. And oh, what a view! The coastline from Half Moon Bay to the Golden Gate National Recreation Area is at your feet.

The panoramic view is a hiker's reward for the rigorous ascent of Montara Mountain, whose slopes form the bulk of the state park. Montara Mountain, geologists say, is a 90-million-year-old chunk of granite (largely quartz diorite) that forms the northernmost extension of the Santa Cruz Mountains.

Alas, what is a beautiful park to hikers is an ideal location for a multi-lane highway to the California Department of Transportation. Caltrans wants to build a Highway 1 bypass through the park to replace the existing landslide-prone stretch of highway known as the Devil's Slide that begins about 2 miles south of Pacifica.

Caltrans and its building plans have been fiercely contested by environmentalists, who fear the highway bypass would completely destroy the ambiance of the park and lead to further development in the area. The two sides have been battling it out in court for several years.

At the moment, it's not cement, but the coastal scrub community—ceanothus, sage and monkeyflower—that predominates on the mountain. The park also boasts several flower-strewn grasslands. Meandering down Montara Mountain is willow- and alder-lined Martini Creek, which forms the southern boundary of the state park.

The park's trail system includes footpaths as well as Old San Pedro Road, a dirt road that's popular with mountain bikers. Little hiker symbols keep walkers on the trail, but since all routes climb Montara Mountain and more or less meet at the top, don't be overly concerned about staying on the "right" trail.

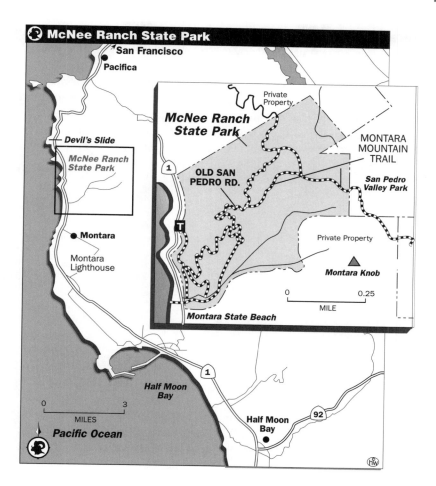

Opposite the state park, across Coast Highway, is Montara State Beach. This half-mile sand strand is a popular surfing, fishing and picnicking spot.

Hikers will note that the nearest spot for provisions is the hamlet of Montara, where there's a café and grocery store. Good accommodations for a hiker on a budget is the Montara Lighthouse Hostel right on the coast. The thirty-bed hostel, which is located right next to a working lighthouse, has kitchen facilities, a volleyball court and even an outdoor hot tub.

DIRECTIONS TO TRAILHEAD Take Highway 1 to Montara and park in the fair-sized lot at the north end of Montara State Beach. Walk carefully 150 yards up-coast and cross the highway. The unsigned trail begins at a pipe gate across a fire road on the inland side of Coast Highway.

THE HIKE Head up the fire road a short distance and join the trail on your left, which swings north, up-coast, over a seasonally flowered grassy slope. The path drops to join a dirt road, then begins ascending once more.

As you climb, you pass two benches, strategically placed for you to catch your breath. The dirt road eventually swings south, but you join a footpath and ascend to a saddle. Two trails lead left to the peak and terrific views.

Below you, up-coast, is the town of Pacifica and beyond that the Golden Gate Bridge and San Francisco Bay. To the east is Mount Diablo, and way out to sea on the far horizon are the Farallon Islands.

CHAPTER **3** THREE

NORTH COAST

San Francisco is a city of walkers. And many of the city's best walks are coast walks along the bay and ocean shores of the Golden Gate National Recreation Area. GGNRA, as its known, extends across the Golden Gate Bridge, and protects the wild headlands of Marin County.

From the "Bridge at the Edge of the Continent," walkers are treated to splendid views of San Francisco Bay, which contains 90 percent of California's remaining coastal wetlands. Other great bay views—and great hikes—can be had from China Camp State Park, Angel Island and Mt. Tamalpais.

The Bay Area is rich in coastal trails. An officially designated Coast Trail heads through Golden Gate National Recreation Area, Mt. Tamalpais State Park, and Point Reyes National Seashore. Coast Trail offers days and weekends of fine hiking to remote backcountry camps. Construction is well underway on two new, 400-mile-long trails—Bay Trail and Bay Area Ridge Trail.

Point Reyes National Seashore, with its densely forested ridges, wild and open coastal bluffs, and deserted beaches, is an unforgettable place to ramble. With its moors, weirs, glens and vales, Point Reyes Peninsula calls to mind the seacoast of Great Britain. When fog settles over the dew-dampened grasslands of Tomales Point, hikers can easily imagine that they're stepping onto a Scottish moor, or wandering one of the Shetland Islands.

North of Marin County is the sparsely populated and little developed coastline of Sonoma and Mendocino counties. As you travel north, you pass from rolling, grass-covered hillsides to steep cliffs and densely forested coastal mountains.

The names on Sonoma's shore are intriguing: Blind Beach, Schoolhouse Beach, Arched Rock, Goat Rock, Penny Island and Bodega Head. These colorfully named locales are the highlight of Sonoma Coast State Beach, which is not one beach, but many.

In Mendocino County, at Van Damme and Russian Gulch State Parks, another very special environment awaits the walker: the Pygmy Forest. A nutrient-poor, highly acidic topsoil has severely restricted the growth of trees to truly Lilliputian size. Sixty-year-old cypress trees are but a few feet tall and measure only a half-inch in diameter.

Few coastal locales are as photographed as the town of Mendocino and its bold headlands. The town itself, which lies just north of the mouth of Big

River, resembles a New England village. Now protected by a state park, the Mendocino Headlands are laced with trails that offer postcard-views of wave tunnels and tidepools, beaches and blowholes.

Sinkyone Wilderness State Park and King Range National Conservation Area are part of California's famed Lost Coast—an area of unstable earth and fast-rising mountains. The San Andreas Fault lies just offshore and touches land at Shelter Cove. So rugged is this country that highway engineers were forced to route Highway 1 many miles inland; as a result, the region has remained sparsely settled and unspoiled. Its magnificent vistas and varied terrain—dense forests, prairies and black-sand beaches—reward the hearty explorer.

California's coastline rises to a magnificent crescendo at Redwood National Park. Redwood Creek Trail travels through the heart of the national park to Tall Trees Grove, site of the world's tallest tree.

The redwoods seem most at home in places like Gold Bluffs in Prairie Creek State Park. Dim and quiet, wrapped in mist and silence, the redwoods roof a moist and mysterious world.

Many beautiful "fern canyons" are found along the north coast. The one in Prairie Creek Redwoods State Park is particularly awe-inspiring. Bracken, five-finger, lady, sword and chain ferns smother the precipitous walls of the canyon.

Lucky hikers might catch a glimpse of the herd of Roosevelt elk that roam the state park. These graceful animals look like a cross between a South American llama and a deer, and convince (if any convincing be necessary) hikers that they have indeed entered an enchanted land.

■ SWEENEY RIDGE

Sweeney Ridge Trail

From Skyline College to San Francisco Bay Discovery Site is
4 miles round trip with 600-foot elevation gain

Unlike most California coastal locales, San Francisco Bay was discovered by walkers, not sailors. The bay's infamous fog and its narrow opening had concealed it from passing ships for two centuries when Captain Gaspar de Portolá sighted it on November 4, 1769.

The actual discovery site is atop Sweeney Ridge above the town of Pacifica. Portolá was at first miffed by his discovery because he realized that his expedition had overshot its intended destination of Monterey Bay. He soon realized, however, that he had discovered one of the world's great natural harbors, and he figured it would be an ideal place for his government to build another presidio. Portolá's discovery aided Captain Ayala, who was then able to sail his *San Carlos* into the bay.

It was quite a conservation battle to save Sweeney Ridge. The late Congressman Phillip Burton, aided by many Bay Area conservationists, succeeded

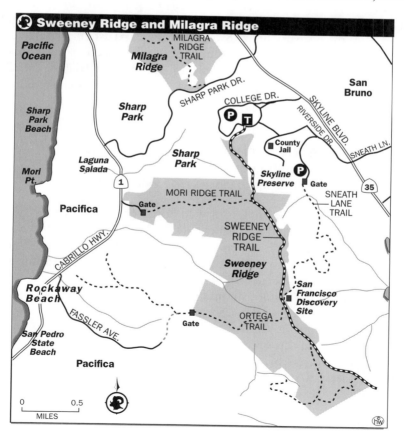

in placing a thousand acres of the ridgetop under protection of the Golden Gate National Recreation Area.

Sweeney Ridge is the name of the trail you'll use while walking the ridge itself. Four trails lead to Sweeney Ridge: Baquiano Trail and Mori Ridge Trail lead eastward to Portolá's discovery site, while Sneath Lane Trail and Sweeney Ridge Trail climb southward to the ridgetop.

DIRECTIONS TO TRAILHEAD Mori Ridge: From Highway 1 at the outskirts of Pacific, turn east at the first opportunity south of Fairway Drive. You'll see a sign for Shelldance Exotic Plant Nursery. Take this road 0.3 mile to its end and park near the nursery.

Fassler Avenue: Take Highway 1 to the Rockaway Beach area of Pacifica. Follow Fassler eastbound to its end at a gate.

Skyline College: Take Highway 35 to San Bruno. Turn west on College Drive, following it to the south side of campus. Look for parking area #2.

Sneath Lane: Take Highways 280 or 35 to Sneath Lane exit in San Bruno. Follow the lane westbound to its end at Sweeney Ridge.

THE HIKE The ridge is often cloaked in morning fog, and in the afternoon, the wind really kicks up. When it's foggy, the coastal scrub and grasslands are bathed in a strange, sharp light. Sweeney Ridge is particularly attractive in spring, when lupine, poppies, cream cups and goldfields color the slopes.

And the view is magnificent: Mount Tam and Mount Diablo, the Golden Gate and the Farallon Islands, plus dozens of communities clustered around the bay.

■ SAN BRUNO MOUNTAIN
Summit Loop Trail
3.1 mile round trip with 700-foot elevation gain

San Bruno Mountain is the last of wild South San Francisco, a 2,700-acre preserve for endangered butterflies such as the Mission blue and San Francisco silverspot, habitat for a dozen endangered plants such as the Franciscan wallflower and the San Bruno Mountain manzanita, and a wonderful place to unwind for stressed out *Homo sapiens.*

Surrounding the 1,314-foot summit of San Bruno are Daly City, South San Francisco, Brisbane and San Francisco. From the top you can see downtown San Francisco and ships in the bay, and you get an air traffic controller's-view of jets zooming in and out of San Francisco's airport.

The park is bisected by east-west running Guadalupe Canyon Parkway. South of the parkway, steep trails climb San Bruno. North of the parkway the terrain is more mellow. The mountains slopes, saved from 1970s subdivision

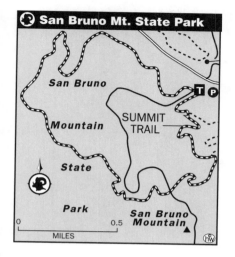

are covered with native grasses and some-times stirring spring wildflower displays.

Summit Loop is the most inspiring hike in the park with terrific clear-day views. Dress warmly. The weather—high winds, frequent fogs—is everything you'd expect of a locale near Candlestick Park.

DIRECTIONS TO TRAILHEAD From Highway 101 a bit north of South San Francisco, take the Cow Palace exit and join Guadalupe Canyon Parkway. Head west 2 miles to San Bruno Mountain County Park. Begin at the trailhead on the south side of the parkway.

THE HIKE Follow the pathway through the eucalyptus grove into somewhat boggy terrain, crossing April Brook Ravine and switchbacking upward to Bitter Cherry Ridge. Views of downtown San Francisco and Daly City are part of the view which also includes a look east-ward at Flower Garden, a meadow festooned with springtime wildflowers.

Atop the ridge, the path meets a paved road. Turn left, for a few minutes walk east, then pick up the trail again on the south side of the road. Look for more spring wildflowers en route as you reach Radio Road and a forest of antennae. Cross the road and begin a northward, switchbacking descent. Soon you'll intersect eastward-bound Ridge Trail (for 5 more miles of hiking pleas-ure, hike out to East Peak and back).

Summit Loop Trail descends past native mats of San Bruno manzanita and serves up excellent Bay views.

When your reach Dairy Ravine Trail, you can veer right down the canyon, then right again on Eucalyptus Loop Trail back to the parking area.

■ LANDS END
Coastal Trail
From Cliff House to Golden Gate Bridge is 6 miles round trip

San Francisco is known as a city of walkers. Whether this reputation is due to its relatively healthy, vigorous upscale population, or to the city's terri-ble traffic and scarcity of parking, is open for debate.

This walk, a scenic and historic journey from Cliff House to the Golden Gate, explores a part of San Francisco's diverse shoreline.

Today's Cliff House, perched above Ocean Beach, is the fourth structure erected on this site. In 1863, the first roadhouse was built; it catered to the

wealthy, high-toned carriage crowd. Along came millionaire and philanthropist Adolph Sutro, who had moved to San Francisco after making his fortune as an engineer during Nevada's silverstrike era. Sutro thought that the city's working-class residents would enjoy a seaside diversion of public pools. He built a steam railway from downtown to the coast; the ride to Cliff House cost a nickel.

After the original Cliff House, called Seal Rock House, burned down, Sutro replaced it with a six-story gingerbread-style Victorian mansion. This, too, burned to the ground in 1907. Sutro again rebuilt, this time constructing a rather utilitarian structure.

After many years of planning and two years of renovation, the latest incarnation of Cliff House re-opened in 2004. This new and greatly updated Cliff House boasts two bars, two restaurants and a terrace available for sunset wedding ceremonies and other private parties. Architectural elements from the 1909 design, as well as some inspiration from the old Sutro Baths, were incorporated into Cliff House IV.

Coastal hikers, and anyone else who takes inspiration from Lands End, will appreciate the expanded panoramic vistas from three publicly accessible observation decks. Seal Rocks, frequented by seals and noisy sea lions, the Marin Headlands and the wide blue Pacific are all part of the wonderful views.

DIRECTIONS TO TRAILHEAD From Highway 101 (Van Ness Boulevard) in the city, turn west on Geary Boulevard and follow it to its end. As the road turns south toward Ocean Beach, you'll see Cliff House on your right.

THE HIKE After you've enjoyed the many attractions of Cliff House, walk northeast a short distance to the Greco-Roman-like ruins of the Sutro Baths. Six saltwater swimming pools and a freshwater plunge were heated by a complex series of pipes and canals. Museums, galleries and restaurants were also part of the complex built by Adolph Sutro in 1890. The popularity of public spas gradually waned and, in 1966, fire destroyed all but the cement foundations of the baths.

Wander north over to the Merrie Way parking area and join Coastal Trail. For a time you'll be walking on the abandoned bed of the old Cliff House and Ferries Railroad. The trail winds through cypress and coastal sage, and hugs the cliffs below El Camino del Mar.

Coastal Trail leads along the Lincoln Park Bluffs. If it's low tide when you look down at the shoreline, you might be able to spot the wreckage of some of the ships that have been dashed to pieces on the rocks below. This rocky, precipitous stretch of coast is known as Lands End.

You'll get great views from the Eagle Point Lookout, then briefly join El Camino Del Mar through the wealthy Seacliff residential area. A quarter-mile of travel (keep bearing left) brings you to sandy China Beach, the site of an encampment for Chinese fishermen a century ago. The beach is also known as James Phelan Beach for the politician-philanthropist, who left part of his fortune to help California writers and artists.

Backtrack to Sea Cliff Avenue, following the westernmost lanes of this fancy residential area, and continue north a short half-mile to expansive Baker Beach. At the south end of the beach is the outlet of Lobos Creek.

In his autobiography, Ansel Adams recalled the many delightful days he spent as a child exploring Lobos Creek. These childhood adventures were the great nature photographer's first contact with the natural world.

At the north end of Baker Beach is Battery Chamberlain, a former coastal defense site, complete with a "disappearing" 95,000-pound cannon. Occasionally park interpreters demonstrate how the cannon could be cranked into its cement, tree-hidden bunker.

Follow the beach service road up through the cypress to Lincoln Boulevard. Coastal Trail is a bit sketchy as it follows the boulevard's guard rail for a half-mile of contouring along the cliffs. The trail meanders among cypress and passes more military installations—Batteries Crosby, Dynamite, and Marcus Miller. Beyond the last battery, Coastal Trail leads under the Golden Gate Bridge. Just after the trail passes under the bridge, you can follow a path to historic Fort Point.

■ GOLDEN GATE PROMENADE
Golden Gate Promenade
From Aquatic Park to Golden Gate Bridge is 4 miles one way

Surely one of the most memorable shore walks in San Francisco is along Golden Gate Promenade. Along the 4-mile path extending from Aquatic Park to Golden Gate Bridge is a rich diversity of historical, architectural and cultural attractions complemented by a sandy beach, vast waterfront green, and inspiring vistas of the Golden Gate Bridge and Marin Headlands.

Golden Gate Promenade even has its own logo: a blue and white sailboat emblem. Along the promenade you can witness several periods of military history from the early airfield at Crissy Field to that Civil War-era brick fortress Fort Point.

The promenade is a popular place to exercise. San Franciscans jog, cycle, walk, run and triathlon here. Some stop at the exercise stations en route. Rare is the time when the area isn't filled with athletic Bay Area residents pursuing their aerobic conditioning.

You can begin this walk from a couple of different locales, ranging from east to west: Fisherman's Wharf, Aquatic Park or Fort Mason. The latter option has much to recommend it for the first-time visitor. Golden Gate National Recreation Area headquarters is at Fort Mason, and the parking is pretty good here, too. Obtain a map from the white, three-story, one of many historic buildings at Fort Mason.

Fort Mason (well worth a walk all by itself) has evolved into the north shore's culture capital. The piers and warehouses of Fort Mason Center host theater performances, live radio shows, environmental education seminars, and many kinds of recreational activities.

Sunbathers enjoy snuggling into one of the hollows of grassy Marina Green to get out of the wind, which is considerable—to the delight of kite flyers. The winds stirring the bay across from Crissy Field have made the waters here a premiere sailboarding locale.

Don't miss another national park system attraction off the promenade. San Francisco Maritime National Historic Park, once part of the Golden Gate National Recreation Area, is now an independent unit that includes a museum and a collection of historic ships.

The maritime museum is housed in a onetime 1930s bathhouse, built in the form of a luxury ocean liner. Stainless steel railings and portholes add to the nautical look of the structure. Inside are exhibits interpreting a century and a half of California seafaring—from the ships that carried gold-seeking '49ers to whaling boats, yachts and ferries.

DIRECTIONS TO TRAILHEAD Park in the large lot at Fort Mason, at the intersection of Marina Boulevard and Beach Street.

THE HIKE From Fort Mason, you may walk along Marina Boulevard or across Marina Green, but the paved pathway along the bay shore is the best way to go.

At St. Francis Yacht Harbor, notice the sea wall, which offers a great stroll; at its end, is a wave organ which (when the tide is right) serenades walkers with the sounds of San Francisco Bay.

The promenade joins Marina Boulevard for a time, passing some Mediterranean-style haciendas and—nearing that glorious reminder of the 1915 Panama Pacific Exposition—the Palace of Fine Arts and its superb, hands-on science exhibits—the Exploratorium.

Resuming a more bay-side route, Golden Gate Promenade leads along Crissy Field. Besides nostalgia for the early days of aviation, Crissy Field also boasts the north shore's most pristine stretch of beach. The low dunes bordering the beach are dotted with native grasses.

The promenade zigzags around a parking lot and fishing pier before nearing Fort Point. With so much to see, your return route will be as fascinating as the first half of your walk.

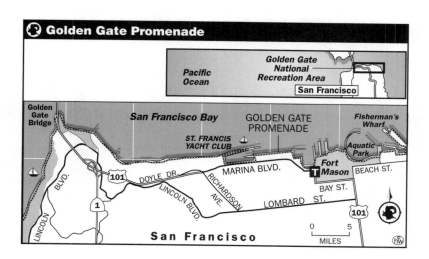

■ PRESIDIO
Ecology Loop Trail
2 miles round trip

S an Francisco's historic Presidio occupies some 1,500 acres of real estate in one of America's most desirable—and expensive—cities. After a century and a half of use as a military post, the U.S. Army transferred ownership of the Presidio to the National Park Service in 1994. Of the many Army bases across the U.S. shut down during the decade of such closures, the Presidio was the only military installation to become part of the park system.

The Park Service manages the Presidio in partnership with the Presidio Trust, a federal government corporation. With the trust managing the interior and the majority of the buildings, and the Park Service responsible for the coastal areas, the agencies team to enhance natural areas, renovate and maintain buildings, upgrade the Presidio trail system, and offer visitor programs.

The Park Service and the Presidio Trust aim to rehabilitate the best of the Presidio's historic buildings, as well as restore the woodlands and native dune vegetation. The Presidio hosts an astonishing number (280) species of native plants. More than 200 species of birds have been sighted in this urban refuge, which offers habitat to a variety of mammals and reptiles.

A little more than a decade after its formation, the urban national park reached a milestone: it began to pay for itself. Some 2,500 residents rent housing ranging from converted barracks to renovated officers' quarters. A free shuttle system connects residents from the Presidio's 21 neighborhoods to nearby public transit.

View of Alcatraz from the Presidio.

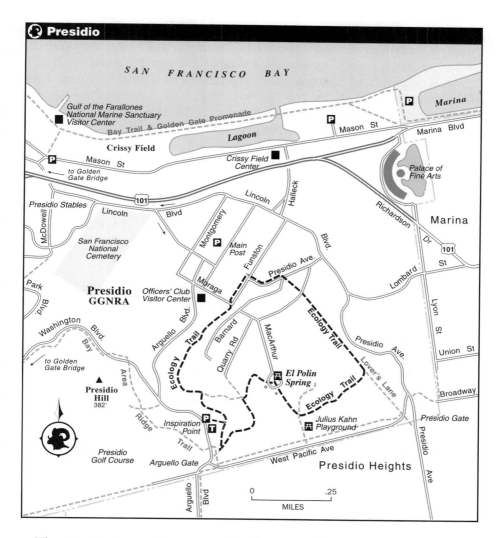

The Presidio is now home to a significant number of quality profit-making and nonprofit enterprises. Filmmaker George Lucas' Letterman Digital Arts Center opened for business in 2005 on the site of the old army hospital. The Thoreau Center for Sustainability houses 50 community and environmental organizations.

Not everyone is altogether pleased by such developments, though most of the local citizenry and visitors seem to be taking the Presidio's extreme makeover in stride. As buildings are restored so, too, are landscapes, including hiking trails, wildlife habitat and the unique urban forest.

One of the most spectacular transformations on the Presidio is the 100 acres of Crissy Field shoreline, consisting of a restored salt marsh, walking and biking paths, and native plants stretching from the foot of the Golden Gate Bridge to the Marina Green. Between 1998 and 2000 individuals and groups from schools, corporations and civic organizations planted more than 100,000 native plants in an area formerly occupied by military buildings and asphalt.

Several periods of architecture are represented in the Presidio, ranging from red brick barracks, circa 1895, built in the Georgian style, to a Spanish Revival-style theater. Some experts rate the Victorian-era officers' homes along Funston Ave. among the best examples of that period in San Francisco.

Environmentally conscious before his time Army Major W.A. Jones is credited with initiating a forestry program in the 1880s that transformed the forlorn, windswept sand dunes into the wooded preserve it is today. Thousands of trees, native and not, were planted under the direction of the Army Corps of engineers: Acacia, eucalyptus, Monterey pine, redwood, madrone and many more species. Some areas were planted in straight rows and now appear like companies of soldiers standing in formation.

Once landscaped, the Presidio proved to be one of the most highly desirable stateside locations for a soldier's assignment. Although the base was used mainly as a medical facility and administration center, during World War II its coastal batteries were activated in order to defend the Golden Gate Bridge against possible enemy attack.

Even before the Presidio became part of Golden Gate National Recreation Area, San Franciscans in the know enjoyed limited public access. Now the walker can wander at will over a 28-mile-long network of paved roads, sidewalks and footpaths.

The Visitor Center, located at the former Officers' Club (Building 50 at Moraga Avenue), is your source for Presidio information, including books, free maps and brochures. It's open daily from 9 A.M. to 5 P.M.

An excellent place to begin a walking tour is near Inspiration Point, at the southeastern corner of the Presidio, on the Ecology Trail. This loop trail explores architecture and military history and also offers a nice walk in the woods. If you have young ones in tow, pick up a copy of "Kids on Trails," a free children's tour guide to activities along the Ecology Trail.

DIRECTIONS TO TRAILHEAD From the Presidio's Arguello Gate entrance, just north of Arguello Blvd. and Jackson St., drive a few hundred yards to the paved parking area on the right, at Inspiration Point. The trailhead is on the east side.

THE HIKE At the parking area walk down a set of wooden steps and turn left to join the Ecology Trail, a wide dirt trail (fire road). After passing Inspiration Point itself, you'll make a gradual descent through groves of Monterey pine and eucalyptus. The buildings of the Main Post lie ahead. The Presidio's oldest existing structures, dating back to 1861 and the Civil War, are found on the Main Post, as is the Visitor Center, located in the former Presidio Officers' Club.

Now the path is paved. Pass Pershing Hall—a bachelor officers' quarters, and continue along the sidewalk on Funston Ave. Officers' Quarters, a splendid row of Victorians that housed officers and their families, is another historic area on Funston Ave.

Turn right at Presidio Ave. and continue over a footbridge. Cross MacArthur and continue on to paved Lovers' Lane. The lane has been a favorite of romantic walkers ever since the 1860s, when it was used by off-duty soldiers to walk into town to meet their sweethearts.

A gradual uphill grade leads near the historic site of El Polin Springs, used by Spanish soldiers more than two hundred years ago. During the summer, archeology students conduct ongoing excavations of the site.

The slope above the springs is serpentine grasslands, and is home to many rare or threatened plants, including the endangered Presidio clarkia. More than two dozen varieties of trees can be seen along the trail. Continue up the trail to the base of Inspiration Point, and follow your route back to the parking lot.

■ SAN FRANCISCO BAY NATIONAL WILDLIFE REFUGE
Tidelands Trail
1.5 miles round trip

San Francisco Bay National Wildlife Refuge is a big one, befitting the west coast's most crucial bay and marsh tidewaters, salt ponds and mudflats. At more than 23,000 acres, it's the nation's largest urban wildlife refuge, critical habitat for the more than 250 species of birds counted here.

Thirty miles of trail trace the bay shore. Some of these pathways use the tops of levees to cross mudflats and salt ponds. (Note that the levees are created of mud dredged from the bay and are sometimes closed for repairs, or for the seasonal use of nesting waterfowl.) Interpretive paths, complete with trailside panels, offer easy-to-follow lessons about the bay's fish, fowl and coastal ecology. One refuge trail even travels to Coyote Hills Regional Park by way of a foot and bicycle bridge over the Dumbarton Bridge toll plaza.

Tidelands Trail is a wide, levee-top interpretive path that visits marsh and bay wetlands. Bay views are grand from a crow's nest observation platform. Tidelands, honored with National Recreation Trail status, loops around Newark Slough, visits a salt

Reflections of life along the bay.

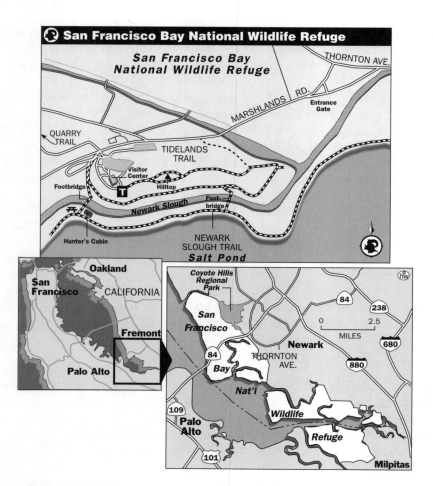

company pumphouse turned picnic site, and offers a duck blind from which to shoot birds (with a camera of course!).

Begin your walk at the attractive visitor center perched on a rise near the eastern approach to the Dumbarton Bridge. Pick up a map and inquire about the refuge's ambitious schedule of guided walks and interpretive programs.

DIRECTIONS TO TRAILHEAD Drive east over Dumbarton Bridge. After the toll plaza, exit on Thornton Avenue. Turn right and drive 0.25 mile to Marshland Road, then turn right to the visitor center.

THE HIKE Join the path at the overlook behind the visitor center. Check out the view of the bay and wetlands from the crow's nest observation platform.

Tidelands Trail descends to the edge of the marsh then crosses a bridge over Newark Slough and intersects Newark Slough Trail (an excellent 5-mile round trip hike if you have the time) and joins a levee. You stroll pass Leslie Salt Company salt evaporator ponds, home to brine shrimp and the birds that eat them. A duck hunter's cabin and a duck blind gives you a chance to learn how ducks were sighted in the pre-refuge past and how they're sighted in the refuge today.

Nearby is a salt industry pumphouse, built on piles over the water. After recrossing Newark Slough on another bridge, the trail returns to the visitor center.

■ CANDLESTICK POINT STATE RECREATION AREA
Candlestick Point Trail
2 miles round trip

To San Francisco baseball fans, Monster Park, formerly known as Candlestick Park, was long the windy home stadium of their beloved Giants. The team relocated to more upscale digs at the new Pac Bell (now SBC) Park in 2001, leaving behind San Francisco's football team, the '49ers, as the sole tenants.

In the shadow of "The Stick" is a state recreation area that beckons other sports-minded visitors. Advanced board-sailers relish the challenge of the wind tunnel off the south shore of the park. Afternoon winds funnelling through Alemany Gap to the Bay often create rides to remember.

Kayakers like to put-in and take-out on the park's sandy beach. Fishermen enjoy the two fishing piers. Some of the best winter bird-watching on the Bay

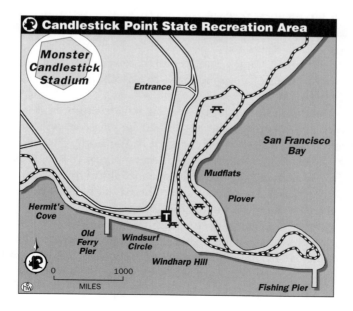

is found at Candlestick Point. And there are plenty of facilities for picnics and barbecues.

The California State Parks Foundation is assisting in the restoration of the point's tidal areas.

DIRECTIONS TO TRAILHEAD From Highway 101, south of San Francisco, take the Candlestick Park exit. Follow the Hunters Point Expressway around the stadium to the state recreation area. There's limited parking along the road, plentiful parking near the main picnic/day use area.

THE HIKE For the walker, a multi-use trail extends a mile or so along the shoreline from the fishing pier to the picnic areas.

Expect a windy walk. Those infamous winds that have long plagued out-fielders, turning even routine fly balls into a challenge to catch, once even blowing a pitcher off the mound, can really slow down a walker.

■ GOLDEN GATE BRIDGE
Golden Gate Trail
Across the Golden Gate from Fort Point to Vista Point is 3 miles round trip

It's known as one of the world's engineering marvels, the proud emblem of a proud city, and "The Bridge at the End of the Continent." The Golden Gate is all of this—and a great walk: it is one of those must-do-once-in-a-life-time adventures.

The technically inclined revel in the bridge's vital statistics: its 8,981-foot length, cables that support 200 million pounds, twin towers the height of 65-story buildings. Statisticians have calculated everything from the number of gallons of International Orange paint required to cover 10 million square feet of bridge, to the number of despondent souls who have leaped from bridge to bay.

For all its utilitarian value, the bridge is an artistic triumph. As you walk the bridge, try to remember how many set-in-San Francisco movies and television shows have opened with an establishing shot of the bridge.

The bridge spans 400 square miles of San Francisco Bay, which is really three bays—San Francisco and the smaller San Pablo and Suisun Bays to the north and northeast. Geographers describe the bay as the drowned mouth and floodplain of the Sacramento-San Joaquin Rivers.

Ninety percent of California's remaining coastal wetlands are contained in San Francisco Bay and its estuaries. Shoreline development and industrial pollutants have damaged fish, shellfish and bird populations; fortunately a great many people care about the bay, and are working hard to save and rehabilitate one of the state's most important natural resources.

"The Bridge at the End of the Continent."

For centuries, high mountains and heavy fogs concealed one of the world's great natural anchorages from passing European ships. It was a coast walker—Sergeant José Francisco Ortega, of the 1769 Portolá overland expedition—who first sighted San Francisco Bay. (See Sweeney Ridge Walk.)

Guarding the Golden Gate is Fort Point, a huge Civil War-era structure built of red brick. The fort, similar in design to Fort Sumter in South Carolina, was built for the then-astronomical cost of $2.8 million, and was intended to ensure California's loyalty to the union.

Fort Point, now part of Golden Gate National Recreation Area, boasts several fine military exhibits, including one emphasizing the contributions of African-American soldiers. Visitors enjoy prowling the three-story fort's many corridors and stairwells. From 1933 to 1937, the fort was the coordinating center for the bridge construction.

While the walk across the bridge is unique, and the clear-day views grand, the trip can also be wearing on the nerves. A bone-chilling wind often buffets bridge walkers, and traffic vibrating the bridge also seems to vibrate one's very being. Anyone afraid of heights should walk elsewhere.

To best enjoy the bridge walk, start well away from it, perhaps even as far away as Fisherman's Wharf, Fort Mason, or Marina Green. It's a pleasing bayside stroll past the yacht harbor and Crissy Field, and along Golden Gate Promenade to Fort Point.

DIRECTIONS TO TRAILHEAD Don't try to drive as close as you can to the bridge. First-time visitors invariably miss the viewpoint parking area just south of the toll plaza and before they know it, end up in Sausalito. Fort Point's park-

ing lot is one good place to leave your vehicle, as are other parking lots along the bay.

THE HIKE From Fort Point, a gravel, then paved, road leads up to a statue of visionary engineer Joseph Strauss, who persuaded a doubting populace to build the bridge.

As you start walking along the bridge's east sidewalk, you'll get a great view of Fort Point. Pause frequently to watch the ship traffic: yachts, tankers, tug boats, ferries, passenger liners. Literally everything necessary for modern life, from California almonds to Japanese cars, passes in and out of the bay by freighter.

Splendorous clear-day views include the cities of the East Bay, and the bold headlands of Marin, which form the more rural part of Golden Gate National Recreation Area. You'll spot Treasure, Alcatraz and Angel islands and, of course, the San Francisco skyline.

The bridge's second high tower marks the beginning of Marin County. Vista Point is the end of your bridge walk. Here you'll witness tourists from around the world photographing each other and proclaiming their admiration for the Golden Gate in a dozen foreign languages.

■ ALCATRAZ ISLAND
Agave Trail
1 mile round trip

Once the island was populated with the likes of Al "Scarface" Capone, George "Machine Gun" Kelly and a couple hundred more incorrigibles. Now the isle's most distinguished residents are the black-crowned night heron, double-crested cormorant and a couple thousand Western gulls.

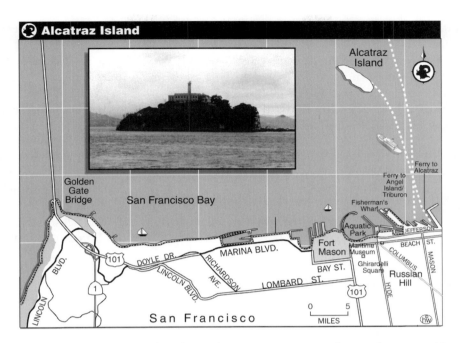

Alcatraz Island

The birds, with National Park Service encouragement, have taken over Alcatraz. Allowing the birds to recolonize "The Rock" is part of a park service program to restore some semblance of the natural world on an island long synonymous with one of America's most infamous maximum-security prisons.

The so-called Bird Man of Alcatraz (Robert Stroud) would certainly be delighted. (The 1962 movie was inaccurate; Stroud raised birds and wrote a book on bird diseases at Leavenworth Prison, but was not allowed to keep birds during the 17 years he was incarcerated on Alcatraz.)

Not everyone is happy with the isle's change from crookery to rookery. The old prison is one of San Francisco's most popular tourist attractions and many visitors (avid bird-watchers excepted) complain about the walls and walkways splattered and splotched with bird droppings, the one-time military parade ground littered with mounds of white and gray feathers, and the malodorous bird guano. National Park officials are faced with the nearly impossible task of managing "historical resources" (the prison), "natural resources" (the birds) and the thousands of tourists who flock to the isle.

The Pacific Coast's first lighthouse was installed on the island in 1854. Alcatraz later served as a military prison for Civil War, Native American and World War I prisoners. From 1934 to 1963 The Rock imprisoned some of America's most infamous "public enemies."

Native American activists took over the island in 1969, claiming sovereignty on the basis of an 1868 U.S. treaty with the Sioux nation and attempting to establish and educational and spiritual center. U.S. Marshals evicted the group in 1971. Alcatraz became part of the Golden Gate National Recreation Area and was opened to the public in 1973. It has been a popular attraction ever since.

Visitors can tour the prison's cell house with the help of a 35-minute audio tour and view a short video shown in the Casement Theater. Ranger-led walks emphasize such topics as natural history, prison guard life and escape attempts.

Agave Trail offers a walk on the wild side of the island. It takes hikers near tidepools and a sea lion haul-out and offers great views of flocks of sea birds.

Agave Trail takes its name from the island's dense population of the spiny succulent. The agaves were strategically planted during the isle's prison era to discourage any would-be rescuers from coming ashore.

Autumn is the best time for a visit. Agave Trail is open only from mid-September through January. The trail is closed the balance of the year in order to protect the nesting sites of the western gull and other fowl. The fall season typically offers the clearest Bay views, as well as relief from the hordes of summer tourists.

DIRECTIONS TO TRAILHEAD Alcatraz Island is accessible by ferries, which depart from Fisherman's Wharf. Reservations (a week ahead), are suggested, especially for weekend visits.

Signed Agave Trail begins just south of the ferry dock.

THE HIKE The path meanders past eucalyptus (favored by nesting black-crowned night herons) and across a hillside spiked with the trail's namesake agave.

Movie fans might recognize locations from Clint Eastwood's *Escape from Alcatraz* and *The Rock,* the latter a 1996 action thriller starring Sean Connery and Nicholas Cage as unlikely heroes who attempt to thwart terrorists who've taken over Alcatraz and are threatening San Francisco with chemical weapons.

The trail descends toward the water and, at low tide, some intriguing tidepools, then ascends sandstone steps to serve up dramatic vistas of the bay, Bay Bridge, Treasure Island and metro San Francisco.

Back up top is a parade ground hewn out of solid rock by military prisoners of the 1870s. Agave Trail passes the ruins of a guard house and junctions the main trail to the cell block. Walkers can continue to the isle's old lighthouse.

■ ANGEL ISLAND STATE PARK
Angel Island Loop Trail
5 miles round trip with 400-foot elevation gain

For an island barely a square mile in size, Angel Island has an extremely diverse history. Over the last two centuries, the island has seen use as a pirate's supply station, a Mexican land grant, an Army artillery emplacement and an Immigrant Detention Center. Now it's a state park, attracting hikers, history buffs and islophiles of all persuasions.

A hundred years of U.S. military occupation began in 1863 when the first gun batteries were installed. The military used the island until 1962, when its Nike Missile Station was deactivated. During wartime periods, particularly during the Spanish-American War, Angel Island was one of the busiest outposts in America. The island served as a processing center for men about to be dispatched to the Philippines, and as a reception/quarantine center for soldiers who returned with tropical diseases.

Not all of the island's attractions are historical. Rocky coves and sandy beaches, grassy slopes and forested ridges, plus a fine trail network, add up to a walker's delight. Perimeter Road takes the walker on a 5-mile tour of the island and offers a different bay view from every turn. From atop Mt. Livermore, a terrific 360-degree panorama unfolds of San Francisco Bay and the Golden Gate.

DIRECTIONS TO TRAILHEAD For information about ferry service to island from Tiburon, call Tiburon Ferry at (415) 435-2131. There is limited ferry service from San Francisco via Red and White Fleet; call (415) 546-2896. The ferries land at Ayala Cove on the northwest side of the island.

Park your car—for a fee—in one of Tiburon's parking lots near the waterfront, or attempt to find some of the scarce free parking.

Angel, the Bay's largest island.

THE HIKE When you disembark, head for the park visitor center, located in a white building that once served as bachelor quarters for unmarried officers assigned to the U.S. Quarantine Station that operated here from 1892 to 1949. At that time, Ayala Cove was named Hospital Cove. At the visitor center, you can check out the interpretive exhibits and pick up a park map.

Walk uphill on the road to the left of the visitor center. You'll intersect Perimeter Road and the Sunset trailhead at the top of the hill.

Sunset Trail switchbacks up steep, coastal-scrub covered slopes, to the top of 781-foot Mt. Caroline Livermore. Picnic tables have replaced the helicopter pad and radio antennae that once stood on the summit. Views of Ayala Cove, Tiburon and the Golden Gate are memorable.

Continuing right (west) on Perimeter Road, you'll soon overlook Camp Reynolds (West Garrison). A side road leads down to the island's first military fortifications. You can walk the parade ground and see the brick hospital built in 1908. Still standing are the chapel, mule barn, barracks and several more structures. Some of the buildings are being restored.

Perimeter Road turns eastward, contouring around chaparral-covered slopes and offering a view down to Point Blunt. You may hear and see the seals gathered around the point. The road curves north and soon arrives at East Garrison, where a collection of utilitarian-looking buildings are a reminder of the many thousands of men who were processed here. East Garrison trained about 30,000 men a year for overseas duty. The hospital, barracks, mess hall and officers' homes still stand.

Continue north. You'll soon come to the Immigration Station, the so-called Ellis Island of the West. From 1910 to 1940, 175,000 immigrants, mostly Asians, were (often rudely) processed. During World War II, German, Italian and Japanese prisoners of war were confined here.

Perimeter Road rounds Point Campbell, the northernmost part of the island, and you'll get a glimpse of the Richmond–San Rafael Bridge, and then a view of Tiburon, before the road descends to Ayala Cove.

■ CHINA CAMP STATE PARK
Shoreline, Bay View Trails
4.5 miles round trip with 400-foot elevation gain

On Point San Pedro Peninsula, only a few ramshackle buildings remain of the once-thriving shrimp fishing village of China Camp. During the 1800s, more than thirty such camps were established on the shores of San Francisco Bay.

The fishermen were mostly Chinese, primarily natives of Kwantung Province. The fishermen staked nets on the shallow bay bottom, in order to capture tiny grass shrimp. The shrimp were dried, then the meat separated from the shell. It was a labor-intensive process, but a ready market for the shrimp existed in China and Japan.

In the early 20th century, competing fishermen helped push through legislation that banned the use of bag nets, and in 1905, the export of dried shrimp was banned entirely, thus ending the San Francisco Bay and San Pablo Bay shrimping business.

In 1977, the state acquired 1,500 acres of bay shore to form China Camp State Park. Some 1890s-era buildings still stand at China Camp Village, and interpretive exhibits tell of the difficult life in this fishing village.

The park's ridge separates the 1890s from the 21st century. While the view south has changed immeasurably, the view down to China Camp on San Pablo Bay is almost exactly what it was in the early 1900s.

Take a fascinating hike into history at China Camp.

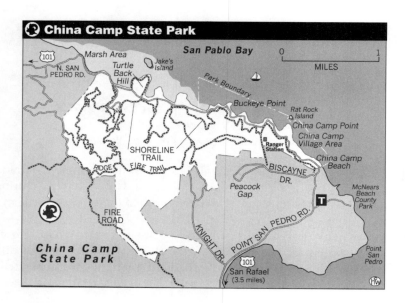

Shoreline Trail is a mellow path that meanders through the forest and grass-land above the miles of marshland that border China Camp. For a grand tour of the park, follow Shoreline Trail to the west boundary of the park. An option-al return route could be on Bay View Trail, which travels through redwoods and stands of bay through the higher (750 feet or so) elevations of the park. Views of upper San Francisco Bay are outstanding. Returning via Bay View and Ridge trails adds up to 6.5 miles; all together that's a 12-mile tour of the park.

A more modest loop, described below, uses parts of Shoreline and Ridge trails for a fine family outing.

DIRECTIONS TO TRAILHEAD From Highway 101 in San Rafael, take the North San Pedro Road exit and head east through a residential area to China Camp State Park. After entering the park, proceed approximately 3 miles to China Camp Village and park in the village lot.

THE HIKE Cross North San Pedro Road and head uphill on the Village Trail. Bear right on the Village Trail where it intersects with Shoreline Trail. As you follow San Pablo Bay from east to west, you'll stay at about a one hundred foot elevation.

Enjoy views of the park's four distinct shoreline hills—Jake's Island, Turtle Back, Bullet Hill and Chicken Coop Hill. When the bay water was higher, these hills were islands.

Two miles out, you'll reach the dirt road leading to Miwok Meadows, a day use area. (Ambitious hikers will continue on Shoreline Trail.) Those opting for a shorter loop will head uphill on the Miwok Fire Trail and join up with the Oak Ridge Trail. Head east on the Oak Ridge Trail, gaining a different perspective with a little elevation compared to the view from Shoreline Trail. When you meet Peacock Gap Trail, turn left, descending briefly back to Shoreline Trail and returning to the trailhead.

Those choosing the longer hike will head left (south) down the Miwok Fire Trail and cross the Miwok Meadows gravel parking lot. At the southwest corner of the lot, you'll find a wooden bridge spanning an intermittent creek. Shoreline Trail picks up again here and you'll continue east until it meets up with Back Ranch Fire Trail. Join this trail and head uphill across slopes forested with oak, madrone and bay laurel. Proceed right (west) at the intersection with Ridge Fire Trail and head to a former Nike missile station to savor terrific views of San Pablo Bay.

For a great loop hike, backtrack on the Ridge Fire Trail and descend on the Back Ranch Fire Trail until it meets up with the Bay View Trail. Follow Ridge Fire Trail left (east) and when it meets up with Miwok Fire Trail, follow this path downhill for a short distance. Miwok Fire Trail meets Oak Ridge Trail, which you'll join heading east. When you reach Peacock Gap Trail, turn left, descend to Shoreline Trail and return to the trailhead.

■ OLOMPALI STATE HISTORIC PARK
Olompali Trail
2.75 miles round trip with 600-foot elevation gain

Olompali State Historic Park in Marin County embraces 4,000 years of a history that is uniquely Californian—from the Miwok of 2,000 B.C. to the Chosen Family Commune of the 1960s, from Spanish missionaries to the Grateful Dead.

For the hiker, Olompali offers a colorful history lesson and a great walk in the park. "You can walk through a couple thousand years of history and get a feel for what the land looked like when the Miwok lived here," explains state park ranger Fred Lew.

From what anthropologists surmise (they've surmised a lot because limited excavation at the park has turned up thousands of artifacts), the Coast Miwok lived in shelters made of sticks, tules and grass. They enjoyed lives, by all evidence, of abundance: they gathered acorns, hunted game in the mountains, fished from the shores of the nearby bay. Olompali (pronounced O-lum-*pa*-lee) was one of the largest villages in the San Francisco Bay area.

The arrival of Spanish missionaries and soldiers ended the Miwok's way of life, though at Olompali they made a valiant effort to adapt. The Miwok learned to make adobe bricks at nearby missions and replaced their tule huts with adobe shelters. They planted crops, raised livestock. In 1843 Franciscan-educated Miwok leader Camillo Ynitia was given Olompali by the Mexican government; he was one of the very few native people to ever receive a land grant.

A decade later, Ynitia sold his land. By 1865, Rancho Olompali, as it was now known, belonged to San Francisco's first dentist, Galen Burdell, and his wife, Mary. The Burdells raised cattle and developed a fabulous estate, complete with imposing mansion and a huge formal garden.

During the 1950s, University of San Francisco Jesuits used the property as a religious retreat. The Chosen Family Commune leased the estate in 1967. The Grateful Dead played here, and one of their album covers of that era features a view of the Olompali hills. After hosting a nude wedding ceremony and celebration that attracted nationwide media coverage, the commune disbanded when a fire destroyed much of the old Burdell mansion.

The state purchased the land in 1977 and opened Olompali State Historic Park in 1990. With the aid of an interpretive booklet, you can take a walk through Olompali history. You'll see Camillo Ynitia's adobe, the ruins of the Burdell mansion, and what's left of Mary Burdell's grand garden, where daffodils, planted here more than a century ago, still bloom each year. A barn, a blacksmith shop, the ranch foreman's house and much more can be visited on this history walk.

DIRECTIONS TO TRAILHEAD From Highway 101, a half hour's drive or so north of San Francisco, and 3 miles north of Novato, get in the left turn lane for San Antonio Creek Road. Make a U-turn and drive south to the park entrance.

A family-friendly history walk is a great introduction to this park.

THE HIKE Pick up the self-guided tour booklet to Olompali and begin your exploration of the park's historic structures. After wandering among the buildings and visiting what's left of the estate's once fabulous formal garden, hit the trail.

The trail's a loop, so it doesn't matter which way you want to hike it. Near the crest of the loop, you'll get glimpses of San Pablo Bay. During spring, such wildflowers as purple iris, pink shooting stars, white milkmaids and orange monkeyflowers brighten park slopes. Keep an eye on the sky for golden eagles.

Olompali is now more than a walk through a historic park. A 2.5-mile trail extension allows hikers to ascend the eastern slope of 1,558-foot Mt. Burdell. The path connects the 700-acre park with another 2,000 acres of Marin County parkland.

■ TENNESSEE VALLEY
Tennessee Valley, Coastal Trails
From Tennessee Valley to Tennessee Cove is 4 miles round trip; to Muir Beach is 9 miles round trip with 800-foot elevation gain

It was a dark and stormy night...when the side-wheel steamship *Tennessee* with 600 passengers aboard, overshot the Golden Gate and ran aground off this isolated Marin County cove. No lives were lost on that foggy night of March 6, 1853, but the abandoned ship was soon broken up by the surf. The vessel is remembered by a point, a cove, a valley and a beach. Very occasionally a bit of the *Tennessee's* rusted remains are visible.

Although only a few miles north of San Francisco, Tennessee Valley, walled in by high ridges, seems quite isolated from the world. Until 1976 when it became part of the Golden Gate National Recreation Area, the valley was part of Witter Ranch.

Tennessee Valley Trail junctions with Coast Trail about a half mile from Tennessee Beach. The walk through Tennessee Valley to the shore is suitable for the whole family. More intrepid walkers will join Coastal Trail for an up-and-down journey to Muir Beach. (See Muir Beach Walk.)

DIRECTIONS TO TRAILHEAD From Highway 101 north of the Golden Gate Bridge, take the Highway 1 offramp. Follow the highway a half mile, turn left on Tennessee Valley Road, and follow this road to the trailhead and parking area.

THE HIKE Tennessee Valley Trail begins as a paved road, farther on becomes gravel, and farther still becomes a footpath. The route descends moderately alongside a willow- and eucalyptus-lined creek. A mile out, take the left-forking trail, which forbids mountain bikes.

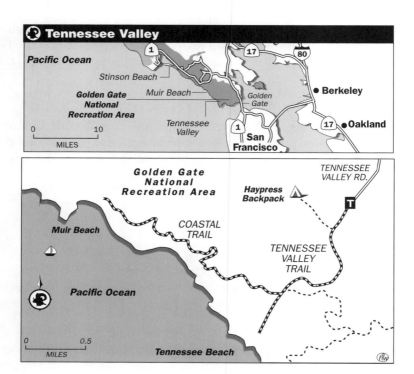

Coastal Trail near Muir Beach.

About 0.5 mile from Tennessee Cove, the trail intersects Coastal Trail. Continuing on Tennessee Valley Trail will take you past a small lagoon, and located just inland from Tennessee Beach. A trail circles the lagoon, and leads back to Tennessee Valley Trail.

Right at the above-mentioned fork connects to Coastal Trail. As you ascend north, pause to look behind at Tennessee Valley. Coastal Trail flattens out a bit, then descends to Pirate's Cove. The trail marches up and down the coastal bluffs, and passes a junction with Coyote Ridge Trail. You'll get a grand view of Muir Beach and Green Gulch. From this junction, you'll descend rather steeply down to Muir Beach.

■ STINSON BEACH
Steep Ravine Trail
From Pantoll to Stinson Beach is 3 miles one-way with 1,100-foot elevation loss

For many walkers, Steep Ravine is a favorite mountain path; it's wet, shaded and remote. The route follows along Webb Creek, which when swollen by winter rains becomes a quite vigorous watercourse, complete with waterfalls. Redwoods, ferns and mosses add to the feeling of walking through a rain forest.

Steep Ravine is, as its name suggests, a steep descent, accompanied by stair steps, and even a ladder in one place. The path intersects Dipsea Trail, which you can use to loop back to the trailhead, or follow to Stinson Beach. Many walkers descend to Stinson Beach and take the bus back up to Pantoll.

DIRECTIONS TO TRAILHEAD From Highway 1, just south of Stinson Beach, turn inland on Panoramic Highway. (Note the signed Dipsea Trail, your exit point for this walk.) Follow the highway up to Pantoll Camp and trailhead. If you're planning to take the bus from Stinson Beach back to Pantoll call the Golden Gate Transit Authority for schedules.

THE HIKE Signed Steep Ravine Trail heads south, descending a series of switchbacks through redwood, Douglas fir and huckleberry. In a half mile, the trail reaches Webb Creek and begins descending Steep Ravine.

Wood ferns, sword ferns and five-finger ferns line the trail, which passes under solemn redwoods. You descend a ladder, originally built by the CCC, and cross a creek a couple of times on footbridges.

One and a half miles from the trailhead, Steep Ravine Trail is joined by Dipsea Trail, coming from the east over a footbridge. Besides retracing your steps, you have three options to consider: You may take Dipsea Trail up to Old Mine Trail, and back to Pantoll. A second alternative is to continue with Steep Ravine Trail to Highway 1, then descend to the Steep Ravine Cabins, built in

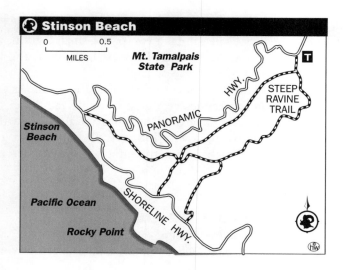

the 1930s as a family retreat for Congressman William Kent, who was instrumental in preserving Mt. Tam and Muir Woods.

Most walkers choose to keep right on Dipsea Trail and head for the town of Stinson Beach. You'll get a bird's-eye view of the strange designs of some of the hillside homes. The trail ends close to the junction of Panoramic Highway and Shoreline Highway. Follow the latter road to Stinson Beach—the tiny town, the sand strand and the bus stop.

■ MT. TAMALPAIS
Railroad Grade, Fern Creek Trails
From Mountain Home Inn to East Peak summit is 6 miles round trip with 1,300-foot elevation gain

For more than century, Bay Area walkers and visitors from around the world have enjoyed rambling on the slopes of Mount Tamalpais. Glorious panoramas of the Pacific coastline and San Francisco Bay were attracting walkers to the mountaintop well before Mount Tam was preserved as a state park in 1928.

If you're lucky, perhaps you'll experience what some Bay Area walkers call "a Farallons Day"—one of those clear days when visibility is greater than 25 miles, thus allowing a glimpse of the sharp peaks of the Farallon Islands.

The Mount Tamalpais and Muir Woods Railroad, known as "the crookedest railroad in the world," was constructed in 1896; it brought passengers from Mill Valley to the summit via 281 curves. Atop Mt. Tam, the Tavern of Tamalpais welcomed diners and dancers.

Dipsea Trail, Mt. Tamalpais State Park.

Redwood-lined creeks, stands of Douglas fir, and oak-dotted potreros are just a few of the great mountain's delightful environments. Thanks to the early trail-building efforts of the Tamalpais Conservation Club, as well as later efforts by the CCC during the 1930s, more than fifty miles of trail explore the state park. These trails connect to two hundred more miles of trail that lead through the wooded watershed of the Marin Municipal Water District and over to Muir Woods National Monument and Golden Gate National Recreation Area.

Mt. Tam's top itself, with its fire lookout tower ringed with barbed wire, isn't quite as nice as the top-of-the-world views it offers. Motorists can drive to within 0.3 mile to the top, which often means a crowd at the summit.

Ah, but getting there is more than half the fun, particularly on trails like Railroad Grade and Fern

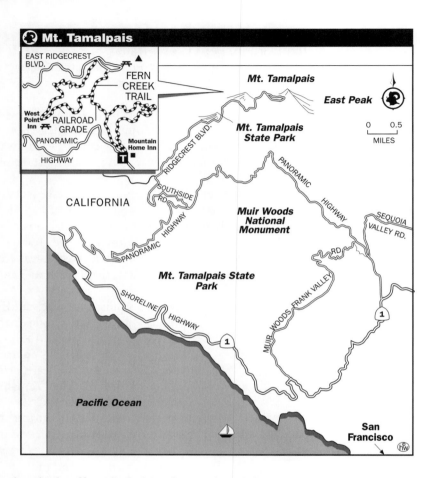

Creek, which offer a little bit of everything: dense stands of laurel, open grassland, oak-dotted knolls, a canyon full of redwoods and ferns.

If you want to stay on the Railroad Grade all the way to the top of Mt. Tam, add 2.5 miles to the ascent plus 2.5 miles to the descent.

DIRECTIONS TO TRAILHEAD From Highway 1 in Mill Valley, veer right on Panoramic Highway, ascending a few miles to Mountain Home Inn and a parking area. The trail begins across Panoramic Highway. A bus stops at Mountain Home Inn, so by all means consider the bus a way to the trailhead.

THE HIKE Begin your steady ascent (7 percent grade all the way) on the Old Railroad Grade. An occasional view opens up among the brush.

Almost 2 miles out, you'll reach a junction with the east fork of Fern Canyon. Take this very steep shortcut a long half-mile to Ridecrest Boulevard just below the East Peak parking lot.

(Dogged railroad buffs will ignore such shortcuts and stay on the Railroad Grade which visits the West Point Inn, originally built by the railroad and now owned by the Marin Water District and run by the West Point Inn Association. Hikers may pause on the veranda and buy some liquid refreshment. You'll circle clockwise around West Point, heading north another 2 miles up the railroad grade).

Once you reach the summit parking lot and picnic area, catch your breath and join the 0.3-mile summit trail to the top of Mt. Tam.

■ MUIR WOODS
Main, Bootjack, Ben Johnson Trails
2-mile and 6-mile loops

A nature trail with numbered stops keyed to the park map begins at Bridge Two, visits Cathedral Grove, crosses Redwood Creek at Bridge Three, and then returns via Bohemian Grove. A pleasant extension continues along Redwood Creek before looping back to the heart of Muir Grove.

DIRECTIONS TO TRAILHEAD Muir Woods is 12 miles from the Golden Gate Bridge. From Highway 101 northbound in Mill Valley, take the Highway 1/Stinson Beach exit. After exiting, stay in the right lane as you go under Highway 101. You are now on Shoreline Highway (Highway 1). Head west 2.7 miles to Panoramic Highway, turn right and drive .8 mile to Muir Woods Road. Turn left and proceed 1.6 miles to the main parking area for Muir Woods on your right. If the main parking lot is full, there is another one about 100 yards southeast.

THE HIKE From the parking area, walk north to the information kiosk and Visitor Center. Pay the small entrance fee. Cross the bridge to the west side of Redwood Creek.

In winter, reflect that your journey up-creek appears to be much easier than that of the steelhead and salmon struggling upstream to spawn.

Your northbound trail soon brings you to Bohemian Grove, where California's premiere men's club retreated in the 1890s. The Bohemians considered building a rough-it-deluxe camp here but opted for the more temperate environs along the Russian River.

Now you embark on the monument's nature trail, keyed to an interpretive pamphlet. Stay with the nature trail to its end, then cross Redwood Creek on a footbridge to the east side of Redwood Creek and Cathedral Grove.

Head north 0.25 mile to reach the William Kent Memorial Tree, which, to most visitors' surprise, is not a redwood but a sky-scraping 273-foot high Douglas fir—the tallest tree in Muir Woods.

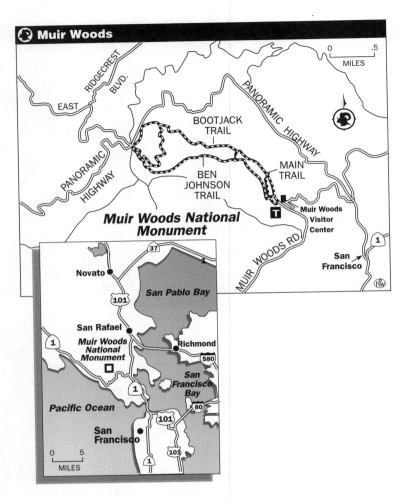

Return to Cathedral Grove and proceed south along Redwood Creek. You'll pass a memorial to pioneer forester Gifford Pinchot, a conservationist in his own right but an extremely utilitarian one, who was often philosophically at odds with the visionary John Muir.

For a longer loop, follow Muir Woods' Main Trail, which becomes Bootjack Trail and continue along Redwood Creek through the forest to Van Wyck Meadow. Here you'll join the historic World War I-era TCC (Tamalpais Conservation Club) Trail heading south, then briefly west to Sapleveldt Trail. Switchback down to Ben Johnson Trail, which leads back to the heart of Muir Woods. Main Trail or Hillside Trail returns you to the visitor center.

■ MUIR BEACH

Coyote Ridge, Green Gulch Trails

5 miles round trip with 800-foot elevation gain

Golden Gate National Recreation Area boasts two major beaches in Marin—Stinson and Muir—the latter a semi-circular strand enclosed by a forested cove.

Both Green Gulch Trail and Coyote Ridge Trail begin and end at Muir Beach and are of approximately the same length. Green Gulch Trail tours an organic farm-Zen center that permits (caring and respectful) hikers to travel its paths. Coyote Ridge Trail climbs the grassy hills above the beach and offer great coastal views.

DIRECTIONS TO TRAILHEAD From Highway 101, 5 miles north of the Golden Gate Bridge, exit for Mt. Tamalpais/Muir Woods. Follow Highway 1 for 9 winding miles to the Muir Beach parking lot. Expect a crowded lot on sunny summer days.

THE HIKE Cross a wooden bridge over the marshy mouth of Redwood Creek and head southward on Coastal Trail. After 200 yards, you'll junction with Green Gulch Trail. Join it if you wish, but I prefer taking a counterclockwise route for this hike and continuing with a mellow climb along Coast Trail, getting a gull's-eye view of Muir Beach.

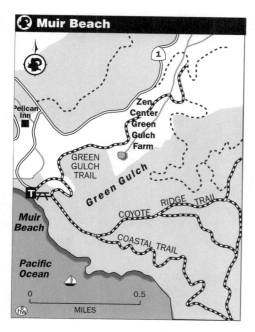

Three-quarter mile from the trailhead, bear left on Coyote Ridge Trail and begin a fairly steep 1.2-mile ascent. Stay left at a fork, curving north then west toward Green Gulch. Descend the gulch past the Zen nursery, organic farm and meditation center, returning to the Coastal Trail and Muir Beach.

■ BOLINAS RIDGE
Bolinas Ridge Trail

To Jewell Trail junction is 2.5 miles round trip; to Shafter Trail Junction is 10 miles round trip with 700-foot elevation gain

Bolinas Ridge, a long finger of land bordered by Highway 1 and Point Reyes National Seashore on the west, is perhaps the Golden Gate National Recreation Area's most remote landscape.

Ridge hikers are treated to dramatic vistas of the wooded slopes to the east and Olema Valley to the west. Bolinas Ridge separates Olema Valley from the forested state parks—Mt. Tamalpais and Samuel P. Taylor to the east.

Olema Valley has the infamous distinction of being the epicenter for the 1906 San Francisco Earthquake. The quake, one of the most severe in American history, resulted from the intense horizontal movement that occurred along the San Andreas Fault.

Long ago, Bolinas Ridge was heavily forested with redwood and Douglas fir; these trees, however, were logged and milled into lumber used to build San Francisco. The ridge these days is mostly grass-covered, dotted with coast live oak and some remnant groves of Douglas fir.

Bolinas Ridge Trail, true to its name, travels the ridgetop some 15 miles from Olema to trail's end at Bolinas-Fairfax Road. You could make this a long one-way day hike with a car shuttle, or do as most hikers do—hike to one of the ridgetop's excellent viewpoints and turn around as time and energy necessitate.

The trail is a popular mountain bike route; however, Bolinas Ridge Road is a wide path and hiker-biker conflicts are minimal on this route.

Get above it all on GGNRA's ridge trails.

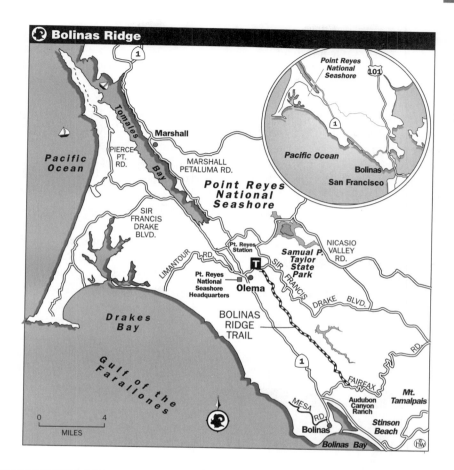

DIRECTIONS TO TRAILHEAD From Highway 101 in San Rafael, exit on Sir Francis Drake Boulevard and drive west 17.5 miles to the trailhead on the left side of the road. Park carefully along the highway.

THE HIKE Join the ascending dirt road, which curves south through rolling grassland. Before long, views open up to the east of Olema Valley and behind you of Tomales Bay and Point Reyes Peninsula.

A mile and a quarter of walking brings you to a junction with Jewell Trail, which drops east to Lagunitas Creek. Continue along the ridgetop a short distance farther for grand views west of forested Inverness Ridge. After another mile along the ridge, you'll walk in the company of Douglas fir growing on eastern slopes.

Four miles out, you'll reach more open terrain, then over the next mile, gain the ridgetop's high point, reach excellent vistas and meet the Shafter Trail. This junction is a good turnaround point.

If you're game, Bolinas Ridge Trail dips and climbs, but is a fairly mellow route all the way to Bolinas-Fairfax Road.

■ PALOMARIN
Coast Trail

From Palomarin to Bass Lake is 5 miles round trip; to Wildcat
Camp is 10.5 miles round trip with 600-foot elevation gain

For the homesick Brit or Scot, Point Reyes peninsula has more than a passing resemblance to the homeland. Inverness, Land's End and Drakes Bay are some of the names on the land that pull on the heartstrings.

Along with its United Kingdom-like moors, weirs, glens and vales, Point Reyes has its "Lakes District." Five lakes—Bass, Pelican, Crystal, Ocean and Wildcat—were created, in part, by movement along the nearby San Andreas Fault. Earth slippage sealed off passage of spring-fed waterways, thus forming the little lakes.

The lakes are reached by a somewhat melancholy stretch of the Coast Trail, forever overhung, it seems, by dark brooding clouds. Springtime travel is a bit more cheery because the route is brightened by wildflowers: foxgloves (causing more nostalgic sighs from our British friends), lupine, morning glory, cow parsnip and paintbrush.

The trail zigs, zags and roller-coasters along as it serves up ocean vistas. Wildcat Beach and the meadowland around Wildcat Camp invite a picnic.

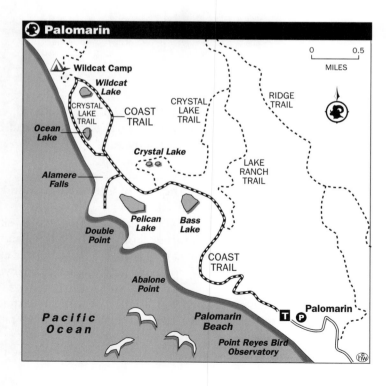

DIRECTIONS TO TRAILHEAD From Stinson Beach, drive 4.5 miles north and take the turnoff (Olema-Bolinas Road) to Bolinas. (This turnoff is rarely signed; Bolinas residents remove it as soon as it's replaced.)

Follow this road to Mesa Road and turn right. You'll pass some *Brave New World*-looking radio towers, and the Point Reyes Bird Observatory, and reach a large trailhead parking area at road's end.

THE HIKE Coast Trail, an old farm road, ascends into a mature stand of eucalyptus, then contours out onto the cliff edge. The trail here, and in the miles to follow, is lined with coastal scrub—coyote bush, black sage, coffee berry. Turning inland, the trail descends into a gully, then climbs again back to the blufftops. Coast Trail soon repeats this maneuver, this time climbing in and out of a larger gully.

You'll pass a junction with Lake Ranch Trail, which leads, among other places to Five Brooks Trailhead off Highway 1. A short distance beyond this junction is Bass Lake, a tranquil spot shaded by Douglas fir.

Another trail junction offers the opportunity to take Crystal Lake Trail to another lake in the "Lakes District."

Triangular-shaped Pelican Lake, perched on a blufftop is the next lake visited by Coast Trail, which descends to another junction. A side trail leads coastward to overlook Double Point, two shale outcroppings that enclose a small bay. Seals often haul out on the bay's small beach. Offshore stand Stormy Stacks, where California brown pelicans and cormorants roost.

Coast Trail crosses Alamere Creek, which cuts through a wild and wooded canyon on its way to the sea. During winter and spring, Alamere Falls cascading over the bluffs is an impressive sight.

A short distance beyond the creek crossing, the trail forks: the left fork, Ocean Lake Trail, and the right fork, a continuation of Coast Trail, both lead a bit over a mile to Wildcat Camp. The two trails skirt Ocean Lake and Wildcat Lake, and form a handy loop. From the camp, there's easy access to Wildcat Beach.

■ BEAR VALLEY
Bear Valley Trail
From Bear Valley Visitor Center to Divide Meadow is 3 miles round trip; to Arch Rock is 8.5 miles round trip

B ear Valley is the busy hub of Point Reyes National Seashore. From the park visitor center, more than 40 miles of trail thread through the valley, and to the ridges and beaches beyond.

The National Park Service's Bear Valley Visitor Center is a friendly place, full of excellent history and natural history exhibits. Film screenings, a seismograph, and dioramas tell the story behind the seashore's scenery.

Outside the visitor center, there is much to see, including a traditional Coast Miwok village. The family dwellings, sweat lodge and other structures, were built using traditional native methods. Near the visitor center is the Morgan Horse Ranch, where park service animals are raised and trained.

Two park interpretive trails are well worth a stroll. Woodpecker Trail is a self-guided nature trail that introduces walkers to the tremendous diversity of the region's native flora. Earthquake Trail uses old photographs and other displays to explain the seismic forces unleashed by the great 1906 San Francisco Earthquake. This well-done and entertaining geology lesson is particularly relevant because most of the land west of the San Andreas Fault Zone is within boundaries of Point Reyes National Seashore.

Bear Valley Trail, a former wagon road, is surely one of the most popular paths in the national seashore. It passes through a very

Bear Valley Trail.

low gap in Inverness Ridge, and follows a nearly-level route to the ocean. First-time visitors will enjoy this easy trail that's highly scenic but sometimes suffers from overuse. (It's a gravel park service road that's traveled by bicycles, too.) Experienced hikers will enjoy Bear Valley Trail for the access it gives to a half-dozen more remote, less traveled trails.

DIRECTIONS TO TRAILHEAD Bear Valley Visitor Center is located just outside the town of Olema, 35 slow and curving miles north of San Francisco on Highway 1. A quicker route is by Highway 101, exiting on Sir Francis Drake Boulevard, traveling through the town of Fairfax and over to Olema. A left turn on Bear Valley Road takes you to the visitor center and trailhead.

THE HIKE Bear Valley Trail, an old ranch road, heads through an open meadow and passes a junction with Mt. Wittenberg Trail, which ascends Mt. Wittenberg. Beyond this junction, the trail enters a forest of Bishop pine and Douglas fir. Your path is alongside Bear Valley Creek.

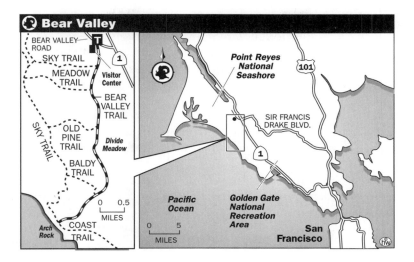

Notice that the creek flows north, in the opposite direction of Coast Creek, which you'll soon be following from Divide Meadow to the sea. This strange drainage pattern is one more example of how the mighty San Andreas Fault can shape the land.

A half-mile along, you'll pass a second trail, Meadow Trail, and after another mile of travel, arrive at Divide Meadow. A hunt club, visited by Presidents William Howard Taft and Theodore Roosevelt, once stood here. During the early part of this century, meadows and nearby forested ridges abounded with deer, bear, mountain lion and game birds.

Well-named Divide Meadow divides Bear Valley Creek from Coast Creek, which you'll soon be following when you continue on Bear Valley Trail. Divide Meadow is a fine place for a picnic.

Shady Bear Valley Trail junctions with a couple more trails, including Old Pine Trail and Baldy Trail that climb Inverness Ridge to the Sky Trail. Near the ocean, Bear Valley Trail emerges from the forest and arrives at an open meadow on the precipitous bluffs above Arch Rock. At low tide, you can squeeze through a sea tunnel at the mouth of Coast Creek.

Unpack your lunch, unfold your map, and plan a return route by way one of Bear Valley's many scenic trails.

■ POINT REYES LIGHTHOUSE

Lighthouse, Chimney Rock Trails

To Lighthouse is 1.2 miles round trip with 400-foot elevation gain; to Chimney Rock is 1.6 miles round trip with 100-foot elevation gain

Some lighthouses welcome sailors to port; some lighthouses warn them of danger. Point Reyes Lighthouse was most certainly built to warn vessels away from a treacherous coastline that was the death of many ships and their crews.

Congress voted construction funds for a light back in 1852 but legal tussles with coastal bluff land owners delayed installation until 1870. Meanwhile, many more ships ran aground.

From past experience, lighthouse keepers had learned that placing a light too high atop California's coastal cliffs diminished the light's fog-penetrating effectiveness; thus, the Point Reyes Lighthouse was built about halfway down the 600-foot bluffs.

The odd placement of the station greatly increased its construction costs, as well as the costs of supplying it during its century of service. Nasty weather, isolation from the world, and the relentless bellow of the foghorn made the lot of the lighthouse keeper a difficult one and contributed to drinking and discipline problems. Some keepers went outright bonkers.

By some accounts, Point Reyes is the foggiest point on the Pacific Coast, and supposedly second only to Rhode Island's Nantucket Island in the entire U.S. When the foggy curtain lifts, however, the lighthouse observation plat-

Approaching the Point Reyes Lighthouse.

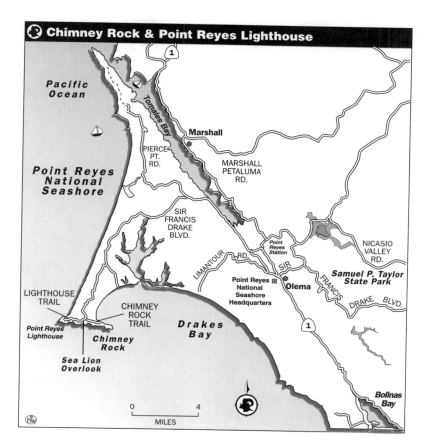

form is a superb place from which to watch for migrating California gray whales. During the winter months, bring your binoculars and scan the horizon for the passing gentle giants.

The lighthouse visitor center is open Thursday through Monday, weather permitting. Inquire at the center about tours of the facility.

A path and 308 stairs (like walking up and down the staircase of a 30-story building) comprise the route to the lighthouse.

So compelling is Point Reyes Lighthouse, most visitors don't bother with the walk to Chimney Rock Overlook, which offers a panoramic view nearly equal to that of the lighthouse. You'll travel a spring wildflower-lined path, glimpsing an old U.S. Coast Guard Lifeboat Station. While you might not be able to discern which offshore rock resembles a chimney, you will be able to view the coastline all the way to San Francisco on a clear day.

DIRECTIONS TO TRAILHEAD From Highway 1 in Olema, drive north a short distance past the turnoff for Point Reyes National Seashore Bear Valley Visitor Center, then turn left on Sir Francis Drake Highway. Follow the highway some 18 miles as it swings west then south. Near its end, the highway splits at a signed junction; the west fork leads a bit more than a mile to the Point Reyes Lighthouse trailhead; the east fork leads about 1.5 miles to the Chimney Rock trailhead.

In 1998, the National Park Service began closing the road to the lighthouse and Chimney Rock on weekends and offered a shuttle service. Tickets may be purchased at the visitor center at Drakes Beach.

■ DRAKES ESTERO
Estero Trail
From Estero Trailhead to Drakes Estero is 8 miles round trip
with 500-foot elevation gain

This coast walk will keep you glued to your field glasses. No, the route isn't difficult to follow; you'll want the field glasses to help you observe the abundant wildlife around Drakes Estero. The many fingers of Drakes Estero, Marin County's largest lagoon, is patrolled by canvasbacks, ruddy ducks and American wigeons. Great blue herons, willets, godwits and many, many more shorebirds feed along the mudflats. You might see deer, either the native black-tailed or the "imported" white fallow browsing the grassy ridges. Harbor seals and sea lion often swim into the estero.

You won't need binoculars to sight the most common animal found in these parts—cows. Both Herefords and Black Angus graze the headlands. This is cow country, and has been since the 1850s. Schooners maneuvered into Drakes Estero, took on a cargo of fine butter, and returned to San Francisco, a ready market for dairy products produced on Point Reyes.

The estero you'll visit, as well as the beach and bay you'll overlook, are named for that pirate/explorer in the service of Queen Elizabeth I, Sir Francis Drake. While walking along the estero, debate that age-old question: Did Sir Francis in June of 1579 sail his *Golden Hinde* into Drakes Bay or into San Francisco Bay? Is he really the discoverer of San Francisco Bay or does that honor fall to other sailors?

The bay where Drake set anchor had chalky cliffs, and reminded the Englishman of the cliffs of Dover. Drake's description of this bay points to Drakes Bay. To mark his discovery, Drake left a brass plate nailed to a post. This plate was supposedly found in 1936 and was originally considered genuine. Metallurgical tests later called in question its authenticity, and in 2003 the plate was confirmed to be a hoax, part of an elaborate and playful scheme dreamed up by local historians.

Old ranch roads form a nice trail system on the west side of Inverness Ridge. Estero Trail is the most dramatic of these pathways, and offers fine vistas and superb wildlife watching opportunities.

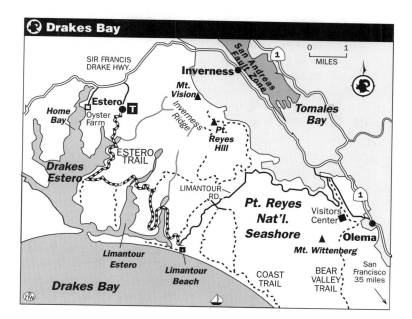

DIRECTIONS TO TRAILHEAD From Highway 1 in Olema (where there's a well-marked turnoff for the Point Reyes National Seashore Bear Valley Visitor Center), proceed 2 miles north and veer left onto Sir Francis Drake Highway. The highway follows the west side of Tomales Bay, passes through a hamlet of Inverness, then heads left (west). You'll pass a junction on your left with a road leading toward Mt. Vision. Keep looking left and you'll see the signed road leading to Estero parking area. Follow this narrow road to the signed trailhead.

THE HIKE Estero Trail, an old ranch road, climbs gently. As you climb look over your left shoulder and admire Inverness Ridge, highlighted by, from west to east, Mt. Vision, Point Reyes Hill and Mt. Wittenberg.

The trail turns to the left, and passes a stand of pine, once the nucleus of a Christmas tree farm. Soon the path crosses a causeway, which divides Home Bay from a pond. Bird-watchers will sight large numbers of shorebirds in the mudflats of Home Bay.

The trail rises above the estero, descends to another pond, and ascends again. About 2.5 miles from the trailhead, you come to a signed junction. Sunset Beach Trail continues well above the estero, and ends at a couple of small ponds, backed by Drakes Bay and the wide Pacific.

Estero Trail swings east and after a half mile comes to a junction. You may head south on Drakes Head Trail down to Limantour Estero, or you may follow Estero Trail all the way to Limantour Beach.

■ TOMALES POINT

Tomales Point Trail

From Upper Pierce Ranch to Lower Pierce Ranch is 6 miles round trip with 300-foot elevation gain; to Tomales Point is 8 miles round trip with 400-foot gain

When the fog settles over the dew-dampened grasslands of Tomales Point, walkers can easily imagine that they're stepping onto a Scottish moor, or wandering one of the Shetland Islands.

The point's rich pasture caught the eye of Solomon Pierce, who began a dairy in 1858. Pierce and his son, Abram, produced fine butter, which was shipped to San Francisco from a wharf they built on Tomales Bay. For seven decades, the point remained in the Pierce family.

The walk begins at Upper Pierce Ranch, where the family house, barn and outbuildings are now maintained by the park service. The path, an old ranch road, wanders over the green hills, which are seasonally sprinkled with yellow poppies and tidy tips, orange fiddleneck and purple iris. A small pond and a eucalyptus grove mark the site of Lower Pierce Ranch.

Be on the lookout for the tule elk herd that wanders the bluffs. A large elk population once roamed the Point Reyes area, but by the 1860s, hunters had eliminated the animals. In 1977, the National Park Service relocated some elk onto Tomales Point from the Owens Valley.

Dramatic views of the Point Reyes area are available from Tomales Point, the northernmost boundary of Marin County and Point Reyes National Seashore.

DIRECTIONS TO TRAILHEAD Drive north on Sir Francis Drake Boulevard past the town of Inverness. Shortly after Sir Francis turns west, bear right

Tule elk roam Tomales Point

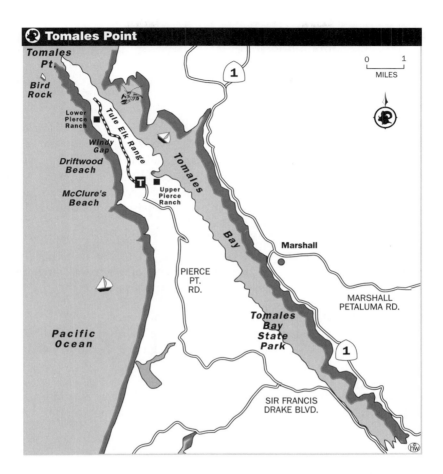

(north) on Pierce Point Road, and follow this road 9 miles to its end at Upper Pierce Point Ranch. Tomales Point Trail shares a trailhead with the 0.5-mile long path leading to McClures Beach.

THE HIKE From the old dairy buildings at Upper Pierce Ranch, the trail climbs north across the coastal prairie. Views of the beach and surf are superb. The wide path climbs and descends at a moderate rate.

As you crest the ridge and meander over to its eastern side, you'll begin to get a view of Tomales Bay, as well as Hog Island and the village of Dillon Beach. The old ranch road descends to the site of Lower Pierce Ranch, and you'll pass a pond and a eucalyptus grove.

Soon the road becomes a trail, and a mile past the ranch, arrives at a high vista point that looks down on Bird Rock, The rock is occupied by cormorants, and by white pelicans.

A faint path and some cross-country travel will take you to the very top of Tomales Point, for stirring views of Bodega Head and Tomales Bay.

■ TOMALES BAY STATE PARK
Johnstone Trail

From Heart's Desire Beach to Jepson Memorial Grove is 3
miles round trip with 300-foot elevation gain; to Shell Beach
is 8 miles round trip

Two lovely trails, named for a professor and a planner, explore Tomales Bay
State Park. Jepson Trail honors Botanist Willis Jepson, founder of the
School of Forestry at the University of California, Berkeley, and author of the
authoritative *Manual of the Flowering Plants of California.* Conservationist
Bruce Johnstone, Marin County planner, and his wife, Elsie, worked hard to
preserve Tomales Bay and place part of it in a state park. Johnstone Trail leads
bayside from Heart's Desire Beach to Shell Beach.

Bay Area walkers have a little secret: When fog smothers Point Reyes and
San Francisco Bay, try heading for Tomales Bay State Park. The park has a
microclimate, and often has sunny days and pleasant temperatures when neighboring coastal locales are damp and cold.

DIRECTIONS TO TRAILHEAD From the town of Inverness, follow Sir Francis Drake Boulevard to Pierce Point Road. Turn right and drive a half-mile to
the entrance to Tomales Bay State Park. Follow signs to the large parking lot
at Heart's Desire Beach.

THE HIKE Near the trailhead are some interpretive displays that tell of clams
and Bishop pine. Signed Johnstone Trail departs from the south end of Heart's

Oysters are sometimes the catch of the day from Tomales Bay.

Desire Beach and immediately climbs into a moss-draped forest of oak, bay, madrone, and wax myrtle.

A half-mile of travel brings you to Pebble Beach. At a trail junction, a short side trail goes straight down to Pebble Beach, but Johnstone Trail swings southwest and begins switch-backing up forested slopes. Some wetter areas of the coastal slope are dotted with ferns. The trail crosses a paved road and soon junctions.

To continue to Shell Beach, you'll bear left on Johnstone Trail. The trail

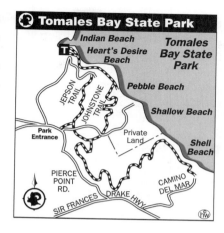

detours around some private property, and contours over the coastal slope at an elevation of about 500 feet. Some strategically placed benches allow walkers to savor the fine bay views afforded by Johnstone Trail. The path leads through Bishop pine and a lush understory of salal and huckleberry bushes. After a few miles, the trail descends through madrone and oak forest to Shell Beach.

Walkers content with looping back to Heart's Desire Beach via Jepson Trail will continue straight at the above-mentioned junction. Bishop pine, along with its similar-looking piney cousins, the Monterey and knobcone, are known as fire pines because they require the heat of fire to crack open their cones and release their seeds. Bishop pines are slow to propagate and are relatively rare in coastal California. (Another nice stand of Bishop pine is located in Montaña de Oro State Park in San Luis Obispo County.) The surest way to distinguish a Bishop pine from its look-alike, the Monterey pine, is by counting the needles: Monterey pines have three needles to a bunch, Bishop pines have two needles to a cluster.

■ BODEGA HEAD

Bodega Head Trail

From Bodega Head to Horseshoe Cove Overlook is 1 mile round trip; to Salmon Creek Beach is 4.5 miles round trip

Anchoring the south end of Sonoma State Beach is the massive granite monolith of Bodega Rock. The great rock lies just west of the San Andreas Fault. Geologists speculate that the inexorable creep of the Pacific Plate along the fault line carried the rock to this location from the Tehachapi Mountains, more than 300 miles away to the southeast.

Bodega's beauty is marred only by a huge hole dug on its harbor side. The "hole in the head," as it's known, is a reminder of the 1960s when Bodega Bay was slated to become the site of one of the largest nuclear power plants in

America. When conservationists protested the desecration of the landscape and geologists raised seismic safety questions, construction of the nuclear power plant was halted.

This walk, from the tip of Bodega Head up the peninsula to Salmon Creek, is a delight. Explore Bodega Dunes, some of the tallest coastal dunes in California, and walk 2-mile long Salmon Creek Beach, longest sand strand in Mendocino County.

DIRECTIONS TO TRAILHEAD From Highway 1 in the town of Bodega Bay, turn west on Bay Flat Road. Follow this road, which veers south and becomes known as Westside Road. The road forks. (The left fork leads to a parking area overlooking the bay side of Bodega Head.) Take the right fork to road's end at the signed Bodega Head Trail.

THE HIKE From the Bodega Head trailhead, the path climbs north. Enjoy good views of Bodega Head and of fishing boats passing through the narrow entrance of Bodega Harbor.

About 0.5 mile of travel brings you to a signed junction. The right fork is the main trail leading to the dunes and beach, but take the left fork 0.1 mile in order to partake of the terrific vistas from Horseshoe Cove Overlook.

Bodega and beyond: not only magnificent, but nuclear-free, too.

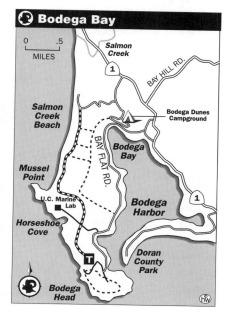

The southern view takes in Bodega Bay, and quite a bit of Marin County coastline, including the northern point of Point Reyes National Seashore. To the north, glimpse Horseshoe Cove, Salmon Creek Beach, and a number of pocket beaches and coves. The building you see is the University of California's Bodega Marine Laboratory, a research and teaching facility. Part of the Bodega Peninsula's ocean-facing coastline and a stretch of bay shore are protected by Bodega Marine Reserve, a unit of the University of California's Natural Reserve System.

Return to Bodega Head Trail, continue north up and over a low rise, and enter Bodega Marine Reserve. The path soon crosses the road leading to the marine lab and reaches the dunes. Wooden posts help you stay on the sandy trail, which is a bit confusing in places.

Once brome grass and rye grass covered the dunes, but these native grasses were grazed—in fact, overgrazed—by livestock. The dunes, naturally unstable and subject to the whims of the wind, were fast blowing away when European beach grass was planted in the early 1950s. This grass, used to protect dikes in the Netherlands, has helped control the drifting sand, and kept it from blowing into the bay.

After climbing the dunes, you'll exit the reserve and descend to a signed junction. A sharp right turn leads over a hill to Westside County Park on Bodega Bay. Proceeding straight ahead, north, will put you on the Riding and Hiking Loop, a trail popular with equestrians, that loops around the dunes and leads 1.5 miles to Bodega Dunes Campground.

Continue on Bodega Head Trail, which veers west 0.5 mile to driftwood-strewn Salmon Creek Beach. You can beachcomb north 2 miles along Salmon Creek Beach, which is fringed with beach strawberry and sand verbena. You can also walk the same distance on the parallel horse path that crosses the dunes above the beach.

■ SONOMA COAST STATE BEACH
Sonoma Coast Trail
From Blind Beach to Shell Beach is 4 miles round trip; to
Wright's Beach is 6.5 miles round trip

The names alone are intriguing: Blind Beach and Schoolhouse Beach,
Arched Rock and Goat Rock, Penny Island and Bodega Head.

These colorfully named locales are some of the highlights of Sonoma Coast
State Beach, 13 miles of coastline stretching from the Russian River to Bodega
Bay.

Sonoma Coast State Beach is not one beach, but many. You could easily
overlook them, because most aren't visible from Highway 1. The beaches are
tucked away in rocky coves, and hidden by tall bluffs.

Sonoma Coast Trail is a pretty blufftop route that connects some of these
secret beaches. During spring, wildflowers brighten the bluff: blue lupine, Indian paintbrush and sea fig.

Sonoma Coast Trail begins on the bluffs above Blind Beach, but the walker
can also begin at Goat Rock, located a half mile north of the trailhead. The rock
is connected to the mainland by a causeway. During the 1920s, Goat Rock was
quarried, and used to build a jetty at the mouth of the Russian River.

A mile north of the trailhead, and 0.5 mile north of Goat Rock is the mouth
of the Russian River. The 110-mile-long river is one of the largest on the North
Coast. At the river mouth, you can observe ospreys nesting in the treetops. The
California brown pelican is one of several species of birds that breed and nest
on Penny Island, located in the river mouth.

DIRECTIONS TO TRAILHEAD From Highway 1, 10 miles north of the
town of Bodega Bay, turn west on Goat Rock Road. Signed Sonoma Coast

Sonoma coastline.

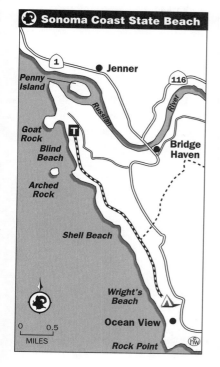

Sonoma Coast State Beach

1

● **Jenner**

Penny Island

116

Russian River

Goat Rock

T

Blind Beach

● **Bridge Haven**

○ *Arched Rock*

Shell Beach

Wright's Beach

△

Ocean View ●

0   0.5
MILES

Rock Point

Trail begins at a small parking lot on the left of the road. If you'd like to begin this walk at Goat Rock, continue to road's end at a large parking area.

THE HIKE Sonoma Coast Trail heads south along the edge of the bluffs. Soon, you'll step over a stile and head across a pasture. The trail climbs to a saddle on the shoulder of Peaked Hill (elevation 376 feet).

You then descend to the flat blufftops, and cross a bridge over a fern-lined ravine. It's a pastoral scene with grassy bluffs and a weathered old barn in the distance.

After crossing another ravine, the path reaches the Shell Beach parking area. A short trail descends the bluffs to Shell Beach. Another trail extends northwest, crosses the highway, and reaches redwood-shaded Pomo Canyon. Picnic tables and walk-in (environmental) campsites are located near the creek.

Sonoma Coast Trail continues south, detouring inland around a private home, then doubling back seaward. The trail plunges into Furlong Gulch, then switchbacks back up to the bluffs. You can follow the trail or the beach to Wright's Beach Campground.

■ FORT ROSS STATE HISTORIC PARK
Fort Ross Trail

To Fort Ross Cove is 0.5 mile round trip; to Reef Point Campground is 4 miles round trip; can extend walk north along park bluffs and south along coast

Fort Ross, the last remnant of czarist Russia's foothold in California, is today a walker's delight. Near the fort, sinuous Highway 1 suddenly straightens. You look out upon a handsome, windswept bluff, and spy a redwood stockade and Russian Orthodox chapel. For the first-time visitor, it's a startling sight.

Napoleon was beginning his 1812 invasion of Russia when Fort Ross—named for *Rossiya* itself—was built. The fort's location ideally suited the purposes of the colony. The site was easily defensible. Tall trees, necessary for the fort's construction and the shipbuilding that would take place in the nearby cove, covered the coastal slopes. The waters were full of sea otters—an attraction for the Russian American Fur Company, which would soon hunt the animals to near-extinction. Wheat, potatoes and vegetables were grown on the coastal terrace, and shipped to Russian settlements in Alaska. All in all, the fort was nearly self-sufficient.

Thanks to the state's replication and restoration efforts, the fort's building brings back the flavor of the Russian's foray into North America. The high stockade, built entirely of hand-hewn redwood timber, looks particularly formidable.

Also of interest are the seven-sided blockhouse, with its interpretive exhibits, and the small, wooden Orthodox chapel. And be sure to stop at the Fort Ross Visitor Center, an excellent facility with Russian, Pomo and natural history exhibits.

When you've completed your walk through history, another surprise awaits: a hike out on the lonely, beautiful headlands.

In 1990, the state park tripled in size; the addition was the former Call Ranch, more than 2,000 acres of wooded canyons and dramatic coastline. From the old fort, you can walk 2 miles north along the coast via old logging roads dipping into Kolmer Gulch, where there's a picnic area, and continue to a stand of redwood and Douglas fir.

You can also walk 2 miles (or more) south along the coast, as detailed below. North- or southbound hikers will enjoy grand views of the fort and up-close looks at the result of earthquake action along the San Andreas Fault.

The chapel at Fort Ross.

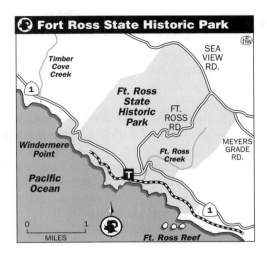

DIRECTIONS TO TRAILHEAD Fort Ross State Historic Park is located off of Highway 1, some 12 miles north of the hamlet of Jenner.

THE HIKE Exit the fort's main gate, follow the stockade walls to the left, and join the downhill path. It's a short walk to secluded Fort Ross Cove, one of California's first shipyards. You'll find an interpretive display and picnic tables here.

Cross Fort Ross Creek on a small footbridge. Earthquake action along the mighty San Andreas Fault has altered the course of the creek by more than a half-mile. Follow the path inland along the creek, which is lined with bay laurel, willow, alder and Douglas iris. After a hundred yards of travel, look to your right for an unmarked, narrow path leading south.

The indistinct path travels onto an open coastal terrace. You'll no doubt see some sheep eating the pastoral vegetation. Follow the undulations of the rye grass- and barley-covered headland, and meander first southeast, then southwest. Continue down-coast until you spot a path descending to a dirt road. (Don't try to climb the sheep fence; use the stile located where the road dead-ends.)

Descend the dirt road to Reef Campground, formerly a private campground, and now a state park facility. It's a good place for a picnic.

Across the road, another stile beckons to the entrance of Sonoma County's "lost coast," so named because high cliffs and high tides keep this 7 miles of beach remote from most hikers.

Should you continue, a mile of walking across boulder-strewn beaches brings you to Fort Ross Reef, which discourages further progress.

■ SALT POINT STATE PARK
Salt Point Trail

From Salt Point, Stump Beach Cove is 2.5 miles round trip; to Fish Mill Cove is 6 miles round trip; to Horseshoe Cover is 10 miles round trip

Sheer, sandstone cliffs and sandy coves highlight Salt Point State Park's 7 miles of coastline. Tidepools, sea stacks, and sea caves add to the coastal drama.

Marine life is abundant in tidepools. One of the first underwater reserves to be set aside in California—Gerstle Cove—is popular with divers.

Several midden sites found within park boundaries suggest that Pomo and Coast Yuki spent many summers camped on this coast. They gathered abalone and salt to preserve seafood.

DIRECTIONS TO TRAILHEAD Salt Point State Park is located about 90 miles north of San Francisco (or 18 miles north of Jenner, 7 miles north of Fort Ross) on Highway 1. From Highway 1, turn west into the state park's campground and follow signs to Marine Terrace Parking Area.

THE HIKE Hike north atop the dramatic bluffs of Salt Point. In 0.25 mile, you'll cross Warren Creek. At the creek mouth is a little cove, one of about a dozen you'll encounter along the state park's coastline.

The coves are quiet now, but in the last century there was much activity. Aleut hunters, brought to nearby Fort Ross by the Russian American Fur Company, hunted otters and seals. Lumber schooners maneuvered into the coves to load redwoods logged from nearby slopes.

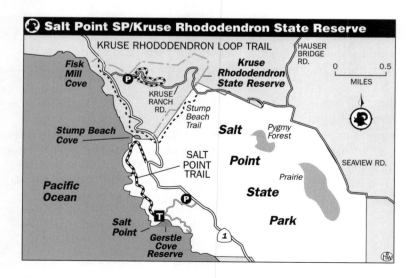

The path reaches the bluffs above Stump Beach Cove, which is not, as you might suspect, named for the remains of redwoods logged nearby; the name honors Sheriff Stump, one-time law-and-order man for Salt Point township.

An old farm road leads down to the cove, where there's a picnic area. Sit a while and watch the terns, cormorants, gulls, osprey and brown pelicans.

If you return to the trailhead from Stump Beach Cove, you'll have hiked a total of 2.5 miles. To continue this hike, follow the trail up the north slope above Stump Creek. Rejoining the bluffs, you dip in and out of Phillips Gulch, Chinese Gulch and other little gullies.

The path is not particularly distinct, and you must devise your own route in places along the edge of the grassy headlands. Photographers will marvel at the spectacle of surf meeting rock. Waterfalls spill into picturesque coves at the mouths of Chinese and Phillips Gulches.

After a time, the trail becomes easier to follow, and alternates between open meadowland and wind-sculpted stands of Bishop pine and Douglas fir.

A good destination is the picnic area south of Fisk Mill Cove, which is about 3 miles from the trailhead. Or you can even continue another 2 miles north to Horseshoe Cove at the northern end of the state park.

See Map
on Page
252

■ KRUSE RHODODENDRON STATE RESERVE
Kruse Rhododendron Loop Trail
2.25 miles round trip with 200-foot elevation gain

One of the annual rites, and fine sights, of spring is a walk amongst the pale pink blossoms of Kruse Rhododendron State Reserve. California rhododendrons festoon the forest floor from about mid-April to mid-June.

The rhododendron's success depends on its struggle for light in a dark world dominated by the tanbark oak, Douglas fir and redwood. A severe forest fire that scorched the slopes of Kruse Ranch was responsible for the sudden emergence of the rhododendrons here. Now, as the tall tree forest regenerates, it restricts the light available to the rhododendrons, thereby diminishing their grand display.

The Kruse family established a ranch here in 1880, raised sheep and extensively logged the coastal slopes. Edward Kruse donated the land to the state in 1933, in memory of his father, who was the founder of San Francisco's German Bank—later, First Western Bank.

DIRECTIONS TO TRAILHEAD Kruse Rhododendron State Reserve adjoins Salt Point State Park. Turn east off Highway 1 onto steep Kruse Ranch Road and travel 0.5 mile to the trailhead.

THE HIKE This is a loop trail; begin from the leg north of Kruse Ranch Road or from the leg to the south.

The trail crosses two gulches—Chinese and Phillips. (You'll explore the mouths of these gulches if you take the Salt Point Trail through the state park.)

Those walkers wishing to stretch their legs a bit may leave the loop trail a mile from the trailhead at the point where the path crosses Kruse Ranch Road. It's possible to follow this dirt road for a mile to Stump Beach Trail, then follow this latter path 1.25 mile back to Highway 1, where it rounds Stump Beach Cove.

■ GUALALA POINT REGIONAL PARK
River, Blufftop, Salal Trails
From Gualala Point Regional Park to Gualala River mouth is 1.5 miles round trip; to Sea Ranch is 4.5 miles round trip

Gualala, the name of a river, a point, a town, and a park located on the northern boundary of Sonoma County offers some fascinating walks. Hurried travelers can exit Highway 1 and stretch their legs with a short walk along the Gualala River. Walkers with more time will enjoy exploring all the environments of Gualala Point Regional Park—ocean, river and forest. Environmental activists and those who observed the two-decade long struggle to open Sea Ranch to public use will relish the chance to hike this stretch of coastline.

The origin of the name Gualala has never been satisfactorily explained. Anthropologists suggest that it is the Spanish rendering of the Pomo word *walali*—"where the waters meet." Some historians speculate that Ernest Rufus, a captain in John Sutter's Indian Company and the 1846 grantee of Rancho German, gave the area its name. Walhalla in Teutonic mythology is the abode of heroes fallen in battle.

Unlike most California coastal rivers and creeks, which cascade westerly from the slopes of coastal mountains, the Gualala flows south to north—along the San Andreas Fault. A sand spit forms at the river mouth in summer, when this area can best be explored on foot. Near the Coast Highway bridge is a freshwater marsh, habitat for water- and shore-birds. A redwood grove, accompanied by rhododendrons and sword ferns, lines an upper stretch of the river. These diverse Gualala River habitats can be explored via the highly recommended 0.75-mile long River Trail.

Be sure to check out the exhibits in the park's visitor center. A wind generator system provides power for the building.

DIRECTIONS TO TRAILHEAD Gualala Point Regional Park is located off Highway 1, a half-mile south of the town of Gualala. (The first left inside the park leads to the trailhead for Salal Trail which you'll pass if you decide to

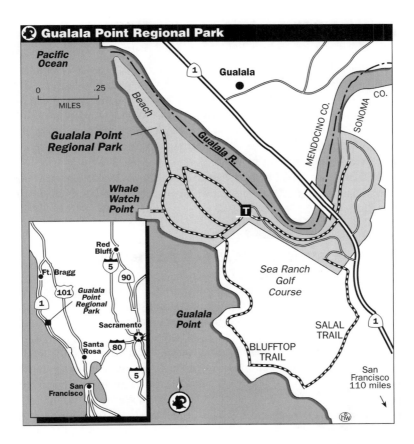

pursue the Sea Ranch option of this walk.) Continue a half-mile through the park to the visitor center.

THE HIKE From the visitor center, follow the paved path for a hundred yards. Join a grassy trail and descend to the river mouth.

After exploring the river mouth, double back to a line of cypress trees and head south on the blufftop trail to Whale Watch Point. At a fence line delineating the park boundary, you can either loop back to the trailhead or walk through the fence into Sea Ranch on the blufftop trail.

The trail into Sea Ranch plunges into a stand of cypress. When you emerge you'll spy the golf course, dotted with deer and golfers. State Coastal Conservancy trail signs keep you on track, which doggedly follows the bluffs.

Near the path are several Bauhaus-inspired homes, done in an architectural style sometimes described as "grain elevator modern." Some architects believe this severe style blends in with the surroundings; others have their doubts.

You round cypress-covered Gualala Point and cross a wooden footbridge. After walking across a grassy headland you reach a junction with Salal Trail on the bluffs above a rocky pocket beach.

Salal Trail crosses a paved path and joins the creekbed. (On brisk days, it's a refuge from the wind.) The path winds past a stand of redwood and through dense berry bushes. Crossing a small bridge and paved road, the trail continues with Salal Creek through a densely vegetated area of ferns, Bishop pine and cypress. You emerge from Salal Creek drainage near Highway 1. Head north on the path paralleling the highway.

About 0.25 mile of travel brings you to the Salal trailhead and the park day-use area. From here, it's a 0.5-mile jaunt along the road back the visitor center.

■ VAN DAMME STATE PARK
Fern Canyon Trail
From Van Damme State Park Campground to Fern Canyon is 5 miles round trip with 200-foot gain; to Pygmy Forest is 7 miles round trip with 400-foot gain

Fern-filled Fern Canyon.

Five-finger and bird's-foot, lady and licorice, stamp, sword and deer—these are some of the colorful names of the ferns growing in well-named Fern Canyon. This lush canyon, the heart of Van Damme State Park, is also rich with young redwoods, red alder, big-leaf maple and Douglas fir, as well as a tangled understory of wild cucumber and berry bushes.

Little River meanders through Fern Canyon, as does a lovely trail which crosses the river nine times. Fern Canyon Trail, paved along its lower stretch, follows the route of an old logging skid road. For three decades, beginning in 1864, ox teams hauled timber through the canyon.

A lumber mill once stood at the mouth of Little River. During the late nineteenth century, schooners, used for shipping logs and lumber, were constructed at a boatworks located at the river mouth. Lumberman and San Francisco businessman

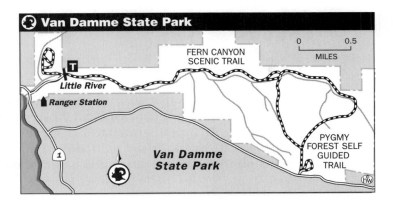

Charles F. Van Damme was born in the hamlet of Little River. He purchased land on the site of the former sawmill and bequeathed the river mouth and canyon to the state park system.

In Van Damme State Park, another very special environment awaits the walker: the Pygmy Forest. A nutrient-poor, highly acidic topsoil, combined with a dense hardpan located beneath the surface that resists root penetration, has severely restricted the growth of trees in certain areas of the coastal shelf between Salt Point and Fort Bragg.

The Pygmy Forest in Van Damme State Park is truly Lilliputian. Sixty-year-old cypress trees are but a few feet tall and measure a half-inch in diameter. The walker has a choice of two trails that lead to the Pygmy Forest. One route loops 3.5 miles through Fern Canyon; another, the mile-long Logging Road Trail leads more directly to the forest. A self-guided nature trail, built upon an elevated wooden walkway, loops through the Pygmy Forest.

DIRECTIONS TO TRAILHEAD Van Damme State Park is located off Highway 1, 3 miles south of Mendocino. Turn inland on the main park road, and follow it through the canyon to a parking area at the beginning of signed Fern Canyon Trail.

THE HIKE The first and second crossings of Little River give you an inkling of what lies ahead. During summer, the river is easily forded; in winter, expect to get your feet wet.

The wide path brings you close to elderberry, salmonberry and a multitude of ferns. Two miles and eight river crossings later, you'll pass the state park's environmental campsites—reserved for walkers and bicyclists.

The road splits into a short loop and the two forks rejoin at the end of the paved road. Both trails lead to Pygmy Forest. To the left, the longer loop continues east through Fern Canyon before joining the old logging road and traveling to Pygmy Forest. For a shorter walk to Pygmy Forest, cross Little River and follow the Old Logging Road Trail a mile.

■ ANGELO COAST RANGE PRESERVE

Walker Meadow Loop Trail

5.75 miles with 500-foot elevation gain

Ancient old-growth forests are more often associated with Washington's Olympic Peninsula than with anything in California, but the Angelo Coast Range Preserve protects a beauty. Along the headwaters of the Eel River's South Fork grows a virgin forest of Douglas fir and redwood accompanied by the many ferns and flowering plants that thrive in the dark world below these tall trees.

Dwelling in this forest primeval are such seldom-seen creatures as the ringtail, mink, bear, spotted owl and the red tree vole, a small, tree-dwelling rodent that lives its whole life high above the ground. More than 90 kinds of moss and some six dozen species of lichen have been identified in this forest.

A veritable rain forest it is with as much as 150 inches of rain falling some years. In shocking contrast to these wettest of Coast Range slopes, some of the preserve's slopes are cloaked in chaparral, a floral community more at home with 15, not 150, inches of rain per year.

In the early 1900s, Wilderness Lodge, a retreat for San Franciscans, was built. The rustic resort closed during the Depression and later many of its buildings burned. A few surviving structures are now used by visiting students and scientists.

During the Depression of the 1930s, Heath and Marjorie Angelo purchased an old homestead, intent on preserving it as wilderness. Alarmed by increased logging in the area, they purchased more land. In 1959, the couple sold their land to the Nature Conservancy; it was the environmental group's first West Coast purchase. The U.S. Bureau of Land Management contributed additional virgin forest to the preserve.

The preserve's best walks follow the South Fork of the Eel River, patrolled by a variety of ducks and waterfowl. River otters are delight to watch. As you hike the Eel's banks you'll travel in the company of redwoods, Douglas fir and madrone, as well as oaks festooned with moss.

Enjoy the loop through Walker Meadow when seasonal bridges are in place (April–October); otherwise make this hike a 7-mile round trip out-and-back to Wilderness Lodge or the preserve's north boundary.

DIRECTIONS TO TRAILHEAD From Highway 101 in Laytonville, turn west on Branscomb Road and drive 17 miles (3 miles past Branscomb) to Wilderness Lodge Road. Turn north and proceed another 3 miles to road's end just beyond the headquarters of the Angelo Coast Range Preserve.

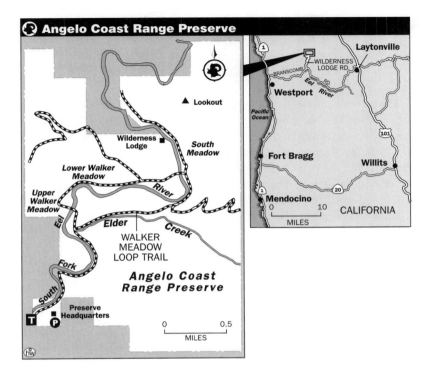

Angelo Coast Range Preserve

Laytonville
WILDERNESS LODGE RD.
BRANSCOMB
Eel River
Westport
Pacific Ocean
101
Fort Bragg
Willits
20
Mendocino
0   10   CALIFORNIA
MILES

Lookout
Wilderness Lodge
South Meadow
Lower Walker Meadow
River
Upper Walker Meadow
Eel
Elder Creek
WALKER MEADOW LOOP TRAIL
Fork
South
Angelo Coast Range Preserve
Preserve Headquarters
T P
0   0.5
MILES

THE HIKE Head northeast on Wilderness Lodge Road, traveling alongside the Eel River. It's a mellow ascent through mixed forest—big Douglas fir and redwood, accompanied by big-leaf maple, madrone and tanoak.

A mile out, you'll pass right-forking Conger Trail, which travels to an old homestead. Our road/trail soon crosses a bridge over Elder Creek, leaving the Eel behind and following the creek. The lower leg of Walker Meadow Loop (your return route) comes in from the left, but you continue another quarter-mile to the caretaker's residence.

Climb some more through oak woodland, passing right-forking Black Oak Mountain Trail, then descend back down to the Eel River and a junction with the north end of Walker Meadow Loop.

(If you continue with the road and Eel River a short half-mile you'll reach Wilderness Lodge, one-time rustic resort now overnight quarters for researchers and students.)

Walker Meadow Trail visits both the upper meadow, where remains of homesteads intrigue the hiker (how did anyone live out here?) and the lower meadow, a grassy expanse interrupted with clumps of manzanita.

Rejoin Wilderness Lodge Road and retrace your steps back to the trailhead.

■ MENDOCINO HEADLANDS STATE PARK
Mendocino Headlands Trail
2 to 5 miles round trip

Few coastal locales are as photographed as the town of Mendocino and its bold headlands. The town itself, which lies just north of the mouth of Big River, resembles a New England village, no doubt by design of its Yankee founders. Now protected by a state park, the headlands are laced with paths that offer postcard views of wave tunnels and tidepools, beaches and blowholes.

Today Mendocino may be familiar to fans of the television series "Murder She Wrote;" it stands in for Cabot Cove, sleuth Jessica Fletcher's hometown.

Like the town, the headlands have a storied past. *Booldam* ("Big River") is what the Pomo called their village here. Wave tunnels, one measuring more than 700 feet long, penetrate the Mendocino Bay bluffs. By some fanciful accounts they've been the death of ships—particularly during the days of sail, when a number of vessels were reportedly blown into the tunnels and never seen again.

Despite rough surf conditions, one of California's first "doghole ports" was located here. A railway, built in 1853, carried redwood lumber from a nearby mill to a chute located on the point. It was a tricky loading operation, to say the least.

In this 1907 view, quaint Mendocino resembles a New England fishing village.

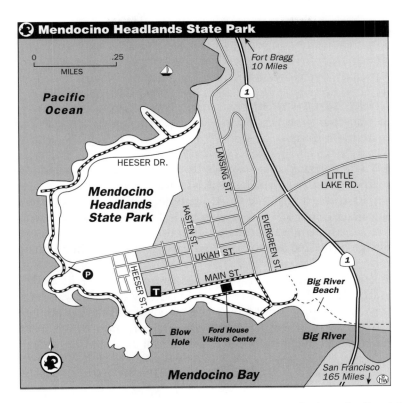

Mendocino Headlands State Park

Once the most cosmopolitan of little ports, Mendocino declined in economic and cultural importance as the logging industry came to a halt in the 1930s. The town revived in the 1950s when a number of San Francisco artists established the Mendocino Art Center. What was bohemian and cheap in the 1950s and 1960s is now upscale and pricey, but the town's Maine village look has been preserved.

Mendocino's citizenry not only preserved the town in a historical district, but succeeded in placing a portion of the majestic bluffs, threatened with a modern subdivision, under the protection of Mendocino Headlands State Park in 1972.

Mendocino is a great town for the walker to explore. Grand Victorian houses and simple New England saltboxes mingle with a downtown that includes several fascinating nineteenth-century buildings. Among the architectural gems are the Masonic Hall, built in 1866 and topped with a redwood sculpture of Father Time, the Mendocino Hotel with its antique decor and the Presbyterian Church, constructed in 1867 and now a state historical landmark.

Be sure to check out the historic Ford House perched above the bay on the south side of town. Inside the house are exhibits interpreting the human and natural history of the Mendocino coast, as well as the State Park Visitors Center.

A summer or weekend walk onto the headlands allows you to escape the crowds, while a winter walk, perhaps when a storm is brewing offshore, is a special experience indeed. From the end of town you can walk down-coast to Big River or up-coast to a blowhole.

DIRECTIONS TO TRAILHEAD From "downtown" Mendocino, follow Main Street up-coast past the Mendocino Hotel to Heeser Street. Park wherever you can find a space.

THE HIKE The unsigned trail leads southwest through a fence and soon forks; the route down-coast to Big River Beach is described first.

Heading east, the trail delivers you to some blufftop benches and a coastal accessway leading down to Portuguese Beach, known as Point Beach by locals. Wooden steps cross a gully and the trail soon forks again—offering both a route along the edge of the bluffs and another heading on a straighter course toward Big River.

Notice the cross-ties, remains of the old oxen-powered railway that hauled lumber to the bluff edge, where it was then sent by chute to waiting ships.

Wildflowers seasonally brightening the grassy headlands include lupine and Mendocino Coast paintbrush. More noticeable are non-native species gone wild—nasturtiums, calla lilies, hedge rose—as well as Scotch broom, an unwelcome pest that thrives along the north coast.

After meandering past some Bishop pine, the path descends moderately to steeply to the beach where Big River empties into Mendocino Bay. The quarter-mile-long beach is also part of Mendocino Headlands State Park. Upriver is a marsh, Big River Estuary, a winter stopover for ducks and geese. Salmon and steelhead spawn upriver.

Return the same way or detour through town to admire some of Mendocino's historical buildings.

To the Blowhole and beyond: Bearing right at the first trail junction from the trailhead leads to the blowhole. While no aqueous Vesuvius, the blowhole can at times be a frothy and picturesque cauldron.

The path continues north along the edge of the headlands for another mile. You'll pass a plaque dedicated by the sister cities of Mendocino and Miasa, Japan, "to the peaceful pursuit of the peoples of the Pacific and to the protection of the environment that all living things therein may exist in perpetual harmony."

■ RUSSIAN GULCH STATE PARK
Russian Gulch Trail
From Campground to Falls is 6.5 miles round trip with 200-foot elevation gain

Russian Gulch is a lush coastal range canyon filled with second-generation redwoods, Douglas fir and California laurel. Beneath the tall trees grows an understory of ferns, berry bushes, azaleas and rhododendrons.

By some accounts, Gulch and State Park take their name from the Fort Ross-based Russian fur hunters who trapped in this area. Historians speculate that the gulch was one of the places where the hunters cached otter skins.

Russian Gulch offers walkers the chance to experience several distinct biotic communities. The mouth of the canyon is framed, as if in a photograph, by a handsome Coast Highway bridge. A beach offers swimming and sunning; however, the cold waters here are more popular as an entry point for wetsuit-clad divers. Urchins and abalone populate the rich subtidal area.

Above the river mouth, the park headlands offer great north and south coastal views, as well as glimpses of Russian Gulch itself. Out on the headlands, seasonally bedecked with Douglas iris and poppies, is The Punchbowl, a collapsed wave tunnel that forms a 100-foot-diameter hole. This blowhole, while too large to blow very much, is nevertheless an inspiring sight when the surf wells up inside the hole.

The trail system through Russian Gulch State Park offers a number of alternatives. You may take a direct or a more roundabout route through the canyon and either a longer or shorter route to the waterfall. It's possible to combine all trail options into a delightful 9-mile tour of the park.

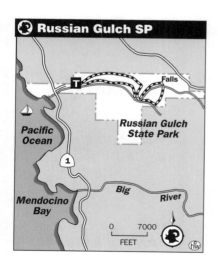

DIRECTIONS TO TRAILHEAD Russian Gulch State Park is located just off Highway 1, 2 miles north of the town of Mendocino. Fern Canyon Trail, a continuation of the park road closed to vehicle traffic, departs from the east end of the campground.

THE HIKE The paved trail, suitable for bicycles, is nearly flat for the first mile as it winds along with the stream. Along the bottom of the gulch grow alder, willow and big-leaf maple. On higher canyon slopes are western hemlock, Douglas fir and second-growth redwoods. The forest was even thicker before early loggers cleared the canyon.

One and a half miles of travel brings you to a small picnic area, where you'll find a couple of picnic tables beneath the redwoods. A short distance past the picnic area, you'll spot signed North Trail, which leads northwest back to the park campground; consider this path as an alternate return route. Hikers may continue about 100 feet past this trail junction to the signed beginning of the waterfall loop.

Russian Gulch forks here and so does the trail. Take the left, shorter, route and climb by trail, wooden steps and footbridges 0.75 mile to the falls. The falls cascade 36 feet into a small grotto.

If you continue on the loop trail (this adds 2.3 more miles to your walk), you'll climb stone steps above the falls, then switchback away from the creek through tanoak forest. After topping a ridge, the trail drops into the south fork of Russian Gulch and returns you to the lower trail junction and the return route to the trailhead.

■ POINT CABRILLO PRESERVE
Point Cabrillo Trail
To lighthouse and around preserve is 3 miles round trip

Two miles north of Mendocino is a scene that will stir the heart of any seascape painter: a rocky shored, wave-battered peninsula, a picturesque lighthouse, three red and white Victorian houses, a ragged line of wind-sculpted cypress. Add an omnious horizon, dark clouds, white-capped ocean and you have a tableau to remember.

Even visitors without paint and canvas will savor Point Cabrillo Preserve and enjoy a walk over the dramatic blufftops.

Point Cabrillo Lighthouse was constructed by the U.S. Lighthouse Service in 1908 in order to aid navigation by the north coast steam-powered lumber schooners, known for their maneuverability in small coves known as doghole ports. Lighthouse keepers and their families lived on the point until the late 1960s when the light was automated.

Thanks to the considerable two-decade long efforts of the California Coastal Conservancy, the lighthouse and 300 surrounding acres were acquired and recently opened to the public. P.t Cabrillo Preserve is jointly managed by the Conservancy and the nonprofit North Coast Interpretive Association.

Point Cabrillo Lighthouse.

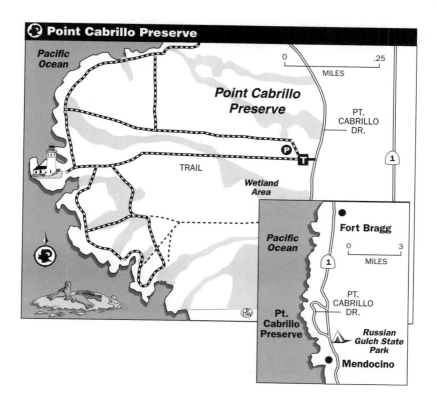

The preserve is bounded by private residences north and south, Point Cabrillo Drive to the east, the restless Pacific on the wild west side. Some 300 acres of wind-tossed grassland tilts toward the water. Watch for the long ears of the coast mule deer poking above the grass.

A farmhouse on the eastern edge of the preserve is all that remains of the Pine Grove, a community that by all accounts knew how to have a good time. A racetrack, brewery, hotel and a dance hall entertained travelers and timber workers from the 1870s to the 1920s.

DIRECTIONS TO TRAILHEAD From Mendocino, drive north on Coast Highway 1 a few miles to signed Point Cabrillo Drive. Drive a mile and turn left into the brand-new parking area for Point Cabrillo Preserve.

THE HIKE Take the main lighthouse road (closed to vehicles) leading coastward. It proceeds in straightforward fashion a short mile to the lighthouse.

After admiring the lighthouse and the historic nearby homes of its former keepers, walk north on the blufftop path over the grassy headlands. Watch for black-shouldered kites, northern harriers, and marsh hawks swooping over the grasslands, and for the long ears of the coast mule deer poking above the grass.

Ocean views are spectacular. Black oyster-catchers, cormorants and pigeon guillemots nest on the rocks offshore from Point Cabrillo. Otters and harbor seals bob in the waters adjacent to the point, which has been designated a reserve by the Department of Fish and Game.

The path bends eastward with the coast and reaches the northern boundary of the preserve. At an unsigned junction join the trail heading due south. This path leads to another east-west trending road. Turn left (east) follow this partly-dirt–partly-paved road back to the upper end of the parking area.

■ JUG HANDLE STATE RESERVE
Jug Handle Ecological Staircase Trail
5 miles round trip with 300-foot elevation gain

The watershed of Jug Handle Creek holds a rare natural phenomenon—an "ecological staircase"—that attracts scientists and nature lovers from all over the world. The staircase is composed of five terraces, each about 100,000 years older and about 100 feet higher than the one below it.

The terraces were sculpted into the sandstone cliffs by wave action. As a result of tectonic action—our North American plate crunching against the offshore Pacific plate—the terraces were uplifted. In fact, today the terraces continue their inexorable uplift at the rate of an inch per century. Wave action is slowly forming a sixth terrace at the mouth of Jug Handle Creek.

Terraces, and the forces forming them, are by no means unique to Jug Handle Creek; however, in most California coastal locales, the terraces are eroded and indistinct. Only at the state reserve are the evolutionary sequences so distinguishable, and so well preserved. Your walk up the staircase will be greatly aided if you pick up an interpretive pamphlet from the park office.

DIRECTIONS TO TRAILHEAD
Five miles south of Fort Bragg, turn west off Highway 1 into the Jug Handle Reserve parking area.

"Just my size," youngsters say of the Pygmy Forest.

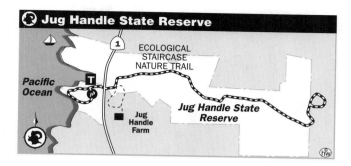

THE HIKE Head west on the signed trail out onto the grassy blufftops. The trail loops toward the edge of the bluffs, offers a view of Jug Handle Cove, then returns east to dip under the highway bridge.

The first terrace supports native grassland and wind-sculpted Sitka spruce. Second-growth redwoods are the most noticeable feature of the second terrace.

The upper terraces are the site of the Mendocino Pygmy Forest. Cypress and pine are but 5 to 10 feet tall, and shrubs such as rhododendron, manzanita and huckleberry are also dwarf-sized.

Adding to the somewhat bizarre natural world of upper Jug Handle Creek are a couple of sphagnum bogs—layers of peat standing in water—which support mosses and an insectivorous plant called sundew that uses its sticky leaves to capture its victims.

When you reach the end of the trail, you can rejoin Gibney Fire Road for a quick return to the main trail leading back to the parking area.

■ TEN MILE BEACH
Ten Mile Beach Trail
From Laguna Point to Ten Mile River is 10 miles round trip; shorter hikes possible

Ten Mile Dunes and Inglenook Fen, Laguna Point and Cleone Lake. These are some of the intriguing names on an intriguing land—MacKerricher State Park. Extending from just north of the Fort Bragg city limits to Ten Mile River, this park offers the walker a chance to explore headlands and wetlands, sand dunes, forest and meadowland.

In 1868, Scottish immigrant Duncan MacKerricher paid $1.25 an acre for a former Indian reservation, *El Rancho de la Laguna*. MacKerricher and his heirs worked the land until 1949 when they gift-deeded it to the state. The vast redwood forests of the coast range in the areas bordering Ten Mile River were heavily logged. An early coast railroad connected the mills of the town of Cleone with a landing at Laguna Point. Lumber was loaded onto flatcars which rolled by gravity to waiting schooners; horses hauled the cars back to the mill. At the point, anchor pins and other signs of the old landing can be seen.

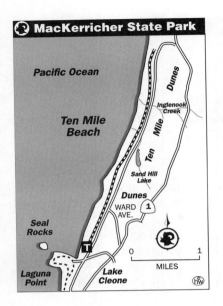

A more obvious reminder of this coast's logging history is the old haul road that crosses the park. In 1949, the road replaced a railway, which for three decades carried timber from the Ten Mile River Area to the Union Lumber Company in Fort Bragg. In 1982, winter storms washed out sections of the road, closing the 5-mile stretch from Cleone Lake to Ten Mile River. The road is closed to motor vehicles and is a superb path for walkers.

The old haul road travels the length of Ten Mile Beach to the mouth of Ten Mile River, so named because it's 10 miles north of Noyo River. The beach is backed by one of the California coast's longest dune systems.

DIRECTIONS TO TRAILHEAD From Highway 1, 3 miles north of Fort Bragg, turn west into the main entrance of MacKerricher State Park. Follow the signs to the Laguna Point Parking area.

THE HIKE Immediately west of the underpass, a short gravel road leads up to the paved ex-logging road. Walk north on the high embankment. You'll soon observe Cleone Lake, a tidal lagoon cut off from the sea by the road. Many shore- and water-birds visit the lake. Mill Creek, which feeds the lake, is a winter stopover for ducks and geese. Bird-watchers will enjoy the mile-long walk around the lake.

Soon you'll pass some squat shore pines—a coastal form of the much better-known lodgepole pine. You'll also walk past a side trail leading to the state park campground. A quarter-mile later another side trail beckons; this one leads over the dunes, which are covered with grasses, sand verbena and beach morning glory.

About a 1.5 miles north of the trailhead, you'll encounter a washed-out section of road and, a few hundred yards farther, another bad section.

Two miles north of Laguna Point, tucked in the dunes, lies Inglenook Fen; it's a sensitive area and not open to the public. A botanist studying this unique ecosystem gave it the Old English word *fen*—meaning something like a bog or marsh. Sandhill Lake and the marshy area around it support many rare plants such as marsh pennywort and rein orchid, as well as many endemic varieties of spiders and insects.

After walking 3 miles, you'll pass a couple of small creeks and begin crossing the widest part of the sand dunes, which at this point are about a mile wide and measure more than 100 feet high. About 4.5 miles from the trailhead, the road turns inland with Ten Mile River. You can continue walking north a short distance if you wish down to the mouth of Ten Mile River. The marsh area is inhabited by lots of waterfowl.

The main route travels inland above the east bank of Ten Mile River. A side trail leads southeast to a parking area beside Highway 1, while the paved road continues under the highway bridge.

■ USAL BEACH
Lost Coast Trail
From Usal Beach Campground to Anderson Gulch is 5 miles round trip with 1,100-foot elevation gain

Usal is a Native American word meaning south; it was used by nineteenth century settlers to describe the native Sinkyone, who lived in a village at the mouth of what we now call Usal Creek. Usal Creek and Beach mark the southern boundary of Sinkyone Wilderness State Park, and the southern end of the magnificent Lost Coast Trail that travels the length of the park.

In 1889, J.H. Wonderly built a redwood mill, logging railway, and wharf at Usal. The operation was purchased by Captain Robert Dollar in 1894. The property sold cheap because ship captains were quite reluctant to call at Usal; it had a reputation as one of the north coast's most dangerous doghole ports. But Captain Dollar had his own fleet, including the custom-built schooner, *Newsboy,* which braved Usal Landing.

Usal Mill closed in 1902 and soon burned to the ground, along with the town. (No trace of town remains today.) Captain Dollar went on to build a worldwide shipping empire with his Dollar Line passenger and freight vessels.

A rustic state park campground is situated along Usal Creek Campground near the beach. Surf fishing, beachcombing and abalone diving attract many visitors. Good sightings of osprey diving into the surf can be enjoyed from the 2-mile sand beach. A seasonal waterfall, which tumbles over the cliff edge to the beach, can be reached by walking (during low tide) 2 miles up-coast.

A park ranger pauses with his son on Lost Coast Trail.

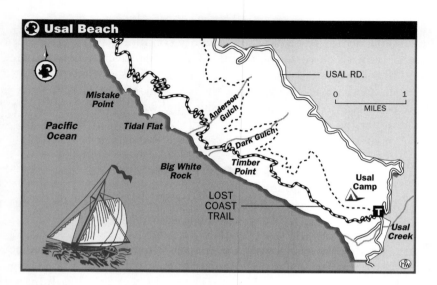

This walk samples Lost Coast Trail, which extends some 50 miles north through Sinkyone Wilderness State Park and the King Range National Conservation Area. It's not a gentle trail, and the up-and-down nature of the southern portion is typical of its entire length. Prominent ridges offer spectacular vistas of up to 100 miles of Lost Coast.

DIRECTIONS TO TRAILHEAD To reach the south portion of Sinkyone Wilderness State Park at Usal Beach, take Highway 1 three miles north of the hamlet of Rockport and turn west on unsigned, unpaved County Road 431 (Usal Road). Follow this road 6 miles as it rises to a thousand feet, then descends to Usal Beach Camp.

THE HIKE From the signed trailhead, Lost Coast Trail rises steeply above the Usal Creek drainage. The path switchbacks through redwoods up onto a ridgeline, gentles, then resumes climbing to a notch just below 1,320-foot high Timber Point.

From Timber Point, Lost Coast Trail descends precipitously to fern-choked Dark Gulch. The gulch was once "dark" with redwood and Douglas fir, but was heavily logged. The trail climbs out of Dark Gulch and contours on grassy slopes. As the path approaches Anderson Gulch, it swings east, then descends to a stream and a small campsite set in a meadow. There's a good view down-gulch to the ocean.

■ BEAR HARBOR
Lost Coast Trail

From Orchard Creek Camp to Bear Harbor is 0.8 mile round trip; to J. Smeaton Chase Grove is 4 miles round trip with 600-foot elevation gain; to Wheeler Camp is 9 miles round trip with 800-foot gain

Just before the turn of the century, Bear Harbor was the scene of one of the most unusual railroad lines in history. In order to transport logs from Harvey Anderson's timber holdings, the Bear Harbor and Eel River Railroad began construction of tracks from Bear Harbor to Piercy on the Eel River. A winch lowered and raised the locomotive and cars over the first very steep stretch of narrow-gauge track near Bear Harbor. Past Usal Road, the train ran on its own power.

Disaster plagued the railroad from the start. A Pacific storm destroyed Bear Harbor wharf in 1899; owner Harvey Anderson was killed in an industrial accident in 1905, and the 1906 San Francisco Earthquake caused major damage to the track and trestles.

Today, rusted rails dangling down the cliffs at Bear Harbor, and faint traces of the railbed in Railroad Canyon, are all that remain of the railroad. (Railroad history buffs may view the steam engine used during the brief life of the rail line at Fort Humboldt State Historic Park.)

Lost Coast Trail visits a second historical site—the ghost town of Wheeler. Established in 1950, this company town and its modern sawmill stood for ten years. Big trucks hauled the cut lumber to Willits.

This stretch of Lost Coast Trail is interesting for more than historical reasons. Steep canyons shelter stately redwood groves, which stand tall above a lush understory of ferns, calypso orchids and Douglas iris. Grassy meadows are seasonally bedecked with lupine, buttercup, and Indian paintbrush. The trail offers terrific vistas, too. Although it marches up and down quite a bit, it never strays too far from the incessant roar of the surf.

DIRECTIONS TO TRAILHEAD Follow directions for the Needle Rock Hike in Sinkyone Wilderness State Park. Stop at the park visitor center and inquire about the condition of the park road (Briceland Road or Bear Harbor Road). Except after heavy rains, most vehicles with good ground clearance can make the 2.5 mile distance to Bear Harbor. At road's end is Orchard Creek Camp and a parking area.

THE HIKE Cross Orchard Creek on a small wooden bridge. The trail meanders creekside and soon passes a path that leads leftward to some giant eucalyptus that shelter Railroad Creek Camp.

The path crosses Railroad Creek and joins the old railroad bed of the Bear Harbor Railroad. At one time, the tracks angled up and over the ridge to your

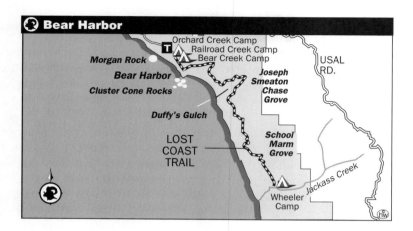

right, and met up with a loading chute. Look carefully, and you'll spot some rusted rails sticking out of the clifftop.

If it's low tide, pick your way over the driftwood piled at the mouth of Railroad Creek. The guano-covered, flat-topped rock you see offshore supported a loading pier that reached to shore.

To pick up the Lost Coast Trail, double back from the beach a short distance. The path heads east up the canyon cut by Railroad Creek. Bay laurel, red alder, and maple shade the way.

The trail crosses the creek and begins climbing out of the canyon. You join an old logging road—one of several utilized by the Lost Coast Trail as it snakes along from Bear Harbor to Usal—for a short distance. About 1.5 miles from the trailhead, as you top a grassy ridge, you'll get a superb view of Bear Harbor and its offshore Cluster Cone rocks.

The path descends into Duffy's Gulch, which embraces a lovely creek and a redwood grove. Woodwardia and sword ferns, as well as redwood sorrel, complement the thousand-year-old redwoods. The grove is named for J. Smeaton Chase, long-overlooked trail rider/nature writer, whose 1913 book, *California Coast Trails,* is a classic. In it, Chase recounts his 1912 horseback ride along the California coast from Mexico to Oregon. Quite an adventure in those days!

The trail climbs out of Duffy's Gulch and heads south along the grassy, wind-blown bluffs. An astute walker might detect a pattern to the "Lost Coast Trail" lots of ups and downs.

The route alternates between mixed conifer forest and blue-eyed grass meadowland. A half-mile from Wheeler, you approach another redwood grove—School Marm Grove. The fern-lined trail descends with Jackass Creek to the bottom of the canyon, then over to the grassy flats where the town of Wheeler once stood.

Cement foundations are about all that remain of the town of Wheeler. Walk past Wheeler Camp and the old town site, and follow Jackass Creek down to the beautiful black sand beach.

■ SINKYONE WILDERNESS STATE PARK
Lost Coast Trail
To Jones Beach is 2 miles round trip; to Whale Gulch is 4.5 miles round trip

The land we now call Sinkyone Wilderness State Park, located about 225 miles north of San Francisco, has long been recognized as something special. During the late 1960s, the great Catholic theologian Thomas Merton believed that the Needle Rock area would be an ideal place for a life of prayer and contemplation, and talked of establishing a monastic community there.

The state park, along with the U.S. Bureau of Land Management's King Range National Conservation Area to the north, comprise California's Lost Coast, 60 miles of wild shoreline located in northern Mendocino and southern Humboldt counties. One reason the coast is "lost" is because no highways cross it. So rugged is this country, highway engineers were forced to route Highway 1 many miles inland from this coast—and the region has remained sparsely settled and unspoiled. Its grand vistas and varied terrain—dense forests, prairies, coastal bluffs, beaches—reward the hardy explorer.

The sea is an overwhelming presence here, and its rhythmic sounds provide a thunderous background for a walk along land's end. The sky is filled with gulls and pelicans, sea lions and harbor seals gather at Little Jackass Cove, and the California gray whale migration passes near shore during winter and early spring.

A herd of Roosevelt elk roams the park. These magnificent creatures were once common here and in the King Range, but were exterminated in the last

Bull Roosevelt elk lock horns in Sinkyone Wilderness State Park.

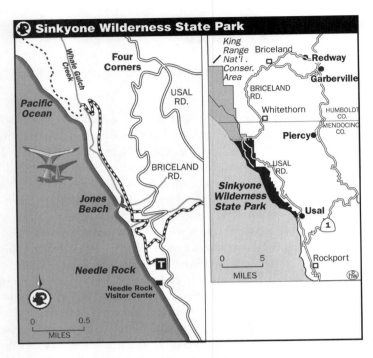

Sinkyone Wilderness State Park

century. The Roosevelt elk that lucky visitors see today are "extras" relocated from Prairie Creek State Park.

Lost Coast Trail travels the length of Sinkyone State Park north through King Range National Conservation Area. The sixty-mile trail would make an ideal week-long backpacking adventure. The portion of the Lost Coast Trail detailed here explores the northernmost, and most easily accessible, portion of the state park. It's a relatively easy introduction to a challenging trail.

DIRECTIONS TO TRAILHEAD From Highway 101, take either the Garberville or Redway exit and proceed to "downtown" Redway, located 3 miles north of Garberville on Business 101. Turn west on Briceland Road. After 12 miles of travel, fork left to Whitethorn. A mile or so past the hamlet of Whitethorn (don't blink or you'll miss it), the pavement ends, and you continue on a potholed dirt/mud road for 3.5 miles to a junction called Four Corners. Leftward is Usal Road, rightward is a road climbing into the King Range National Conservation Area. Proceed straight ahead 3.5 miles to the Sinkyone Wilderness State Park Visitor Center.

The park road is steep, winding, and only one lane wide. Maps and information are available at the visitor center.

THE HIKE Begin at the Needle Rock Visitor Center. During the 1920s, a small settlement and shipping point were established at Needle Rock. The

Calvin Cooper Stewart family were the main residents of Needle Rock, and today their ranch house serves as the park visitor center.

Walk up the park road toward the old barn. Notice a trail leading to the bluff edge, then down to the beach. Famed Needle Rock is a short distance up the dark sand beach.

Join Lost Coast Trail, which leads behind the barn and dips in and out of a gully. You'll pass Barn Camp, one of the state park's primitive, or walk-in, campsites. A quarter mile of travel brings you to Streamside Camp, another of the park's primitive, but superb, camps.

You'll soon reach a junction with a trail climbing to the east. This is Low Gap Trail, which ascends the coastal bluffs and crosses the park road. The trail plunges into the forest, travels along Low Gap Creek, and, after a stiff climb, reaches Usal Road. Lost Coast Trail, your route, continues along the lovely bluffs to Low Gap Creek, heads inland briefly, then crosses a bridge over the creek. The path heads toward a stand of eucalyptus, which shelters the Jones Beach campsites.

The trail forks. The left fork leads 0.2 mile to Jones Beach. If it's low tide, you can walk back to the trailhead via the beach.

Lost Coast Trail proceeds with the right fork and soon descends into a canyon. You cross two creeks, which drain an area that can be very marshy during the rainy season. You walk near the edge of a cattail-lined pond, climb to higher ground, and pass a second pond.

Soon you are treated to a bird's-eye view of Whale Gulch. A rough, unmaintained path descends to the mouth of Whale Gulch, where there's a small lagoon and piles of driftwood logs. After sitting on a driftwood log for a while and contemplating the Lost Coast, return to the trailhead the way you came.

■ KINGS PEAK
Lightning, King Crest Trail
4 miles round trip with 1,000-foot elevation gain

The King Range seems to rise straight from the sea; this abrupt rise is unsurpassed on California's coast, and is found in few places in the world. Kings Peak at 4,087 feet the highest summit in the range, is less than 3 miles from the ocean.

The King Range is one of the most geologically active mountain ranges in America. The North American plate grinds over the Pacific plate, fracturing the bedrock as the mountains lift skyward. Scientists believe that tectonic movement has caused the shoreline to lift more than 60 feet over the last 6,000 years.

King Crest Trail stretches about 8 miles over the dramatic ridgetops of the King Range. This walk explores the geologically fascinating signature peak of the King Range, and offers grand views of the Lost Coast.

Kings Peak lords over land and sea.

DIRECTIONS TO TRAILHEAD From Redway, take Briceland Road past the hamlet of Briceland. Veer right on Shelter Cove Road, which ascends a 2,000-foot pass. Shelter Cove Road descends to Shelter Cove, but you turn right and proceed 7 miles. Just before Horse Mountain Campground, turn left onto King Range Road and follow it 6.5 miles to the Lightning Trailhead and a small parking area north of the trailhead.

THE HIKE The narrow trail leads along the sharp spine of the ridge, which has a particularly dramatic fall-off on the west side. You travel through a madrone forest and tackle some fairly steep switchbacks.

As you walk through an area of low-lying brush, you'll get your first view of Kings Peak, companion sharp ridges and, off in the distance, North Side Peak. You might be pulling off sweaters and jackets on this next stretch of trail; there's about a 20-degree difference in temperature between the cool tanoak and madrone woodland and the exposed ridgetop.

At a signed junction, one fork leads to Maple Camp, which has water—a consideration if you're planning a long hike or backpack on King Crest Trail. A final half-mile ascent brings you to Kings Peak.

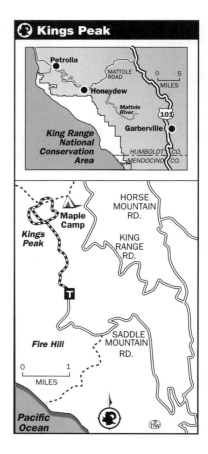

On a clear day you'll see Mattole Valley and grassy Cooksie Ridge and Spanish Ridge. To the east is the Eel River drainage and the peaks of the Yolla Bolly Wilderness. To the south is Sinkyone Wilderness State Park. To the west lie the canyons cut by the various forks of Big Flat Creek, as well as the wide blue Pacific.

■ MATTOLE RIVER
Lost Coast Trail
From Mattole River mouth to Punta Gorda Lighthouse is 6 miles round trip

The Mattole River marks the northern boundary of the Bureau of Land Management's King Range National Conservation Area. From the trailhead at Mouth of Mattole Recreation Site, the Lost Coast Trail travels 24 miles along the beach to Shelter Cove. Shipwrecks, a variety of marine life, and magnificent black sand beaches are some of the attractions of what many walkers consider the wildest coastline in California.

The sleepy, storybook hamlet of Petrolia, located near the river mouth, was the site of the state's first producing oil wells, drilled here in 1865. Leland Stanford's Mattole Petroleum Company had the most successful well—Union Well—which produced a hundred barrels of oil at a one barrel a day pace.

After the oil boom ended, settlers came to the Mattole Valley to take advantage of the fertile farmland and rich pasture. Mattole Valley is one of the wettest places on the Pacific Coast. The town of Honeydew, immediately to the north of the King Range, records an average of more than a hundred inches of rain a year. During extremely wet years, more than two hundred inches of rain may fall on the Lost Coast.

Punta Gorda Lighthouse.

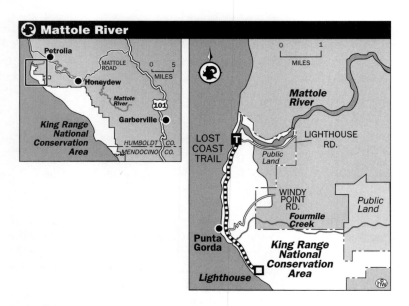

Adjacent grazing and logging have unfortunately taken their toll on the Mattole River. As heavy rains washed the denuded hillsides to the sea, millions of cubic yards of rock and gravel were dumped into the Mattole. Gravel bars formed, which altered the course of the river. Time and nature are slowly healing the Mattole, but the river will continue to meander off-course for many more years.

California's best beach backpacking trip is the trek from the mouth of the Mattole to Shelter Cove. A more moderate journey of 3 miles along the Lost Coast Trail takes the walker to the abandoned Coast Guard Lighthouse at Punta Gorda.

In 1911, after several ships were wrecked on the rocks and reefs off the King Range coast, a lighthouse was built a mile south of Punta Gorda—the name means "massive point." The lighthouse, which shined its warning beacon for four decades, shut down in 1951 due to high maintenance costs.

Petrolia, jump-off point for the Lost Coast Trail, got a rude awakening in April 1992 when a severe earthquake shook the community. The quake rattled residences and destroyed Petrolia's general store and post office.

DIRECTIONS TO TRAILHEAD From Highway 101 in Fortuna, take the Ferndale exit and follow the signs to Petrolia. Turn west on Lighthouse Road, following it 5 miles to its end at the mouth of the Mattole Recreation Site.

THE HIKE Before heading south, walk a quarter-mile north to the mouth of the river. Seagulls and ospreys circle overhead. Harbor seals frequent the tidal area where the Mattole meets the Pacific.

Walk south along the wild coast. The low dunes at the back of the beach are dotted in spring with sea rocket and sand verbena. Thin waterfalls cascade over the steep cliffs to the beach.

Two miles from the trailhead, you'll round Punta Gorda, which serves as a rookery for the Steller's sea lion. A mile south of the point is the old Punta Gorda Lighthouse. Beyond is another 20 miles of beach, the wildest in California.

■ FERNDALE'S RUSS PARK
Lytel Ridge, Francis Creek, Village Trails
2-mile loop

Ferndale is nothing if not quaint: a handsomely restored 1890s Victorian village—plus some fine art galleries, museums, shops and B&Bs. Ferndale's 1850s-founded dairy industry produced a famed butter and the "butterfat palaces" of its successful citizens. Main Street merchants hand out brochures that detail a walking tour of Ferndale's Victorian homes and buildings rendered in Eastlake, Queen Anne, Gothic Revival and variety of other styles.

Within the tiny city's limits is wild Russ Park, a preserve that gives a glimpse into another kind of nineteenth-century life—plant and wildlife. The park preserves the area's natural history just as the Ferndale Museum at Third and Shaw streets displays the town and country memorabilia of its early pioneers.

Russ Park is a preserve of tall trees—towering Sitka spruce, grand fir, redwood and western red cedar. Beneath the trees thrive the licorice, lady and leather ferns that gave Ferndale its name.

When pioneer Zipporah Patrick Russ donated the park to the city in 1920 she stipulated that the land be used for recreation and as a refuge and breeding place for birds. Birding, by the way, is pretty good in Russ Park. More than 60 species have been identified. (Such near-to-Ferndale locales as Cape Mendocino and the eastern Eel River Delta also attract lots of birds and their watchers.)

A short walk in 105-acre Russ Park, the pride of Ferndale, is a treat, and much wilder than you might expect.

DIRECTIONS TO TRAILHEAD From Highway 101, some 15 miles south of Eureka, take the Ferndale exit and drive 5 miles west to the town. Follow Ferndale's Main Street to its south end. Turn left on Ocean Street and proceed to Russ Park and an unpaved parking area.

THE HIKE Lytel Ridge Trail ascends slopes shaded by maple and Sitka spruce, soon reaching a wooden trail map, and continuing amidst thickets of berries—salmonberries, and thimbleberries.

A half-mile along, you'll reach a trail junction. A short right-forking connector leads to Zipporah's Pond and a small Redwood Grove. Continue with

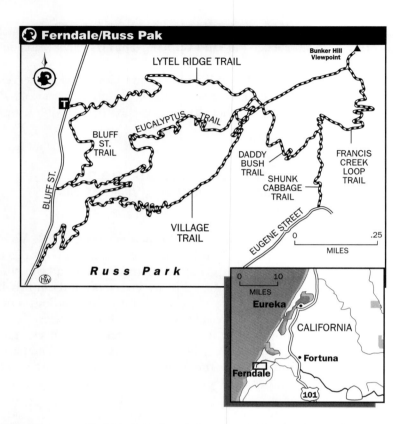

the left fork now called Francis Creek Loop, which travels southeast, soon forking again. A left-forking path ascends briefly to Bunker Hill Viewpoint, the park high point, for views of Eel River.

The main path tops the ridge, then descends north, switchbacking down into a ferny canyon, and completing the loop back toward Zipporah's Pond. This time fork left and visit the tranquil pond. Explore William Crane Grove, a mixture of Sitka spruce, fir and redwoods on the pond's north shore.

Descend from the pond, either on Eucalyptus Trail or Village Trail. Near the bottom of the hill, Bluff Street Trail returns you east to the trailhead.

■ PATRICK'S POINT STATE PARK
Rim Trail
From Palmer's Point to Agate Beach Campground is 4 miles round trip

Though Patrick's Point State Park is positioned in the heart of the redwoods, other trees—Sitka spruce, Douglas fir and red alder—predominate on the park's rocky promontories. The state park takes its name from Patrick Beegan, who homesteaded this dramatic, densely forested headland in 1851.

For hundreds of years the Yurok spent their summers in the Abalone Point area of the headlands. The Yurok gathered shellfish and hunted sea lions. A variety of game and a multitude of berries were plentiful in the surrounding forest.

The area now called Patrick's Point also had some spiritual significance to the native people. According to the Yurok belief, Sumig, the spirit of the porpoises, retired to Patrick's Point when humans began populating the world.

Rim Trail follows an old Indian pathway over the park's bluffs. Spur trails lead to rocky points that jut into the Pacific and offer commanding views of Trinidad Head to the south and Big Lagoon to the north.

Agate Beach vista from Patrick's Point.

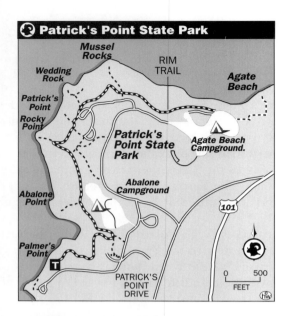

DIRECTIONS TO TRAILHEAD Patrick's Point State Park is located 30 miles north of Eureka and 5 miles north of Trinidad. Exit Highway 101 on Patrick's Point Drive and follow this road to the park. Once past the park entrance station, follow the signs to Palmer Point.

THE HIKE The trail plunges into a lush community of ferns, salmonberry and salal. The scolding *krrrack-krrrack* of the Steller jay is the only note of dissent heard along the trail.

Abalone Point is the first of a half-dozen spur trails that lead from Rim Trail to Rocky Point, Patrick's Point, Wedding Rock, Mussel Rocks and Agate Beach. Take any or all of them. (These side trails can sometimes be confused with Rim Trail; generally speaking, the spurs are much more steep than Rim Trail, which contours along without much elevation change.)

From Patrick's Point and the other promontories, admire the precipitous cliffs and rock-walled inlets. Gaze offshore at the sea stacks, a line of soldiers battered by the surging sea. Seals and sea lions haul out on the offshore rocks, which also double as rookeries for gulls, cormorants and pigeon guillemots.

Rim Trail meanders through a tapestry of trillium and moss, rhododendron and azalea. Sword ferns point the way to a grove of red alder.

Rim Trail ends at the north loop of the Agate Beach Campground road.

Hikers wishing to explore Agate Beach should continue a short distance along the road to the signed trailhead for Agate Beach Trail. This short, steep trail switchbacks down to the beach.

In marked contrast to the park's rocky shore that you observed from Rim Trail, Agate Beach is a wide swath of dark sand stretching north to the state parks at Big Lagoon.

Beach-combers prospect for agates in the gravel bars and right at the surf line. These agates are a nearly transparent variety of quartz, polished by sand and the restless sea. Jade, jaspar and other semiprecious stones are sometimes found here. One more noteworthy sight is the huge quantity and unique sea-sculpted quantity of the driftwood on this beach.

■ TALL TREES GROVE
Redwood Creek Trail
To Tall Trees Grove is 8.2 miles one way with 500-foot elevation gain

Redwood Creek Trail travels through the heart of Redwood National Park to Tall Trees Grove, site of the world's tallest measured tree. After one of the 1960's classic conservation battles, a narrow corridor of land along Redwood Creek was acquired to protect the world's highest tree, a coast redwood measuring 365.5 feet. This giant was discovered in 1963 by a National Geographic Society expedition.

The 9-mile stretch along Redwood Creek known as "the worm" was downslope from private timberlands, where there was extensive and insensitive clearcut logging. Resulting slope erosion and stream sediments threatened the big trees, so to protect this watershed, the National Park Service purchased an additional 48,000 acres, mostly in Redwood Creek basin. For more than a decade, the park service has been rehabilitating scarred slopes.

Redwood Creek Trail follows an abandoned logging road on a gentle ascent from the outskirts of Orick to Tall Trees Grove. From the Tall Trees, walkers may follow Redwood Creek Trail back to their vehicles.

One word of caution: The three bridges that cross Redwood Creek are in place only during the summer. Use your best judgment and inquire at the visitor center before attempting this hike during the wetter seasons.

DIRECTIONS TO TRAILHEAD From Highway 101, about 3 miles north of Redwood Information Center and 2 miles from the town of Orick, turn east on Bald Hills Road. Take the first right to the Redwood Creek trailhead. A free permit is necessary for overnight camping along this trail and can be obtained at Redwood Information Center.

THE HIKE The first 1.5 miles of trail, from the trailhead to the first bridge crossing of Redwood Creek, passes through regenerating forest as well as old growth Sitak spruce and redwood. The trail also passes a meadowland that flanks the river.

Occasional clearings and the bridge crossings allow the walker to get the "big picture" of Redwood Creek. Three distinct communities of flora can be discerned: Extensive grass prairie, emerald-green during the wet season and

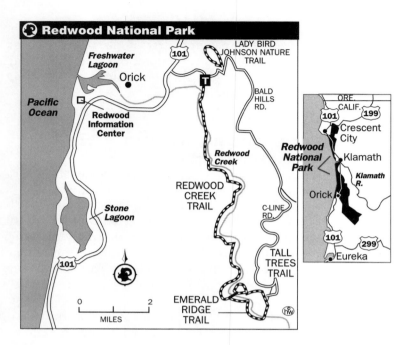

golden brown during the drier months, dominates the eastern slopes above Redwood Creek. Down-slope of the grassland are vast clear cuts, slowly recovering as new-growth red alder forest. Near the creek are the groves of old-growth redwoods and a lush understory of salmonberry, oxalis and sword fern.

During the summer months, the walker may descend to Redwood Creek and travel the creek's gravel bars nearly to Tall Trees Grove. The river bars are fine pathways and also serve as campsites for backpackers.

Continue through the forest primeval. The redwoods congregate in especially large families on the alluvial flats along the creek.

Enjoy the loop trail through the Tall Trees Grove before returning back the way you came or, if you have a vehicle waiting, take the Tall Trees Trail up to C-Line Road.

■ PRAIRIE CREEK REDWOODS STATE PARK

Fern Canyon, James Irvine, Clintonia, Miners Ridge Trails

Loop through Fern Canyon 1 mile round trip; via Gold Bluffs, Gold Bluffs Beach is 6.5 miles round trip with 500-foot elevation gain

Dim and quiet, wrapped in mist and silence, the redwoods roof a moist and mysterious world. Park trails meander over lush ground and the walker is treated to the cool feeling and fragrance of wood and water.

The Fern Canyon in Prairie Creek Redwoods State Park is undoubtedly the most awe-inspiring of all the fern canyons found along the North Coast. Five-finger, deer, lady, sword, and chain ferns smother the precipitous walls of the canyon. Bright yellow monkeyflowers abound, as well as fairy lanterns, those creamy white, or greenish, bell-shaped flowers that hang in clusters. Ferns are descendants of an ancient group of plants which were much more numerous 200 million years ago. Ferns have roots and stems similar to flowering plants, but are considered to be a primitive form of plant life because they reproduce by spores, not seeds.

In this spectacular state park, Roosevelt elk roam the meadows and even the beaches.

Gold Bluffs was named in 1850 when prospectors found some gold flakes in the beach sand. The discovery caused a minor gold rush. A tent city sprang up on the beach but little gold was extracted.

Gold Bluffs Beach is a beauty— 11 miles of wild, driftwood-littered shore, backed by extensive dunes. Sand verbena, bush lupine, and wild strawberry splash color on the sand.

This walk explores some of the highlights of Prairie Creek Redwoods State Park—Fern Canyon, magnificent redwood groves, and Gold Bluffs Beach.

DIRECTIONS TO TRAILHEAD

From Highway 101, 3 miles north of Orick, turn west on Davison Road. The dirt, washboard road (suitable only for vehicles under 24 feet in length) descends logged slopes and through second-growth

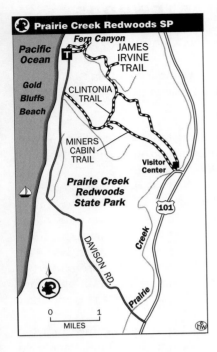

redwoods to the beach. The road heads north along Gold Bluffs Beach. One and a half miles past the campground, the road dead-ends at the Fern Canyon Trailhead.

THE HIKE The path leads along the pebbled floor of Fern Canyon. In the wettest places, the route follows wooden planks across Home Creek. With sword and five-finger ferns pointing the way, you pass through marshy areas covered with wetlands grass and dotted with a bit of skunk cabbage. Lurking about are Pacific giant salamanders.

A half-mile from the trailhead, the path climbs out of the canyon to intersect James Irvine Trail, named for a man who contributed much to the formation of redwood parks.

The James Irvine Trail crosses to the south side of the canyon and proceeds southeast with Home Creek. The trail reaches the upper neck of Fern Canyon and junctions with Clintonia Trail. (James Irvine Trail continues ascending through dense redwood forest to a trailhead near the park visitor center.) Clintonia Trail leads a mile through virgin redwood groves to a junction with Miners Ridge Trail. Bear right.

Part of Miners Ridge Trail is an old logging road, once used by mule-drawn wagons. The trail was also a pack train route for the Gold Bluffs miners. You'll descend with Squashan Creek to the ocean.

It's a 1.5-mile beach walk along Gold Bluffs Beach back to the trailhead.

Lucky walkers might catch a glimpse of the herd of Roosevelt elk that roam the park. These graceful animals look like a cross between a South American llama and a deer and convince walkers that they have entered an enchanted land.

■ LAGOON CREEK

Redwood Coastal Trail

From Lagoon Creek to Hidden Beach is 2 miles
round trip; to Requa Overlook is 8 miles round trip
with 200-foot elevation gain

The Coastal Trail—or Redwood Coastal Trail as national park rangers often refer to it—is a 40-mile pathway that connects state and national parklands. One of the more spectacular sections of the trail is the 4 miles between Lagoon Creek and the mouth of the Klamath River.

Lagoon Creek empties into a pond, formed in 1940 when the lumber mill dammed the creek to form a log pond. The creek and pond became part of Redwood National Park in 1972. Heart-shaped yellow pond lilies float in the tranquil pond, which is habitat for ducks, egrets, herons and red-winged blackbirds.

Adding to the pleasure of a walk in this area is the Yurok Loop Nature Trail which explores the lagoon area. The walker may use one half the loop on departure and the second half on the return. Interpretive brochures are (sometimes) available at the parking area or information centers.

DIRECTIONS TO TRAILHEAD Lagoon Creek Fishing Access is located west of Highway 101, 5 miles north of the town of Klamath.

THE HIKE Head south along the Yurok Loop Nature Trail, which travels through a dense canopy of oak, alder and willow. From the blufftop are occasional views of the beaches below.

Enjoy an easy meander along the lagoon, or a
more strenuous walk to Requa Overlook.

Coastal Trail veers right from the nature trail and follows a fern-lined path to a grove of red alder. During spring and summer, hikers may observe hummingbirds extracting nectar from pink-flowered salmonberry bushes.

About a mile from the trailhead is the turn-off to Hidden Beach, a driftwood-piled sandy beach that's ideal for a picnic.

From the Hidden Beach turn-off, the trail ascends into Sitka spruce forest. Halfway to Requa Overlook, Coastal Trail crests a divide and continues on through thick forest. A few overlooks allow the walker glimpses of the bold headlands north and south, and of the wave-cut terraces below. Sea lions and seals may haul out on offshore rocks.

Coastal Trail bears southeast to Requa Overlook, which offers picnic sites and striking views of the mouth of the Klamath River. The overlook is also a good place to watch for migrating California gray whales.

■ DEL NORTE COAST REDWOODS STATE PARK
Last Chance Trail
From Enderts Beach Road to Highway 101 is 7 miles one way; shorter and longer round trip hikes possible

Sometimes we hikers become so enamored by the majestic coast redwoods in Redwood National Park, we overlook the park's magnificent coast. The national park and adjoining state parks are linked by a series of coastal trails that present panoramas of both a spectacular shoreline and some of the world's tallest trees.

Like Redwood National Park, Del Norte Coast Redwoods State Park delivers the scenery in its name: an impressive coastline, as well as magnificent old-growth redwoods. The combination of redwoods—as well as a mixed forest of Sitka spruce, Douglas fir and red alder—with the coast, adds up to a hike to remember.

What is now the park's campground area, on the inland side of Highway 101, was once owned and logged by the Hobbs Wall Company. Land logged during the 1920s is now a thriving second-growth redwood forest, but much evidence of the logging operation remains, in the form of stumps and machinery. Decaying ties and trestles found in the park are reminders of the old Crescent City & Smith River Railroad—quite an engineering project visitors will surmise after taking a look around at the steep terrain in the vicinity of Mill Creek.

The majority of the state park is located on the ocean side of Highway 101; in fact, what is now a splendid hiking trail used to be the Redwood Highway (101). The old highway was abandoned in 1935 for its present route. Part of the old road is on the National Register of Historic Places.

The Last Chance Trail is the northernmost stretch of the California Coastal Trail; this is the "last chance" to walk part of the California Coastal Trail (part hiker's dream, part reality) before joining the Oregon Coast Trail.

Don't think you're lost if you see Redwood National Park signs (easy to recognize because the agency seems to be the last proponent of the metric system in America) instead of Del Norte Redwoods State Park signs. The National Park Service has jurisdiction over the Enderts Beach trailhead and a fine backpack camp; however, much of Last Chance Trail is on state park land.

DIRECTIONS TO TRAILHEAD From Highway 101, about 2 miles south of Crescent City, turn west on Enderts Beach Road and wind 2.5 miles to road's end at Crescent Beach Overlook and the beginning of Last Chance Trail.

THE HIKE As you hike south on the old coast highway, you'll get grand views behind you of the Crescent City coastline and in a short while will be treated to good views south of Enderts Beach; a quarter-mile from the trailhead a short side trail on the right offers the opportunity to descend to this pocket beach.

Last Chance Trail drops into Nickel Creek Canyon, where another side trail leads to a walk-in campground. A half-mile out, Last Chance Trail begins a very steep climb of a bit more than a mile, ascending through old-growth redwoods. Two miles along, you top out and begin a descent, entering Del Norte Coast Redwoods State Park.

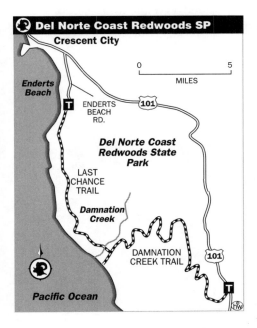

Three miles along are the magnificent redwoods thriving in the headwaters of Damnation Creek. Another mile of travel and a short descent brings you to a ford of Damnation Creek. (This is a good turnaround point; an 8-mile round-trip hike by the time you get back to the trailhead.)

Those hikers continuing with Last Chance Trail will cross (use caution, the log "bridges" are slippery) Damnation Creek and travel another mile through the forest. The path nears Highway 101 at mile 5, junctions with Damnation Creek Trail at the 6-mile mark, leads through some more redwood forest primeval and reaches Highway 101 seven miles from the trailhead.

■ HUMBOLDT LAGOONS STATE PARK

Big Lagoon Beach Trail

Along the sand spit is 6 miles round trip; to Big Lagoon County Park is 8.5 miles round trip; to Patrick's Point State Park is 10 miles round trip

Big, Big Lagoon is 3.5 miles long, walled off from the power of the Pacific by a 600- to 700-foot-wide strip of sand. The lagoon's marshy habitat is an important rest stop for migratory birds on the Pacific flyway.

Long, sandy Big Lagoon Beach, along with Dry Lagoon and portions of Stone Lagoon, comprise Humboldt Lagoons State Park. The park appeals to hikers and fishermen, who enjoy the lonely beauty of the sand spits and wetlands.

The park is much more than marshlands. Sitka spruce thrive on the north and southwest shores, and even some wind-blown old-growth redwoods cling tenaciously to life on the east shore.

Gold-seekers swarmed into the area in 1849 when discoveries were made along the Klamath and Trinity rivers. Prospectors attempted to mine the sand spits along Big and Stone lagoons, but managed to extract very little gold despite considerable effort.

Dry Lagoon State Park was established in 1931. The park expanded over the next half century to more than 1,000 acres, added a couple more lagoons, and in 1981 its name was changed to Humboldt Lagoons State Park. Land acquisitions by the Save-the-Redwoods League further enlarged the park.

The wild, rocky Humboldt coast offers unexpected sights of startling beauty, like these trees stubbornly clinging to their offshore home.

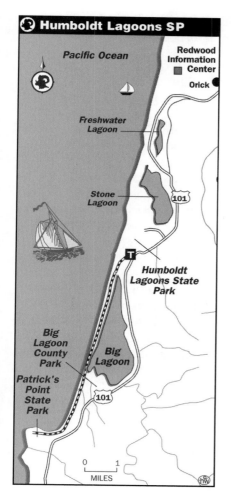

Humboldt Lagoons SP

Pacific Ocean

Redwood Information Center

Orick

Freshwater Lagoon

Stone Lagoon

101

Humboldt Lagoons State Park

Big Lagoon County Park

Big Lagoon

Patrick's Point State Park

101

0   1
MILES

Walking Big Lagoon Beach means paying attention to the tides. Several times each winter, Big Lagoon's barrier beach is breached by waves; the beach at these times is impassable. During other seasons, best hiking is at lower tides. Consult a local tide table.

(More about the local lagoons: Dry Lagoon offers a mile-long beach hike north of the lagoon, plus a 1-mile loop trail around the environmental campsites. You can take a 2- to 3-mile hike along the barrier beach fronting Stone Lagoon.)

DIRECTIONS TO TRAILHEAD From Highway 101, some 7 miles south of Orick, turn west onto the signed state park road and travel a mile to road's end at a beach parking lot.

THE HIKE From the parking lot, follow the beach south. Atop the nearby wooded bluffs are some excellent environmental campsites. About a half-mile along, the mixed black- and white-sand beach broadens. You'll reach the north end of Big Lagoon about 0.75 mile from the trailhead.

Now you'll walk the crest of the barrier beach, dotted with sea rocket, dune tansy and sand verbena. Two miles out, you'll notice a couple of low spots in the sand spit. During very high tides, waves crest the sand spit, spilling into the lagoon.

Three miles along, you'll get a good view of Big Lagoon at its widest—more than a mile across. On the east side grows a forest of Sitka spruce and some wind-sculpted redwoods.

Rest awhile on the driftwood logs scattered on the beach. Down-coast is a nice view of Agate Beach and the dramatic, wooded bluffs of Patrick's Point State Park; it's another 2-mile walk, if you're in the mood.

Return the same way, or, if you want to extend your walk a bit more, curve around the lagoon to the south shore where you'll find Big Lagoon County Park.

■ PELICAN BAY
Pelican Bay Trail
From Radio Road to Point St. George is 2 miles round trip; to
Lake Tolowa is 8 miles round trip

Extending between Pyramid Point at the mouth of the Smith River south to Point St. George, Pelican Bay is one of California's most bountiful fisheries. Salmon, rockfish and sole are caught offshore, while the Dungeness crab is taken along the coast.

Attracted by the ocean's abundant harvest, the native Tolowa camped in the Pelican Bay area as early as 300 B.C. The Tolowa fished salmon from the Smith River mouth, gathered mussels and clams, and hunted sea lions.

Two coastal lagoons—lakes Earl and Tolowa—are separated from the bay by a sandbar. The mostly freshwater Lake Earl and the more saline Lake Tolowa host more than 250 species of birds. The lakes are a crucial stopover for birds traveling the Pacific Flyway, the west coast bird migration route. Sometimes as many as one hundred thousand birds can be sighted here. Surrounding the lakes are saltwater marshland and freshwater wetlands, as well as far-reaching sand dunes.

Point St. George on the south end of Pelican Bay is a dramatic headland, at the foot of which are rich tidepools. Extending west from the point is St. George Reef, which includes Seal Rocks, a seal and sea lion rookery. At the end of the reef, some 7 miles from the mainland, stands St. George Lighthouse, abandoned in 1975 due to extraordinarily high maintenance costs. The lighthouse was built in 1892, in tardy response to the 1865 wreck of the Pacific Mail steamer *Brother Jonathan,* a tragedy that claimed the lives of 213 passengers. Crescent City's Brother Jonathan Park has a cemetery and memorial honoring those who perished.

Point St. George.

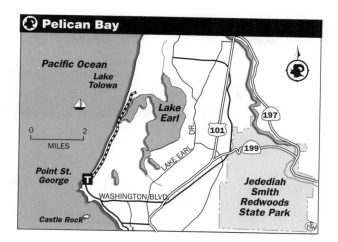

This walk offers two different ways to explore Pelican Bay. A walk south takes you to the rich tidepool area of Point St. George while beach walking north leads to Lakes Earl and Tolowa, and trails exploring Tolowa Dunes State Park.

DIRECTIONS TO TRAILHEAD From Highway 101 just north of Crescent City, exit on Washington Boulevard and drive west. Washington becomes Radio Road, which you follow to its terminus at a parking area.

THE HIKE From the parking lot of a former Coast Guard station, follow the trail 100 yards down grass-covered hillocks toward the shore.

(Head south to reach the Point St. George tidepools. The crashing sea has gouged pockets into the sandstone and shale point. The unusually rich tidepools, fringed with kelp and sea palms, are filled with a myriad of life. Walkers may stalk the amazing 24-armed sunflower starfish—at 2 feet across, it's one of the largest and fastest stars found on the California coast.)

The journey northward from the trailhead takes you along a beach backed by dunes. About a half-mile inland is Dead Lake, a small freshwater lake that, like so many bodies of water along the redwood coast, was formerly a lumber mill pond. The lake, now state property, is habitat for wood ducks.

Continue along the driftwood littered beach to Lake Tolowa, which is surrounded by a marshland. Opportunities for exploration of Lake Tolowa and its larger neighbor, Lake Earl, are limited by the marshy terrain and mudflats, which are better suited to the needs of soft-shelled clams than hikers; nevertheless, there are a few trails that lead inland to explore the dunes and wooded ridges of 5,000-acre Tolowa Dunes State Park. After observing the multitude of waterfowl, including canvasbacks and the endangered Aleutian goose, return along the beach to the trailhead.

THE TRAILMASTER'S TOP TEN

1. SAN DIEGO'S NORTH COUNTY
California Coastal Trail
25 miles

Ever since enjoying an "Inn to Inn" walk along the Dorset Coast in England, I've pondered how—and where—coast walkers could enjoy a similar experience along the California coast. Sunny San Diego—in particular its north county shoreline—is certainly one good place for a long walk.

Twenty-five miles of unobstructed beach await the hiker in north San Diego County. Extending between Del Mar and Oceanside is a coastline of black and white sand beaches, backed by bluffs and dotted with lagoons.

The towns and beaches here are quiet, giving the illusion of being off the beaten track. Until 1964, the coastline was busier because Coast Highway—then the main thoroughfare between Los Angeles and San Diego—sent motorists whizzing right alongside the coast. However, when Interstate 5 routed travelers inland, the Coast Highway—and the small towns—were left to residents and beach-goers.

To some casual visitors, the towns of Del Mar, Solana Beach, Encinitas and Leucadia all look alike, though residents are quick to dispute this, and to point out the superiority of their own particular town and beach. And, in truth, when you walk (as opposed to drive) through these towns, you'll find each has a distinct personality.

The walker will find camping at San Elijo State Beach and South Carlsbad State Beach, plus plenty of motels in all price ranges—from semi-seedy bungalows in Leucadia to Automobile Association of America-approved accommodations in Encinitas and Carlsbad.

A superb weekend walk would be the 25-mile stretch from Del Mar to Oceanside. For a 35-mile, 3-day jaunt, walk the shore from La Jolla to Oceanside.

Feeling a bit leg-weary or want to bring along some pint-sized hikers? No problem. Hike until you're tired, then hop on one of the many North San Diego County Transit buses that run up and down the coast.

For more information: San Diego Visitors and Convention Bureau at (619) 232-3101.

2. SANTA MONICA BAY
California Coastal Trail
20 to 40 miles

Fringed by palm trees, with the Santa Monica Mountains as dramatic backdrop, the wide sandy beaches along Santa Monica Bay draw visitors from around the world. Locals tend to get a bit blasé about this beauty in their backyard, and often fail to take advantage of what is, in my opinion, one of the world's great beach walks.

Favorite bay walks enjoyed by tourists include Venice Beach and the Venice Boardwalk, the Santa Monica Pier and Palisades Park in Santa Monica. These are pleasant enough excursions, but I would suggest something more ambitious: a walk around the entire bay.

Such a walk will surely be a very long day—or a weekend—to remember. You'll get a real feel for the bay, not only as a collection of beaches and seashore sights, but as a living, dynamic ecosystem whose health and well-being depends heavily on government and citizen action.

Geographically, Santa Monica Bay is a mellow intrusion by the Pacific Ocean into the western edge of the Los Angeles lowlands. The bay's magnificent curving beaches are cooled by a prevailing ocean breeze, which protects the coast from the temperature extremes—and smog—that are characteristic of the interior.

Alas, all views along Santa Monica Bay are not picture-perfect; huge smokestacks from power plants tower over some South Bay beaches, while jets departing LAX fly low and loud over others. And the bay has its share of well-documented environmental problems, too. Sewers and storm drains empty into the bay. Organizations such as Heal the Bay have undertaken the Herculean task of educating the public and public officials that the bay is not merely a series of sand strands, but a complex ecosystem.

Pick a brisk fall or winter weekend to walk the bay and you'll be surprised at how much shoreline solitude you'll enjoy. It's possible to walk the bay from Torrance to the Santa Monica Pier in a very long day, but the 20-mile beach hike is more comfortably completed in 2 days.

If bay walking agrees with you, consider walking the rest of the bay—another 20 miles from the Santa Monica Pier to Point Dume.

You can arrange a car shuttle or use the bus system to return to your day's start point. Better yet, leave a bicycle at the end of your walk and cycle back to the trailhead along the South Bay Bicycle Path. Super-jocks will relish the challenge of what I call the Triathlon Trail: Walk the 20 miles from Torrance County Beach to the Santa Monica Pier, cycle the South Bay Bicycle Path, then take a long refreshing swim.

For more information: Call Heal the Bay at (310) 453-0395 for updates on Santa Monica Bay environmental issues and educational programs.

3. SANTA MONICA MOUNTAINS
Backbone Trail
65 miles

The day will soon come when the final miles of the 65-mile long Backbone Trail will finally be completed and the path will extend across the spine of the Santa Monica Mountains from Will Rogers State Historic Park to Point Mugu State Park. After some three decades of often frustrating work on the part of conservationists and government agencies, the trail is about 95 percent complete; in 1998, Congress appropriated the necessary funds to complete land purchases to bridge the gaps between trail segments and, ultimately, to complete the Backbone Trail.

The Backbone Trail network is a rich blend of footpaths, fire roads and horse trails, leading through diverse ecosystems: meadows, savannas, yucca-covered slopes, handsome sandstone formations, seasonal and all-year creeks. When finished, the Backbone Trail will literally and symbolically link the scattered beauties of the Santa Monicas.

The hiker who wants to get away from it all (L.A.) for the weekend can find enough completed trail for a 2-day trek. One section extends 11.5 miles from Will Rogers State Historic Park to Topanga State Park. Spend the night in Topanga, and then head another couple mile into Hondo Canyon, one of the most intriguing in the Santa Monicas.

The longest uninterrupted stretch (some 20 miles) is from the Saddle Peak area to Malibu Creek State Park. You can then follow the Backbone along Malibu Creek through the park or take a "high road" along Mesa Peak Motorway to the Castro Crest area, then on through Newton Canyon to trail's end at Corral Canyon Road. Total distance: about 12 miles.

A third stretch of Backbone worth a weekend leads from the shoulder of the range's highest summit, Sandstone Peak, into the heart of Point Mugu State Park. Hikers can overnight at Camp Herbert Allen in the National Park Service's Circle X Ranch, then begin a long descent into the Boney Mountain Wilderness in Point Mugu State Park. It's about 8 miles to Danielson Camp, plus another 8 to the Ray Miller Trailhead at the mouth of La Jolla Canyon on the coast.

For more information: Santa Monica Mountains National Recreation Area at (805) 370-2301.

4. BIG SUR BACKCOUNTRY
Ventana Wilderness Trails
20 to 40 miles

Geographically, and some would say spiritually, Big Sur is the heart of California. The Big Sur backcountry, under the administration of the Monterey District of Los Padres National Forest, is not gentle wilderness, but a dramatic, enchanted land, explored by more than 300 miles of trail.

Trails climb the Santa Lucia Mountains, and probe the headwaters of the Arroyo Seco and the Little Sur and Big Sur rivers, which originate in the Ventana Wilderness. The Ventana Wilderness, expanded by federal legislation to nearly 200,000 acres in 1992, offers some challenging backcountry adventures.

In 1978, the Marble Cone Fire extensively damaged the backcountry. Much of what was then forest is now brush land and may not regain its timbered beauty for many more years. A number of steep canyons and watersheds, however, escaped devastation. In many places Big Sur is as beautiful as ever, an attractive hiking destination for Southern Californians, Bay Area residents and walkers from around the world.

Three of my favorite trails include paths along the Big Sur and Carmel rivers and a high country route up one of the tallest peaks in the Santa Lucia Mountains.

The Big Sur River hike in this guide describes a 10-mile jaunt through the Big Sur River watershed along Pine Ridge Trail to Sykes Hot Springs. From the hot springs, the trail climbs another 12 miles to China Camp. (If you want to go the easy way, join Pine Ridge Trail at its China Camp trailhead off Chew's Ridge Road (also called Jamesburg-Tassajara Road). The 22-mile trail drops 4,000 feet in elevation on its way to Big Sur Station.

Ventana Double Cone Trail travels 13 miles and climbs 3,000 feet from Bottcher's Gap to Ventana Double Cone. Because the trail travels exposed, sun-drenched slopes, this can be kind of a hot hike, but offers grand coastal views. Pat Springs Camp, halfway along, is a superb trail camp.

The Carmel River area is a great place to hike, too. It's 19 miles from China Camp to Los Padres Dam via Church Creek, Pine Valley and Carmel River Camp. The Carmel River has some small waterfalls and deep pools. Plan to get wet; there are lots of river crossings en route.

For more information: Big Sur Multi-Agency Facility (831) 667-2315.

5. SANTA CRUZ MOUNTAINS
Skyline to the Sea Trail
35 miles

As its name suggest, Skyline to the Sea Trail drops from the crest of the Santa Cruz Mountains to the Pacific Ocean. The Big Basin Redwoods State Park walk in this guide describes an 11-mile one-way day hike on the Skyline to the Sea Trail through Big Basin Redwoods State Park to the ocean at Waddell Beach. Another stretch of Skyline Trail (19 miles long) connects Castle Rock State Park with Big Basin. And yet another length travels through Sanborn Skyline County Park.

A vigorous 2-day weekend hike or a more moderate 3-day weekend hike is the 35-mile trek (mostly a descent) from Saratoga Gap, at the junction of Highways 9 and 35, down through Big Basin Redwoods State Park to Waddell Beach.

Castle Rock State Park is a good one to get to know. Perched high on the western slope of the Santa Cruz Mountains among frequent fogs (and just above occasional smogs), the park offers dramatic rock formations and quiet forest paths.

From Castle Rock State Park the path closely parallels Highway 9. As the trail continues past Waterman Gap, hikers descend from chaparral to deep woods and enjoy great views of Big Basin. As the trail enters the state park, it winds along with Opal Creek and descends into the redwoods.

Castle Rock State Park has two overnight walk-in trail camps. Castle Rock Trail Camp, tucked in a knobcone forest in the heart of the park, has 23 sites. Waterman Gap Trail Camp, a 6.5-mile hike from Saratoga Gap, has six sites in the redwoods.

For more information: Big Basin Redwoods State Park, (831) 338-8860. Ask for the fine trail maps published by the Santa Cruz Mountains Natural History Association.

6. SAN FRANCISCO BAY
Bay Area Ridge Trail
500 miles

Bay Area Ridge Trail is a 500-mile trail-in-the-making that will eventually connect 75 parks scattered around San Francisco Bay. The multi-use path (hikers, mountain bicyclists, equestrians) follows the main ridgelines closest to the bay, and offers many glorious bay views.

The late William Penn Mott is credited with coming up with the idea for the Bay Area Ridge Trail in the 1960s when he was the general manager of the East Bay Regional Parks District. Mott later served with distinction as California state parks director and as national parks director.

The trail is testimony to what makes the Bay Area one of America's most outstanding natural areas and places to hike. Rolling meadows, rocky peaks, redwood forests and tumbling creeks are a few of the many diverse environments the trail crosses.

The trail, in its conception, design and implementation, is an outstanding example of the spirit of volunteerism that makes the Bay Area one of the world's premier places to walk. Thanks to the coordinating efforts of the Bay Area Ridge Trail Council and hundreds of volunteers, the path has rapidly progressed from dream to signed trail in record time. (In contrast, many long-distance trails are infamous for their slow progress.)

More than half of the route is now accessible to hikers. Completed stretches of trail travel through the Santa Cruz Mountains redwoods, the dramatic Marin County headlands and the rolling hills of the Napa-Sonoma wine country. Some campsites and accommodations are found along the way and more are planned, spaced a day's walk apart.

The Bay Area Ridge Trail tours such well-known parks such as Tilden Regional Park and Redwood Regional Park in the East Bay hills, Mt. Tamalpais State Park and the Marin Headlands and Castle Rock State Park in the Santa Cruz Mountains. Less pastoral sections of the trail skirt the cities of Martinez, Benicia and Daly City.

For more information: Call the Bay Area Ridge Trail Council at (415) 561-2595. More than a dozen pamphlets that map out various segments of the trail are available, along with a guidebook, *The Bay Area Ridge Trail* (Wilderness Press).

7. SAN FRANCISCO BAY
Bay Trail
400 miles

To the area's 6.5 million residents and to visitors from around the world, San Francisco Bay often appears to be both everywhere and nowhere at the same time. California's largest (by far) bay seems everywhere in the background, in view from freeways, office buildings, and from neighborhoods where a "Bay View" adds value to housing that is among the most expensive in the nation. But the bay might as well be nowhere, too, obscured as it is by highway sound walls, billboards and industrial developments.

San Francisco Bay has long inspired the somewhat incongruous views of a shimmering natural wonder when viewed from afar, and a homely and inaccessible waterfront when viewed up-close. On foot, walkers can experience the bay shore environment in segments that are nearly pristine and others that are, ecologically speaking, all but obliterated.

The new Bay Trail aims to make the many faces of San Francisco Bay accessible to the sojourner afoot, and to make the bay as pedestrian-friendly as the city and its surrounding park lands. When completed, the 400-mile trail will encircle the bay and link wildlife refuges, city parks, historic sites and urban and residential areas, as well as a diversity of waterfronts ranging from the trendy and boutiqued to the commercial and industrial.

The trail will connect all nine Bay Area counties and provide links to other long-distance trails—most notably to the California Coastal Trail that extends both north and south of San Francisco, and to the Bay Area Ridge Trail, the region's 500-mile pathway that forms a second, wider ring around the Bay. By the dawn of the twenty-first century, about 50 percent of the bay's shoreline was accessible to hikers and about 50 percent of the trail was completed.

Conservationists and trail advocates credit State Senator Bill Lockyer of Hayward with providing both the creative inspiration and crucial funding legislation to launch Bay Trail. California's State Coastal Conservancy has played a leading role in the trail's development and is the path's chief financial supporter. The nonprofit Bay Trail Project now coordinates completion efforts. For more information: Call the Office of Bay Area Governments at (510) 464-7900.

8. GOLDEN GATE NATIONAL RECREATION AREA
Coastal Trail
8 to 60 miles

Coastal Trail extends through Golden Gate National Recreation Area, Mt. Tamalpais State Park and Point Reyes National Seashore. The path (sometimes called Coast Trail, California Coastal Trail or Pacific Coast Trail) offers some fine hiking to surprisingly remote backcountry camps.

Hikers from around the world have been drawn here, and with a blossoming of accommodations ranging from fine inns to budget hostels, an ideal opportunity for European-style walking has been created. By crossing the Golden Gate Bridge from San Francisco and using a combination of coastal trails, it is possible to take a guided walk of some 60 miles to the hamlet of Inverness.

You can begin your walk in San Francisco, cross the Golden Gate Bridge, and head for the Golden Gate Hostel or one of several hike-in camps.

Coastal Trail begins on the San Francisco side of Marin Headlands and more or less follows the shore northwest, from Rodeo Beach to Tennessee Valley to Muir Beach. The path crosses Mt. Tamalpais State Park and enters Point Reyes National Seashore. From Palomarin, a major jump-off point for explorations of the point, Coastal Trail winds past a number of lakes and backcountry camps as well as Point Reyes Hostel, before reaching its end in the Drakes Estero/Inverness Ridge area.

If your idea of a vacation is eating-staying-walking in a beautiful place and leaving the organization to somebody else, a 6-day tour such as the one offered by the Berkeley-based Backroads might be for you. The accommodations (rustic elegance in a majestic setting) and food are first-rate on these tours, which attract walkers from across the nation and around the world.

Those hikers planning their own walking tour can plan an itinerary (and lodging) to fit their own budgets. Walkers creative with a bus map will figure out how to arrange transit back to San Francisco.

A modestly paced, 6-day walk might include:

Day 1: Over Golden Gate Bridge to Sausalito (7.5 miles) or to Golden Gate Hostel (8.5 miles).

Day 2: Coastal Trail to Tennessee Valley, then on to Muir Beach (6-9 miles).

Day 3: Muir Beach to Stinson Beach, with a detour to Muir Woods (9 miles).

Day 4: Stinson Beach across the slopes of Mt. Tamalpais, down to funky Bolinas (10.5 miles).

Day 5: From Bolinas, a walk along the San Andreas Fault line to Olema (12 miles).

Day 6: Olema through Bear Valley, over Mt. Wittenberg, to Inverness (9.5 miles).

For more information: Call Golden Gate National Recreation Area at (415) 561-4700.

9. LOST COAST
Lost Coast Trail
50 miles

When it comes to coast walking, it doesn't get any wilder than California's Lost Coast, where towering shoreline cliffs rise abruptly like volcanoes from the sea. California has a very long coastline, and millions of acres of wilderness, but it has only one wilderness coast.

The Lost Coast. And you can explore California's wildest shore with the Lost Coast Trail, which crosses and connects Sinkyone Wilderness State Park and King Range National Conservation Area.

Lost Coast Trail, as it travels through Sinkyone Wilderness State Park, provides a strenuous, yet rewarding experience. The 22-mile trail alternates between deep forested canyons and prominent ridges, and offers spectacular vistas up to 100 miles of coastline. I recommend 2 nights and 3 days to hike the rugged coast between Usal and Bear Harbor.

North of Bear Harbor the terrain is gentler for a time; the going is much easier as you meander over coastal terraces, past the park's visitor center at Needle Rock, and on to Whale Gulch.

Beyond the waterfalls of Whale Creek, the mellow path again becomes a rugged mountain track as you ascend Chemise Mountain and intersect the trail network of the King Range National Conservation Area, which is administered by the U.S. Bureau of Land Management.

Lost Coast Trail through the King Range is primarily a beach route. The 24-mile long wilderness beach is one of the most attractive features of the Conservation Area, along with the abandoned Coast Guard lighthouse at Punta Gorda, relics of early shipwrecks, and abundant marine life.

For more information: Call Sinkyone Wilderness State Park (707) 986-7711, King Range National Conservation Area at (707) 825-2300. *California's Lost Coast* (Wilderness Press), an authoritative map by John McKinney, charts and interprets the trail highlights.

10. REDWOOD NATIONAL PARK
Coastal Trail
40 miles

The namesake redwoods are obviously what draw most travelers to Redwood National Park, but it is often the region's spectacular coast that prompts a return visit.

Dramatic bluffs, hidden coves, tidepools and wilderness beaches are linked by a 40-mile length of Coastal Trail.

Coastal Trail explores the coast of Redwood National Park as well as Prairie Creek Redwoods and Del Norte Redwoods state parks. Linking forest footpaths, the beach and a few miles of paved road, Coastal Trail offers a splendid hike of some 30 miles.

A good place to begin is Skunk Cabbage trailhead located just north of the Redwood Information Center and the hamlet of Orick. The path descends a few miles to 11-mile Gold Bluffs Beach. A superb campground is located on the beach and a smaller trail camp, Butler Creek, is located toward the north end of the beach.

Coastal Trail joins Coastal Drive (a dirt road) for a few miles, then heads east to Douglas Memorial Bridge and crosses the Klamath River. After a little more road-walking, Coastal Trail resumes at Klamath Overlook.

Coastal Trail passes through Sitka spruce forest and brings hikers within easy reach of two hostels—one near Lagoon Creek, the other, Redwood Hostel, a mile north. For a few miles, the trail parallels the east side of Highway 101, then resumes on the west side as it probes the virgin redwood forest in the Damnation Creek area. A few more miles of walking bring the hiker to trail's end at Crescent Beach.

For more information: Call Redwood National Park at (707) 464-6101.

INFORMATION SOURCES

Adopt-A-Beach Program
(800) COAST-4U

California Coastal Commission
45 Fremont Street, Suite 2000
San Francisco, CA 94105
(415) 904-5200

California Dept. of Parks & Recreation
P.O. Box 942896
Sacramento, CA 94296
(916) 653-6995

California State Coastal Conservancy
1330 Broadway, Suite 1100
Oakland, CA 94612
(510) 286-1015

Alcatraz Island Ferry
  (The Blue and Gold Fleet)
(415) 705-5555

Andrew Molera State Park
(831) 667-2315

Angel Island State Park
(415) 435-1915

Año Nuevo State Reserve
(650) 879-0227

Arroyo Burro Beach County Park
(805) 687-3714

Asilomar State Beach
(831) 372-4076

Bay Area Ridge Trail Council
(415) 561-2595

Bay Trail Project
(510) 464-7900

Big Basin Redwoods State Park
(831) 338-8860

Big Sur Multi Agency Facility
(831) 667-2315

Border Field State Park
(619) 575-3613

Butano State Park
(415) 874-0173

Cabrillo Marine Aquarium
(310) 548-7562

Cabrillo National Monument
(619) 557-5450

Candlestick Point State Recreation Area
(415) 671-0145

Carmel River State Beach
(831) 624-4909

Carpinteria State Beach
(805) 684-2811

Catalina Island Chamber of Commerce
  and Visitors Bureau
(310) 510-1520

Catalina Island Conservancy
(310) 510-2595

Channel Islands National Park
(805) 658-5700

China Camp State Park
(415) 456-0766

Crystal Cove State Park
(949) 494-3539

Del Norte Coast Redwoods State Park
(707) 464-6101

The Dune Center
(805) 343-2455

El Capitan/Refugio State Beaches
(805) 968-1033

Elkhorn Slough
(831) 728-2822

Fitzgerald Marine Reserve
(415) 363-4020

Forest of Nisene Marks State Park
(831) 763-7062

Fort Ross State Historic Park
(707) 847-3286

Garrapata State Park
(831) 624-4909

Golden Gate National Recreation Area
(415) 561-4700

Hearst San Simeon
  State Historic Monument
Information: (805) 927-2020
Reservations: (800) 444-7275

Henry Cowell Redwoods State Park
(831) 335-4598

Humboldt Lagoons State Park
(707) 677-3132

Jacks Peak County Park
(888) 588-2267

Jedediah Smith Redwoods State Park
(707) 464-9533

Jug Handle State Reserve
(707) 937-5804

Julia Pfeiffer Burns State Park
(831) 667-2315

King Range National Conservation Area
(707) 825-2300

Leo Carrillo State Park
(805) 488-1827

Limekiln State Park
(831) 667-2403

Long Beach Aquarium of the Pacific
(562) 590-3100

MacKerricher State Park
(707) 937-5804

Malibu Lagoon State Beach
(818) 880-0350

Marina State Beach
(831) 649-2976

McGrath State Beach
(805) 654-4744

McNee Ranch State Park
(650) 726-8819

Mendocino Headlands State Park
(707) 937-5804

Mission Bay Visitor Information Center
(619) 276-8200

Montana de Oro State Park
(805) 528-0513

Monterey Bay Aquarium
(800) 840-4880

Monterey State Historic Park
(831) 649-7118

Morro Bay State Park
(805) 772-2560

Moss Landing Wildlife Area
(831) 649-2870

Mt. Tamalpais State Park
(415) 388-2070

Natural Bridges State Beach
(408) 423-4609

Ocean Beach County Park
(805) 934-6123

Oceano Dunes SVRA
(805) 489-2684

Olompali State Historic Park
(415) 892-3383

Patrick's Point State Park
(707) 677-3132

Pfeiffer Big Sur State Park
(831) 667-2315

Pismo State Beach
(805) 473-7220

Point Cabrillo Light Station
(707) 937-0816

Point Lobos State Reserve
(831) 624-4909

Point Mugu State Park
(805) 488-1827, 488-5223

Point Reyes National Seashore
Point Reyes, CA 94956
(415) 464-5100

Point Sal State Beach
(805) 733-3713

Point Sur State Historic Park
(831) 625-4419, 667-0528

Prairie Creek Redwoods State Park
(707) 464-6101

Redwood National and State Parks
(707) 464-6101

Russian Gulch State Park
(707) 937-5804

Salinas River State Beach
(831) 649-2976

Salt Point State Park
(707) 847-3221

San Clemente State Beach
(949) 492-3156

**Santa Barbara Conference
and Visitors Bureau**
(805) 966-9222

Santa Barbara County Parks Dept.
(805) 568-2461

Santa Monica Mountains NRA
(805) 370-2300

Sinkyone Wilderness State Park
(707) 986-7711, 247-3318

Sonoma Coast State Beaches
(707) 875-3483

Sweetwater Marsh NWR
(619) 409-5900

Tijuana River National
(619) 575-3613

Tolowa Dunes State Park
(707) 464-6101

Tomales Bay State Park
(415) 669-1140

Topanga State Park
(310) 455-2465

Torrey Pines State Reserve
12000 N. Torrey Pines Park Rd.
San Diego, CA 92008
(858) 755-2063

Wilder Ranch State Park
(831) 429-2850

INDEX

A
Adams, Ansel, 1, 159
Adopt a Beach, 11-12
Agate Beach, 281-283
Alamere Falls, 234-235
Alamitos Bay, 45-47
Alcatraz Island, 206, 214-216
Anacapa Island, 84-85
Andrew Molera State Park, 151-154
Angel Island State Park, 217-219
Angelo Coast Range Preserve, 258-259
Año Nuevo State Reserve, 186-189
Arch Rock, 36-37
Arroyo Burro Beach, 99-101
Asilomar Conference Center, 168
Asilomar State Beach, 167-168
Avalon, 54-59
Avila Beach, 119-121

B
Backbone Trail, 296
Balboa Island, 38-41
Bay Area Ridge Trail, 298-299
Bay Trail, 299-300
Bean Hollow State Beach, 189-190
Bear Harbor, 271-272
Bear Valley, 235-237
Belmont Shores, 46
Berry Creek Falls, 179-181
Big Basin Redwoods State Park, 179-181
Big Sur River, 146-147, 151-152
Black Jack Junction, 56-57
Black's Beach, 24
Bodega Head, 245-247
Bolinas Ridge. 232
Bolsa Chica Lagoon, 42-44
Border Field State Park, 14-17
Burton, Phillip, 199-200
Butano State Park, 174-175

C
Caballero Canyon, 65-66
Cabrillo Beach, 47-50
Cabrillo Marine Aquarium, 47-48
Cabrillo National Monument, 21-22
Cabrillo, Juan Rodriguez, 21,
Calafia Beach Park, 32, 34
California Coastal Trail, 4-5, 132
Camp Pendleton, 29-31

Candlestick Point State Recreation Area, 211-212
Cannery Row, 164-167
Carmel River State Beach, 161-163
Carmel Valley, 161
Carpinteria State Beach, 93-95
Cascade Creek, 188-189
Catalina Island, 54-59
Channel Islands Harbor, 78-81
Channel Islands National Park, 84-92
Cherry Cove, 59
China Camp State Park, 219-221
Chula Visa Nature Center, 19-20
Cliff House, 201-203
Coal Oil Point Preserve, 101-103
Coastside Trail, 192
Cone Peak, 139-141
Coral Beach, 105
Corona del Mar, 36-38
Corral State Beach, 64
Crystal Cove State Park, 34-37
Cypress Grove, 159

D
De Anza Trail, 105
Del Cerro Park, 52-53
Del Mar Beach, 28-29
Del Norte Coast Redwoods State Park, 288-289
Devereux Slough, 103
Dipsea Trail, 225-226
Drakes Estero, 240-241

E
East Beach, 97-99
El Capitan State Beach, 103-105
Elephant seals, 2, 186-188
Elkhorn Slough, 170-172
Ellwood Beach, 101-103
Emma Wood State Beach, 83
Enderts Beach, 288-289
Ewoldsen Trail, 144

F
Fern Canyon (Prairie Creek Redwoods SP) 285-286
Fern Canyon (Van Damme SP) 256-257
Ferndale, 279-280
Fisherman's Wharf (Monterey), 166
Fisherman's Wharf (San Francisco) 216

Fitzgerald Marine Reserve, 193-194
Forest of Nisene Marks State Park,
  175-177
Fort Point, 212-214
Fort Ross State Park, 249-251
Four Mile Beach, 185

G
Garrapata State Park, 156-159
Gaviota State Beach, 104
Gazos Creek Coastal Access, 189
Golden Gate Bridge, 201-205, 212-214
Golden Gate Promenade, 202-205
Goleta Beach, 101-103
Guadalupe Dunes, 109-112, 115-117
Gualala Point Regional Park, 254-256

H
Half Moon Bay, 192-193
Hearst Castle, 130
Hearst, William Randolph, 131
Heart's Desire Beach, 244-245
Henry Cowell Redwoods State Park,
  177-179
Hermit Gulch, 54-56
Hidden Beach, 287-288
Humboldt Lagoons State Park, 290-291
Huntington Beach, 39

I
Imperial Beach, 18-19

J
Jacks Peak County Park, 163-164
Jade Cove, 136-137
Jalama Beach, 105-107
Jones Beach, 273-275
Jug Handle State Reserve, 266-267
Julia Pfeiffer Burns State Park, 141-144

K
Kendall-Frost Marsh Preserve, 23-24
King Crest Trail, 275-277
King Range National Conservation Area,
  275-279
Kings Peak, 275-277
Kirk Creek Trail, 136-137
Kruse Rhododendron State Reserve,
  253-254

L
La Jolla Canyon, 74-76
Lagoon Creek, 287-288
Lands End, 201-203
Last Chance Trail, 288-289

Leffingwell Landing, 128-129
Lemming Trail, 65-66
Leo Carrillo Beach, 71
Leo Carrillo State Park, 68-70
Limekiln State Park, 138-139
Little Harbor, 57-60
Little River, 256-257
Long Beach Aquarium of the Pacific,
  44-47
Long Beach, 44-47
Los Liones Canyon, 60-62
Lost Coast Trail, 269-275, 277-279,
  301-302

M
Malaga Cove, 50-51
Malibu Beach, 62-64
Malibu Lagoon, 63-64
Marina State Beach, 170
Marvin Braude Mulholland Gateway
  Park, 65
Mattole River, 277-279
McGrath State Beach, 80-81
McKerricher State Park, 267-269
McNee Ranch State Park, 194-196
McWay Falls, 141-144
Mendocino Headlands State Park,
  260-262
Mission Bay, 22-24
Molera Beach, 153-154
Monastery Beach, 163
Montaña de Oro State Park, 119,
  122-126
Montara State Beach, 195-196
Monterey Bay Aquarium, 164-167
Moonstone Beach, 128-129
Mori Ridge, 200
Moro Canyon, 34-36
Morro Bay State Park, 125-128
Morro Bay, 125-128
Moss Landing Wildlife Area, 172-173
Mott, William Penn, 299
Mount Tamalpais, 226-229
Mount Wittenberg, 236
Mountain Home Inn, 227-228
Muir Beach, 223-225, 231
Muir Woods, 226, 229-230
Mussel Rock, 109-112

N
Naples, 46
Natural Bridges State Beach, 183-184
Newport Beach, 38-
Nicholas Flat, 68-70
Nixon, Richard, 31

O
Ocean Beach County Park, 105-107
Ocean Beach, 202
Oceano Dunes Natural Preserve,
117-119
Oceano Dunes State Vehicular
Recreation Area, 117-119
Olema Valley, 232
Olompali State Historic Park, 221-223
Orizaba, Mount, 57
Oso Flaco Beach, 115-117
Oso Flaco Lakes, 115-117

P
Pacific Valley, 135-136
Palomarin, 234-235
Palos Verdes, 50-53
Partington Cove, 145-146
Paseo Miramar, 60-62
Patrick's Point State Park, 281-283,
290-291
Pebble Beach, 189
Pecho Coast Trail, 119-121
Pelican Bay, 292-293
Pescadero Marsh Natural Preserve,
190-192
Pfeiffer Beach. 150
Pfeiffer Big Sur State Park, 141, 148-149
Piedras Blancas Lighthouse, 129,
131-132
Pismo Beach, 117-119
Pogonip, 181-183
Point Cabrillo Preserve, 264-266
Point Conception, 105-107
Point Dume, 67-68
Point Fermin Park, 49
Point Lobos State Reserve, 159-1661
Point Loma Lighthouse, 21-22
Point Mugu State Park, 72-76
Point Pedernales, 105-107
Point Reyes Lighthouse, 238-240
Point San Luis Lighthouse, 119-121
Point St. George, 292-293
Point Sur Light Station, 154-156, 165
Point Vicente Lighthouse, 50-51
Port Hueneme Beach, 76-78
Portuguese Bend, 52-53
Prairie Creek Redwoods State Park,
285-286
Presidio, 206-209
Punta Gorda Lighthouse, 277-279
Pygmy Forest (Jug Handle SR) 266-267
Pygmy Forest (Van Damme SP) 256-257

Q
Queen Mary, 44

R
Rancho del Oso, 181
Refugio State Beach, 103-105
Rocky Ridge, 158-159
Roosevelt, Theodore, 178
Royal Palms County Beach, 49
Russ Park, 279-80
Russian Gulch State Park, 263-264

S
Salinas River State Beach, 169
Salmon Creek Trail, 133-135
Salt Point State Park, 252-254
San Bruno Mountain, 200-201
San Buenaventura State Beach, 81-82
San Clemente State Beach, 31-34
San Francisco Bay Discovery Site,
199-200
San Francisco Bay National Wildlife
Refuge, 209-211
San Francisco Maritime Historic Park,
204-105
San Mateo Point, 31-33
San Miguel Island, 89-91
San Onofre State Beach, 29-31
San Simeon State Park, 129-130
Sand Dollar Beach, 135-136
Sand Dollar Picnic Area, 136
Santa Barbara Island, 91-93
Santa Cruz Island, 86-87
Santa Lucia fir, 140
Santa Maria River, 109. 115-117
Santa Monica Bay, 295
Santa Rosa Island, 88-89
Santa Ynez River, 107
Scripps Institute of Oceanography, 24
Sea Lion Point, 160
Sea Ranch, 255
Seaside Wilderness Park, 83
Shelter Cove, 277-278
Silver Peak Wilderness, 133-135
Silver Strand, 78-79
Sinkyone Wilderness State Park, 269-275
Sinkyone Wilderness State Park, 273-275
Skyline to the Sea Trail, 179-181, 298
Soberanes Canyon, 158-159
Soberanes Point, 156-158
Sonoma Coast State Beach, 248-249
Stearns Wharf, 97-99
Steep Ravine Trail, 225-226
Steinbeck, John, 1

Stinson Beach, 225-226
Summerland Beach, 95-96
Sutro Baths, 202
Sweeney Ridge, 199-200
Sycamore Canyon, 72-74
Sykes Camp, 146-147

T
Tall Trees Grove, 283-284
Ten Mile Beach, 267-269
Tennessee Valley, 223-225
Tijuana River National Estuarine
    Reserve, 17-19
Tijuana River, 14-17
Tolowa Dunes State Park, 293
Tomales Bay State Park, 244-245
Tomales Point, 242-243
Topanga Overlook, 60-62
Topanga State Park, 60-62, 65-66
Torrey Pines State Beach, 24-27
Torrey Pines State Reserve, 25-29
Trail Springs Camp, 140
Trestles Beach, 31-33
Two Harbors, 57-59

U
UC Santa Barbara, 101
UC Santa Cruz, 181-182
Upper Newport Bay Ecological Reserve,
    41-42
Usal Beach, 269-270

V
Vacation Island, 22-24
Van Damme State Park, 256-257
Ventura Pier, 82
Vicente Flat Trail, 136-137

W
Waddell Beach, 181
Waddell Valley, 181
Whale Gulch, 273-275
Whale Peak, 157-158
White Point Natural Preserve, 48
White Point, 47-49
Wildcat Beach, 234-235
Wilder Ranch State Historic Park,
    184-186
Will Rogers State Historic Park, 66
William Randolph Hearst State Beach,
    131-132
Wrigley, William, 54-55

Y
Yurok Loop Nature Trail, 287

Z
Zuma Beach, 67-68

John McKinney is the author of a dozen books about walking, hiking, and nature, including *The Joy of Hiking: Hiking The Trailmaster Way*. The Trailmaster writes articles and commentaries about walking for national publications, promotes hiking and conservation on radio and television, and serves as a consultant to a hiking vacation company. Contact him at: www.thetrailmaster.com.

California Parks Books from Wilderness Press

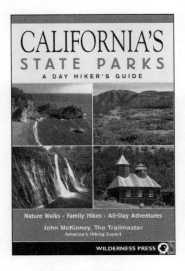

ISBN 0-89997-386-8

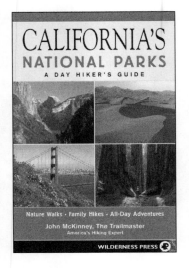

ISBN 0-89997-387-6

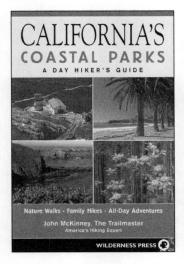

ISBN 0-89997-388-4

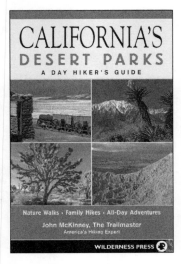

ISBN 0-89997-389-2